PRAISE FOR *FINTECH REGULATION IN PRACTICE*

'This book brings the reader closer to the reality of working in a regulated environment and busts some of the myths that often circulate, limiting beliefs and potentially stifling innovation. *Fintech Regulation in Practice* tackles some of the key questions we're all asking about technology in financial services, providing a much-needed contribution to the discussion and bringing a sense of transparency that will only help progress the debate. This is one of those books that will only enrich the reader's knowledge leaving them informed and energised.'
Nicola Anderson, CEO, FinTech Scotland and former FCA regulator

'Regulation is not bad for business. It is necessary for any resilient long-term business. *Fintech Regulation in Practice* emphasizes the mindset and conduct culture needed to foster an innovative environment where customer protection is a default. Maha El Dimachki highlights the importance of proportionate regulation and how to ensure that regulatory measures are balanced for the business's scale and scope. Her regulatory background reassures us that we are in this together, making the implementation of these measures feel achievable.'
Camilla Bullock, CEO, Emerging Payments Association Asia

'As would be expected from Maha El Dimachki, this book is a must for any fintech that is looking to start and scale. It is an excellent guide to how innovation meets regulation and how regulators have embraced new opportunities to drive industry-led innovation with regulatory oversight.'
Charlotte Crosswell, Chair, Centre for Finance Innovation and Technology and Non-Executive Director

T0295619

'Fintech is a key component of the financial services industry today, and its impact and the benefits will continue to grow. This book provides fintechs around the world with insights into the 'whys' of regulation as well as a guide on how to navigate the regulatory framework for fintechs from start-up to scale-up to maturity. Maha El Dimachki expertly takes readers through the fintech and regulatory lifecycle, breaking down the breadth and complexity of regulation into digestible chapters.'
Nilixa Devlukia, CEO, Payments Solved and former regulator

'Right-sized regulation is key to a strong and stable economy. One that creates a solid foundation for innovation to thrive. To enable that, all parties in the ecosystem from regulators to investors to fintechs of all sizes should play their role in upholding high standards. *Fintech Regulation in Practice* is a must for anyone operating in this ecosystem. A very readable book, it offers a practical approach to fintech regulation; one that promotes a conduct culture and is embedded in the business from early stages right through its lifecycle. The ideas here are more than interesting, emanating as they do from an industry insider turned regulator whose passion for safe and sound fintech growth permeates every page.'
Lord Holmes of Richmond, Member of the House of Lords Select Committee on Democracy and Digital Technologies

'Fintech regulation can be scary. Maha El Dimachki cuts through the noise and guides readers through the complex world providing a simple guide for both students and those working in the industry. Written by the former Head of Early and High Growth Oversight at the Financial Conduct Authority, you could not have a more authoritative voice!'
David Parker, CEO, Polymath Consulting and investor

'As fintech becomes mainstream, we need guardrails to ensure innovation is sustainable and prioritizes the needs of the end customer. *Fintech Regulation in Practice* is a very accessible guide that makes it clear that the way to achieve this outcome is to embed risk management processes in the heart of the business. Drawing on Maha El Dimachki's extensive public and private sector experience, this book offers nuanced perspectives, rejecting a one-size-fits-all approach to regulation. Covering company culture, technology strategy, operations and investor relations - deftly illustrating how these aspects are interlinked - it provides the tools and mindset needed for success.'
Victoria Richardson, COO, Meeco and author of *Money in the Metaverse*

Fintech Regulation in Practice

*Navigate the complexities and
opportunities of regulation*

Maha El Dimachki

First published in Great Britain and the United States in 2024 by Kogan Page Limited

2nd Floor, 45 Gee Street
London
EC1V 3RS
United Kingdom

8 W 38th Street, Suite 902
New York, NY 10018
USA

www.koganpage.com

Kogan Page books are printed on paper from sustainable forests.

ISBNs

Hardback   978 1 3986 1632 5
Paperback   978 1 3986 1569 4
Ebook   978 1 3986 1633 2

British Library Cataloguing-in-Publication Data
A CIP record for this book is available from the British Library.

Library of Congress Control Number
2024940338

Typeset by Integra Software Services, Pondicherry
Print production managed by Jellyfish
Printed and bound by CPI Group (UK) Ltd, Croydon CR0 4YY

CONTENTS

FOREWORD

Fintech plays an important role in the UK. It is not a niche or a subsector. The digital economy is here to stay and with it comes the digitizing of financial services. Fintech has been at the forefront of innovative new ideas that have disrupted traditional financial services, thus creating better outcomes for consumers, more jobs and attracted investment into the UK.

The UK is second only to the United States in fintech investment. It's a position that has been held for a number of years now and one that is important that we continue to defend. But fintech is no longer confined to new innovative firms. It is becoming mainstream and many existing long-term incumbent financial institutions are embracing the digital economy and are using new technologies and innovations such as artificial intelligence, open banking and digital assets or distributed ledger technology to enhance their services and create more efficiency in their businesses.

When I was asked to lead the review into UK fintech by the then UK Chancellor of the Exchequer Rishi Sunak, the team and myself very quickly realized that regulation needed to be prominent in our report. We needed to ensure that policy and regulation performed its role in protecting consumers but also enabled competition and innovation to thrive. That is why we dedicated a whole chapter to it.

The UK has led the way in regulation that fuels competition and creates space for innovation and new ideas. Examples include open banking which was born out of the UK's Competition and Market Authority's review of competition in the retail banking market. The UK's Financial Conduct Authority (FCA) has long been a trend setter in its innovation friendly initiatives. The FCA Sandbox has been replicated many times over the world. More recently, as an outcome of our review, the FCA set up the 'Scalebox' which is oversight of fintechs that are starting up and scaling up in the UK thus helping them to embrace regulation early to support a safe growth trajectory. This particular initiative was led and implemented by the author of this book.

Maha El Dimachki is very familiar with the UK fintech market, has an international background in private and public sector and is a strong advocate for high standard regulation that is proportionate to ensure innovation can thrive without compromising a strong market for fintechs to thrive.

It's a vision I also share. Fintechs should think of regulation and risk management at every stage of their business. Looking at how to embed regulation early, but crucially understanding why regulation is there and how it serves as an enabler for growing a strong and resilient business will serve the fintech in the long term. The strength of the ecosystem is due to the high quality and strength of each of its participants. Without a doubt, fintechs are crucial participants which have matured a lot over the years and their business models and leadership approach have proven to be credible.

Fintech Regulation in Practice is written in a practical and logical way. It attempts to break down a lot of the technical aspects of regulation to the spirit in which they are intended and calls on everyone to embrace regulation and risk management as their friend and while it has a UK focus, the approach applies to many markets outside UK shores.

So, I invite you all, fintechs large and small, regulated or unregulated, investors and regulators from your diverse purviews, to play your part in a strong and thriving fintech ecosystem and hope this book is one resource that can support you in that mission.

Sir Ron Kalifa

FOREWORD

Born out of the banking crisis of 2007–8, when new entrants stepped in to rebuild trust and resilience in the sector, the fintech industry continues to power forward, driving a more inclusive, a more effective and a more democratic financial services sector that works better for everyone. And the UK stands at the forefront. In 2023, despite difficult economic conditions, more than $5.1 billion was invested into the UK fintech ecosystem, second only in the world to the United States, and ahead of the next 28 European countries combined. The UK boasts 10 per cent of the global fintech market share. More than 55 per cent of all SME lending across the UK is being done by fintech and alternative lenders, and today 8 out of every 10 adults in the UK are using at least one fintech tool on a regular basis. There is no doubt that fintech is having a huge impact on our everyday lives.

While the UK is currently a global leader (and the European leader) in fintech, other countries are catching up fast. As CEO of Innovate Finance, the industry body for UK fintech, part of my role is to advocate and lobby for an environment here that cements the UK as the best place in the world to build, scale and grow a fintech business.

I have had the privilege of holding senior roles at Innovate Finance since the organization first launched in 2014, and I took over as CEO in 2021. I feel incredibly honoured to be able to represent a sector that has moved from strength to strength while supporting the UK economy and consumers across the country – and I believe that collaboration between industry, government and regulators is necessary if we are to continue this positive momentum forward. Increasingly from my conversations with government at all levels, including 10 and 11 Downing Street, it is clear that fintech is recognized as the jewel in the UK's tech crown, and that our ongoing leadership in fintech is a critical component of the UK's continued global leadership in financial services more broadly.

Nurturing a successful fintech environment requires a number of components: brilliant entrepreneurs who can move from vision to action; access to an outstanding pool of diverse talent; a flow of investment and capital; government support; and proactive regulation. This final component – regulation – is arguably one of the most important in fully unleashing the power of financial technology and innovation, and it is one of the reasons I was so excited when Maha El Dimachki approached me about this book.

I have known Maha El Dimachki for many years. She has been a lynchpin of the UK fintech ecosystem, and with her uniquely broad and deep background in both regulation and industry, she understands the space in a refreshing - and illuminating - way. The insights she shares in this book with regards to embracing regulation and risk management are vital to any new company looking to grow.

Maha's clear and concise writing, paired with her in-depth understanding of the sector, make this book a mandatory handbook for fintech of all sizes, and from all over the world, as they seek to successfully scale – and a mandatory handbook for anyone looking to better understand the foundation underpinning the exciting growth of this fantastic industry.

Janine Hirt
CEO, Innovate Finance

PREFACE

Innovation. A necessity for any society to advance. The economist Joseph Schumpeter believed that innovation drives economic growth and that the economy goes through waves of technological innovations that move it forward. While it's hard to pinpoint a particular start and end to a wave of technological innovation, with Web3, cryptography, artificial intelligence, and quantum all dominating the technology conversation everywhere including in financial services, there is no question that we're in one of those waves.

With constant change, sometimes at quite a fast pace, the role of the regulators is more important than ever. And so is the need to get regulation right. And the need for a balance of risk management against resources, regulation and rules against innovation and maintaining high standards without stifling growth.

The topic of innovation versus regulation is a fascinating one for me. Working in the private sector, in large financial institutions, with smaller financial institutions and fintechs then moving to the public sector working for a regulator, I could see the interpretation of regulation across both sides. My first role in regulation was one that set me on the path to study the balance of risk and innovation. Setting up the Payments Department at the Financial Conduct Authority, and subsequently the Early and High Growth Oversight Department (or Scalebox), gave me great insight into both sides, the tension that exists and the way in which it can be managed.

The driver for this book has been based on two key principles.

The first is that all parties in the ecosystem benefit from strong regulation. The objectives of a strong sector that is built on foundations of open and free markets but high-quality regulation will ensure that all participants in that sector will thrive. Strong regulation builds confidence. With it, investors invest, and consumers consume with confidence.

The second is that the spirit in which regulation is intended is a real benefit to businesses. Regulation and risk management practically strive for the same outcomes and embedding it in a business from the early stages in a way that is proportionate, is possible. The mindset of risk management and regulation can be an ally to entrepreneurship and innovation, even when clear rules and standards are not drawn.

The book is a practical guide that taps into those principles and links them together. By no means do I claim to be an expert on new technologies, nor do I suggest that the role of fintech founders and CEOs is an easy one. Neither is the role of the regulators and policymakers. I aim to offer a perspective on how to use regulation as a tool to protect your business, your customers and contribute in a positive way to a strong financial services sector. One that continues to thrive which means all participants thrive. That has to be the outcome we all want to achieve.

In this book, I focus on the UK. The UK has long been seen as one of the leaders in financial regulation with a proportionate approach. It is also a market with strong investment in fintech and innovation. However, many of the ideas and principles apply across the world and Chapter 9 talks about some of the global initiatives. While it's not possible to cover every market, I hope it offers a guide to how to consider regulation in other markets or those where regulation is still forming.

I don't believe that one formula for dealing with regulation is possible and I don't offer it. Instead, I offer principles and a mindset in which a fintech can embed the right regulation in the various stages of business growth. It is a guide that allows you to make decisions on what is important. The companies that provided case studies, to whom I am incredibly grateful for their generosity, were important to put this to life. They are live examples of how innovative companies care about regulation and how to embed it in their operations.

This is an exciting time to be in this sector and I'm passionate about how fintech can grow and contribute to real economies around the world. I am lucky to be part of this ecosystem. I feel incredibly lucky to be given the opportunity to share my thoughts, which I'm sure I'll continue to develop with you. If you have decided to read this book, I offer you my deepest gratitude and I hope you find it a useful resource.

1

Financial services and fintech

CHAPTER SUMMARY

- An introduction to financial services and the importance to the economy
- A definition of fintech
- The 'fin' and the 'tech' in fintech and how they interact
- The benefits of fintech to the economy and the drive of policymakers to fuel innovation and competition
- Why it's important to get regulation right

Financial services – a core industry

Financial services, undoubtedly, is one of the economy's most important and influential sectors. After all, financial transactions are at the heart of everything we do. We define financial services as a sector, but it underpins all economic activities. It's the industry that underpins how we live our lives. Businesses, no matter what sector they operate in need to think of cash flow, working capital, investments, profits and financial ratios of all sorts. Research and innovation in medicine, agriculture, engineering, education, space and many other fields need funding.

Deposits, investments, insurance, loans and payments are consumed by every single person or entity in the economy from people to small business to corporates and governments. The ability for everyone in society to access financial services is a key driver of growth in economic activity, and thus growth and prosperity in the economy. Studies have shown how the benefit of a ubiquitous payment system can increase trade and transactions across the economy, how the availability of micro credit can lift many out of poverty and how financial inclusion leads to prosperity.

Many governments are starting to consider financial inclusion. They have implemented various ideas around financial inclusion depending on the economic and political structure of each country. Across the world, a bank account is a basic need to be able to be an active part of the economy. It's the same as an address or a national insurance, social security or digital identification number is needed. A credit score is becoming an important indicator of a person's ability to take part in economic activity and to build individual prosperity. However, globally, there are many people who lack access to these essentials.

In 2014, The UK government announced an agreement with all major banks to offer a basic bank account free of fees.[1] The initiative ensured that these accounts did not incur transactions fees which took the account into overdraft. The initiative incentivized everyone to open a bank account without this fear and uncertainty. We may take some of this for granted in places like the UK but if we cast our minds to the past in the UK or even the recent past in other parts of the world, we will find that getting a loan or having an account with a bank was a service only offered to the wealthy. Recognizing the benefit of financial inclusion and ensuring everyone has access to the financial services they need is a key contributor to growth, prosperity and success of individuals, households and businesses.

In other parts of the world, governments have considered and implemented programmes to make access to financial services available to everyone in society. Micro loans are a familiar example of this. Thinking about micro loans, we can see how the development of a strong universal finance sector can drive prosperity. Micro loans allow an individual to provide for their family. This is particularly important when there is an adverse event or shock on the family. When a person is finding it difficult to make ends meet, microfinance offers the opportunity of reducing the disruption to build wealth while ensuring the stability of the household. They can break cycles of poverty. When given a loan, the ability to put it to good use and create some additional income can be a significant benefit to many. It encourages people to save. At the same time, additional income can be used for additional consumption, which helps in growing the economy and can allow people to save for a rainy day or to cover a life event. One such event is children's education. Educating a person will have significant positive outcomes for an individual, household and ultimately society. The ability to extend an education to those who normally would not be allowed the opportunity can have significant positive outcomes for the individual and society from social mobility, income growth, health-care outcomes and breaking the cycle of poverty and deprivation. Microfinance can create real investment opportunities and create jobs. As entrepreneurs use their loan to establish commercial enterprises a cycle of investment and job creation starts which is a key contributor to economic growth.

From micro loans, we can examine another very important part of economic activity and financial inclusion: payments. A familiar example here is M-PESA. M-PESA in Kenya is a mobile payments wallet offered to every Kenyan who has a mobile phone and has proven to lift many Kenyans out of poverty. One study has shown that over a six-year period consumption in Kenya has grown, lifting some 2 per cent of Kenyans out of poverty. Worthy of note is that the impact has been twice as high on female-headed households.[2] The M-PESA example is interesting as it is further evidence that enabling the safe and efficient movement of money alone can have an impact on economic prosperity of households and economies.

This story is not dissimilar, fundamentally, to the importance of finance in any economy and we will see a similar theme in the emergence and growth of fintech. In many parts of the world, innovative ways to allow everyone to access a bank account, trade and transact, and get access to credit have been seen as a key contributor to the growth of the country and its economic prospects. In fact, there is a recognition that financial literacy and understanding how money must be managed is an important focus for government, NGOs and industry alike. We see this in various economies and markets across the world. Despite their differences, the overarching recognition of the value of financial services, both existing long-standing infrastructure and innovative new solutions, is the same.

Financial services in the UK are a particularly important sector: 8.3 per cent of total UK economic output came from financial services in 2021. That is a contribution of £173.6 billion to the UK economy putting it as the fourth largest in the OECD by proportion to the UK's economic output.[3] It is also a significant contributor to jobs. In Q1 2022, it was estimated that there were 1.08 million jobs in financial services which is approximately 3 per cent of all jobs. The UK is also a net exporter of financial services contributing to a surplus of £44.7 billion.

What is a fintech and is it a sector?

It is worth starting with what sounds like a basic question. What is the definition of fintech? Everyone has their own version of the answer. I don't believe it is important that we must agree on a precise definition, but it's important to explain what definition I've used for the purpose of this book.

If we simply ask the question, when did fintech start, we will find many answers, the earliest dating back to 1866 when the first undersea cable was laid between the UK and the US. This arguably provided the infrastructure to develop financial globalization.[4] I am not sure how many in fintech see that as the beginning, but I'll leave this to your own judgement.[5]

Another answer is the creation of Direct Debit in 1964 by Alastair Hanton, British inventor and former executive of Unilever. Hanton created Direct Debit to collect payments from ice cream vendors. Unilever needed a more efficient method than cash or cheques to collect payments from smaller ice cream vendors. Hanton's solution was to get authority from the vendor to debit their account directly. This gave rise to the concept of Direct Debit as we know it today.[6]

Then we have another answer: the creation of the Automatic Teller Machine (ATM) which was first launched by Barclays Bank in 1967.

This is possibly a more realistic answer of when fintech began, but we probably don't really associate the start of fintech in its true sense until after the 2008 financial crisis with the rise of technology companies disrupting large stagnant incumbent players in financial services. At the same time, governments and regulators started paving the way using tools such as investment opportunities and competition remedies that lowered the regulation barriers to entry into the financial services market. Online banking was already in play, and we started to see more adoption with speed of internet access and widespread adoption of smart phones. App-based technology started to take hold of how we live our lives.

So, at a very basic level, fintech is finance and fintech is technology. Together.

Fintech is finance. It's financial services. Firms offer financial services in a digitally empowered way. The delivery channel is only via technology. Modulr, a payment fintech that found a gap in the payments market and looked to close it, and OakNorth, a lending fintech which used technology to offer loans quickly and easily without compromising risk and high standards (see Chapter 10 for further details on both Modulr and OakNorth) are examples of financial services companies using technology as the basis for their financial services proposition to consumers. A fintech is a firm that uses some technology to deliver its financial services regardless of the channel of delivery.

Fintech is technology. It's technology that is used to power financial services. Therefore, fintechs are companies that develop and offer technology to other businesses that offer financial services such as regtech companies or payment processors. Fintech is also technology companies such as Google and Apple looking to offer financial services in addition to other services they offer. Furthermore, a fintech is an innovative firm that operates in or around financial services, with a digital platform as its core service delivery platform such as Amazon or Alibaba. A fintech is any company, large or small, newly created or existing for decades, that uses technology and digital tools to offer or enable the offering of financial services.

For the purposes of this book, and so we don't leave anyone out, fintech is all of those things and more. Fintech is linked with innovation and our constant drive to ensure we have an environment that supports innovation. It's also linked with the digital economy and this book will focus on fintechs in the digital economy rather than an undersea cable in 1866. Fintechs offer new technologies challenging the boundaries and changing the way we live our lives with all parties in the ecosystem playing their part and interested in the benefits this will achieve.

I deliberately wanted to have a broad definition. After all, this book is about regulation and risk management. All the examples I offered above are companies that operate in a wide ecosystem. They are interconnected. They either compete or partner. They collaborate on key topics. The expectation of how the market works and the drive of regulators to ensure that markets work well falls on everyone. Therefore, the regulatory expectation on firms to ensure a market works is an important foundation for all these firms to understand as they offer services to and interact with each other, consumers, investors and suppliers.

The tech in fintech

Let's start with the 'tech' in fintech. Technology and all things digital are the key to this evolution as is the case for many other sectors, such as health care, the biomedical industry, space and many others. We start with technology being the driver of change and harnessing the benefits of technology in our world. This has been the catalyst for fintech. Technology disrupts the status quo. We know that, intuitively, or because we keep reading and hearing it. It stimulates innovation, entrepreneurship, and in turn competition. It can offer solutions to our everyday lives like nothing we've seen before.

We now have the ability to send a picture of a cat from one side of the world to the other in a millisecond. We can share it with millions of people in an instant. Coming from a big family, it means that we can share a news story or organize an event without having to make 50 different phone calls. It also means that I can speak to my family in different parts of the world. I can video call my mother and sister at the same time and have a family conversation while the three of us live in three different countries. I hope you are able to indulge me with this example, but I remember my childhood where we would record a conversation on a tape and send it in the mail halfway across the world to my uncle and wait a couple of months for a response to our recording to come, via tape. There are many profound uses for technology. It has allowed those with limited mobility to do things they never thought they can. Eye gazing technology is one such example. Imagine a world where a quadriplegic can make decisions of all kinds, including financial decisions using their eyes. Another such tool is facial recognition and its use in identity. The UNHCR has deployed a Global Distribution Tool (GDT) in some refugee camps which relies on biometric data to distribute food and cash to refugees in a fair and equitable way.[7]

Technological disruption creates new and interesting propositions across all parts of the ecosystem that make things run more efficiently, give us immediacy, solve problems or give us something we didn't know we needed and now couldn't live without. I never thought there would be a solution to calling 50 members of my family or sending a picture of a cat halfway across the world in an instant. I didn't think it was a problem that needed solving, but now we want it all the time. We take our world now for granted, but it is worth reflecting on how it used to be.

What I'm trying to say is that we need to remember that fintech didn't start it all. Technology did. It took us by storm, and we started thinking of how to use it in a real way across many parts of our lives including in financial services.

The fin in fintech

Now back to fintech and the 'fin' part. Financial services were ripe for disruption. From clunky back-office processes to storage solutions that were costly to run, to processes that were manual and paper based, to the need to walk into a bank branch to get anything done. Something needed to happen. Regulators identified the state of the sector and, observing technology and consumer behaviour, many looked at policy options that would stimulate competition and give space to disruptors to play. The opening up of access to Real Time Gross Settlement (RTGS) to non-bank payments institutions, or the implementation of the first and second payments services directive, and more recently open banking are examples of regulators and policymakers playing their role in stimulating innovation and competition around the world. A very important outcome here is the significant reduction in barriers to entry. Regulators played their part in lowering barriers to entry (more on this in the next chapter) but let's be very clear, technology itself is what lowered those barriers. You no longer needed large teams of people performing manual tasks or costly infrastructure to set up. We started to see disintermediation and breaking up the value chain where parties were able to come in with their unique proposition to make that part of the chain better.

Technology came in to solve some of the obvious painful parts of the financial services chain that we are all familiar with. They started streamlining and supporting back-end processes for large financial institutions. Two examples are Form 3 and Bottomline Technologies.

Form 3 is a fintech that started to offer cloud-based payment technology known as Payments-as-a-Service. Acting as an aggregator, they have developed a platform that integrates with payments schemes thus allowing payments institutions, banks and non-banks, to connect to the country's payments schemes (Bacs, CHAPS, Faster Payments) with ease using cloud technology. Bottomline Technologies, founded in 1989, centralize, automate and digitize the working capital cycle of any institution including cash management efficiencies, document automation, centralization of treasury services and payment simplification.[8]

Today, it is hard to find a large financial institution that is not on a journey to digitize, digitalize, transform, upgrade, automate or change. Some are back-end processes such as transfer from paper to digital, or infrastructure upgrades. Others are app-based, value add or customer facing. Financial services have gone through a period of disruption and change driven by the advancements in technology and the rise of a digital economy which has and continues to bring many benefits to consumers. Financial services and technology interacting and delivering significant benefits have driven the interest in fintech. So many of the solutions that have been implemented for financial inclusion have been based on fintech and innovation. M-PESA in Kenya, as we described above, was an innovative idea replicated in other jurisdictions, and relies on the use of mobile phone accounts and connecting those to digital wallets. From cloud services to fraud detection software, crowdfunding and peer-to-peer lending plat-forms, payment accounts and digital wallets to crypto assets, Digital Ledger Technology and artificial intelligence all these are dominating today's fintech scene.

Payments have played a significant role in the history and develop-ment of fintech. The way we move money has changed. Use of cash has significantly declined in many economies around the world such as the UK, Australia, Sweden and parts of Asia and this trend will only continue. It is well known that the Covid-19 pandemic also played a part in accelerating the decline of cash in many countries. Singaporean hawker centres were largely cash, until Covid and within a very short period of time, they all started accepting electronic payments via a platform called 'PayNow' which is an account-to-account payment instrument using QR codes. New payments firms, e-wallet providers, money services providers all emerged to serve the population with new and better ways of making payments. (It is worth noting here that these are macro trends, but cash is, does remain and, in some areas, can be the only alternative for transacting. This is true for parts of the UK, many parts of the US and many coun-tries in Asia, Africa and the Middle East.)

Access to finance options has increased and loans can be approved in a matter of minutes. Platforms that offer loans online, peer-to-peer lending facilitated by technology and open banking allowing lenders better visibility of spending behaviour all have technology at their heart. Banking platforms are digital, user-friendly and more accessible. An estimated 90 per cent of the UK adult population use online banking.[9] The benefit of all this is noticed and tangible. Peer-to-peer lending platforms offer a solution to link those with funds to those who need them, cutting out the intermediary and creating a new avenue where access to funds can be achieved. This creates a benefit to both retail and smaller investors and retail and smaller borrowers.

A good example that offers multiple layers of how fintech has served the community well is e-money. E-money wallets also known as digital wallets, have taken the world by storm. E-money wallets have been a real disruptor in financial services. These services have been developed to solve a number of problems that existed in traditional financial services. Access to a bank account requires the bank to understand who is opening the account and transacting or moving money to mitigate the risk of financial crime or money laundering. The process of building this information is called Know Your Customer (KYC) and is a requirement by the financial regulators in most countries. Financial institutions collect a large amount of historical information and offer banking services based on a risk appetite which makes it difficult for those on the lower income threshold or some small businesses to open a bank account quickly.

E-money wallets allow an individual to open a bank account with minimal time and just one form of ID. Many of these wallets rely on topping up the wallet. Given these are top-up solutions, credit is not extended and the risk profile of the customer is lower. Transaction data is gathered as the individual transacts and the risk profile builds up as the customer uses the account more and more. As it is app-based, it is flexible in its uses. These apps have been the first to link your location (via phone) to where you spend, and block a transaction if it's suspicious. They have been the first to offer teenage accounts linked to a parent's account with many useful features for teaching children about money. The teenage account solution has also been used for vulnerable individuals who require a guardian or carer to look out for their financial affairs. They have also disrupted other parts of financial services such as foreign exchange, offering lower rates and a better user experience while travelling or transferring money overseas.

Prepaid card wallets have allowed the UK's Home Office to use these cards to pay refugee allowance payments simply, efficiently and with minimal risk. They have allowed the unbanked to access and build a credit history in a way that would have been extremely difficult before. They offer lower fees depending on the service and lower FX rates. The uses have been multiple and varied.

Now we see many large well-established banks adapting their banking apps to offer similar services to these disruptors. Their offers continue to be a bit more clunky and services are added in small steps, but there is no doubt that large traditional banks can see how the industry has been disrupted and that consumers have embraced the benefits of the innovation. From these developments over the last 10 years, we are now moving from solving particular pain points to harness the power of data in new ways to benefit consumers. The key conversations dominating the fintech world now are principally around open banking (open finance), crypto assets and the underlying technology and artificial intelligence.

Open banking

Open banking, which started in the UK, has been one such policy that sets out to encourage innovation around data in the interest of consumers. It has been a fundamental shift in the traditional banking scene, forcing large incumbent banks to allow regulated third-party providers access to consumer data, with explicit consumer consent, to offer value added financial products and services.

Open banking has fundamentally focused on the opening up of data sets in financial services for better consumer outcomes. It has forced disruption and innovation. Today, open banking offers numerous propositions around improved financial decision-making, better borrowing options and more payment options. It offers money management dashboards, bank-to-bank seamless payments options and in one case the ability to measure your carbon footprint to make greener shopping decisions. Adoption in the UK, as an example, continues to grow and an estimated 10 per cent of digitally enabled consumers and small businesses are using open banking amounting to an estimated 21.1 million open banking payments in March 2022.[10] As a result, we can expect better outcomes for consumers, more start-ups and scale-up fintechs, more jobs and more economic activity.

In fact, now the drive is to move from open banking to open finance. The initiative looks at what data sets need to be unlocked that can further fuel innovation and new ideas for the benefit of consumers. How can Small to Medium Enterprises (or SMEs) be better served? How can financial inclusion or better money management for those that need it deliver better outcomes?

The rise of open banking has been replicated around the world and many economies have seen the benefit of implementing such a policy. The UK has largely led the way with the Competition and Markets Authority retail banking market investigation order 2017 to open up payments data housed within the nine largest banks to third-party providers.[11] In Australia, the basis of open banking started with the consumer data rights, an economy-wide initiative, and banking products were the first cab off the rank. In the US, open banking has been a product of the market growing and innovating. It has been market-led and did not wait for regulation to force the issue. However, regulators did catch up and considered policy to support the growth of open banking for the benefit of consumers. Canada has followed the lead of its neighbour and open banking has been market-led.

In other jurisdictions such as Brazil, Colombia, India, Mexico and Saudi Arabia, open banking has been an initiative of the relevant central bank. Central banks and governments have largely been instrumental in opening data sets for the benefit of competition and open banking has been a significant contributor to the rise of fintech of late.

Open banking, open finance, consumer data rights and all their variations have been popular for innovation and finding solutions to solve problem areas in the economy. However, with new innovations come risks that need to be mitigated and open banking relies on opening data sets that can create value for the data owners. Exploitation of this data, how it's collected, stored, used and shared are all areas that raise questions around value, consent, ethics and how data is used for good. For fintech to serve society, we need to ensure that it develops in a safe way and risks that are visible and, in some cases, not so visible must be addressed to avoid consumer harm.

Cryptographic technology

These days, the current conversation around new fintech seems to default to discussions around cryptographic technology or crypto for short. Cryptocurrencies, crypto assets, stablecoins, digital currencies such as central bank digital currencies and any conversation that is based on cryptographic and blockchain technology are dominating current discourse.

There is no doubt that the rise of propositions based on cryptography has taken the fintech space by storm. It is an ideal case study on the rise of a innovation based on new technology and how it develops rapidly with little regulation around it. The uses of crypto are varied and important to discuss. It isn't a technology that will go away, and it can make fundamental changes to financial services as we know it. It is another example of how technology has found its way into financial services. The use of cryptography combined with the rise of decentralization and peer-to-peer transactions has driven new and varying applications in financial services. While a lot of the crypto conversation started and has been on the basis of how it can transform financial services given its decentralised nature, the technology itself has a profound impact generally with multiple applications beyond financial services.

The World Economic Forum[12] has a helpful description of a non-exhaustive list of applications for Distributed Ledger Technology. These include core or base layer, protocol layer, financial products and services and non-financial products and services.

The first of the core layer blockchains started with a white paper after the financial crisis and the creation of Bitcoin as an alternative to the current centralized system of finance. This was in 2008. Bitcoin daily trading volume is estimated at $37bn in 2023 and its price has fluctuated quite significantly from $7,500 at the start of 2020 to an all-time high of $64,000 in 2021 and back to $26,000 in June 2023. Towards the end of 2023 and early 2024 Bitcoin again saw an increase in value. These are approximate figures as the fluctuation is daily and can be significant. The volatility of crypto currencies is something we will return to, but you can see the financial gain that this instrument has created during this time and the challenges it may pose on many levels for the need to maintain a stable financial market.

Another example of base layer blockchains is Ripple. Ripple was established to make payments easier, faster and more efficient with no point of failure. These challenges in cross-border payments are well documented and Ripple's attempt is to make financial market infrastructure for cross border payments better. The G20 most recently indicated that solving faster, secure and more efficient cross-border payments that are accessible to all is a priority to ensure prosperity for economies and citizens, financial inclusion and better trade.[13] The UK's Financial Conduct Authority Sandbox, in its earlier years recorded a large number of fintechs looking at propositions to support better cross-border payments. This has been an interesting and very real application of this technology for the benefit of payments.

The protocol layer allows for further features and applications to be developed using smart contracts. This is where there are many use cases and it is a very useful technology for providing solutions for areas that have common business rule. One example is Uniswap. Uniswap is a decentralized exchange that uses smart contracts to create liquidity pools that will allow seamless and quick exchange on its platform. There is a lot of experimentation in this area and it is starting to gain some momentum. However, the wide application at scale will no doubt take time. This protocol layer offers viable propositions, but with these nascent technologies, and the stickiness of existing processes that have worked over a long period, it may take a while to displace current processes and infrastructure.

Financial product and services referred to here are those that inter-act with traditional financial instruments we know and use today to allow access to digital assets and transact in crypto currencies. Some larger institutions have invested in infrastructure to link digital assets and tokenized digital assets to traditional assets (fiat currency) on one seamless platform. Deutsche Bank proof of concept for custody services offered just that. The proof-of-concept tested interoperabil-ity between traditional custody platforms and Distributed Ledger Technology (DLT) platforms supporting digital assets and asset backed securities.[14]

PayPal allow their customers to buy and sell a limited number of cryptocurrencies in the PayPal wallet. This means that PayPal custom-ers can transact in these cryptocurrencies offering another payment method without the need to move cryptocurrencies back to fiat currencies to make payments.[15] Most recently in 2023, PayPal issued its own 'stablecoin', a crypto currency that is backed by an asset: in the case of PayPal, it is backed by USD. This means its stability is tied to the USD, unlike other stablecoins that are pegged to other asset classes that can be more volatile than fiat currency.[16] This gives more flexibility for PayPal customers to trade and pay in cryptocurrencies. There is general recognition that this market will grow. Particularly tokenized assets and the buying and selling of these assets will become a feature of investor activity. Therefore, we see financial institutions large and small investing in these applications and platforms.

The final category here is one that goes beyond traditional finan-cial services and are native to cryptocurrencies or the blockchain technology. Some examples are the ability to hold and trade rare pieces of art or digital material of an exclusive nature. Other exam-ples power financial activities in an innovative way such as the UNICEF crypto fund and the World Food Programme testing how cryptocurrencies can give enhanced choices to those receiving human-itarian aid.

The movement of money has been central to the rise of digital currencies. Fast, efficient, traceable, and in the case of crypto curren-cies and digital assets, decentralized. However, the characteristic of fiat currency has not been replicated and one of the key areas of uncertainty is the price volatility of a crypto currency. This created the concept of stablecoins, referenced above in the PayPal example. This is a crypto currency that is backed by a tangible real asset, in some cases backed by fiat currency, that ensures as the name suggests, its stability, or lower volatility which in turns offers more certainty when transacting. The stability of the asset to which it is pegged or linked is a very important factor for the actual stability of the currency, much in the same way as different asset classes offer different levels of risk and volatility.

We've so far described private sector applications and innovations around cryptography. The public sector is looking to use the underlying technology to ensure that they are ahead of the game, that they are developing solutions and creating possibilities that have not been seen before. Generally, they are trying to do it with an economy-wide, wholesale and retail financial services lens in mind.

Central bank digital currency (CBDC) is the obvious example here. Central banks have been observing fintech advances with a keen eye and are now active in looking at the merits of introducing a digital currency. The benefits they see with testing the possibilities are faster payments, more efficient payments, financial inclusion, global payments and trade. At this stage it is seen as a complementary payments instrument rather than a replacement of fiat currency and payment methods and the application, including the merits of a wholesale or retail currencies varies from one central bank to the other.

Artificial intelligence

It's difficult to talk about fintech without talking about artificial intelligence, machine learning and more recently the rise of generative AI in the context of financial services. Artificial intelligence or AI has been used extensively in all parts of our lives. It is arguably the evolution of statistical methods. Today, web search, virtual assistants, navigation, streaming service, social media feeds, online shopping and advertising, smart homes and smart cities and natural language processing are only a few examples. The benefit that this technology brings is across our life spectrum and can be quite revolutionary. ChatGPT of course has taken the world by storm and the reviews are mixed. A report by the Alan Turing Institute on AI in financial services describes AI being machine learning, non-traditional data and automation. The application of these can happen on their own or in combination with each other.[17]

Of course, AI at its basic level started with automating processes and creating efficiencies: finding the repetitive tasks that humans do and based on a set of business rules, and performing that role, in many cases more quickly and effectively than humans. However, AI has developed into much more than that. It is becoming creative. With generative AI, ChatGPT being the obvious example, we are starting to see algorithms that take a set of data and create a new set of data. The application of such technology can be revolutionary if developed in a safe and deliberate way that will serve society. Augmented working is another interesting application of AI. Machines and humans working side by side to deliver products and services is starting and will continue to develop.

Generative AI and augmented working will feature heavily in financial services and fintechs are already looking at how this technology can create innovate ideas that will deliver value. It is yet another technology that is coming into financial services in a significant way and has been gaining attention and cautious enthusiasm. The mixed sentiment lends itself to the ethical question around AI and its uses.

There is no shortage of applications of AI in financial services. Some of the key applications of automation in financial services are around decision-making, producing management information and validation. Many of these automation applications have been tested and well documented around robo advice, smart forms that give you an answer on your loan application in seconds, predictive analytics that can flag indicators of financial distress or credit rating scores based on the data it is fed.

Financial institutions are starting to look at how to use structured and unstructured data to help with innovative products and services, thus increasing competition and providing better service and value to consumers. This trajectory will continue with the increased creation of data, and the continued advancement of a digital economy. AI in financial services can start to play a bigger role. While it is understood that AI can drive innovative ways of providing products and services and the potential for better value to consumers and healthy competition to the market, the risks of AI have also been widely documented and debated from bias and harm to consumers with inaccurate outcomes or outcomes that disadvantage a particular group or section of society.

The fintech momentum in the UK on the rise

Fintechs and the benefit of a strong fintech ecosystem in the UK have been a focus for the financial services sector for a number of years. Promoting innovation, entrepreneurship and economic growth are seen as key benefits of a thriving economy and financial services fuels and supports its growth and sustainability. Recognized as such, the UK government commissioned a review of the fintech market in 2021 (the Kalifa Review into fintech) and continues to drive that focus on the growth of this sector.[18]

The sector has grown significantly, having recorded 1,600 fintech companies in 2016, this has grown to 2,500 in 2022.[19] As of late 2023, the UK is estimated to have 3,000 fintechs in a thriving ecosystem. Investment in UK fintech was estimated at $130 billion in 2021 and $95 billion in a difficult year for the global economy. The UK is a very strong fintech market, second only to the US. Despite the slowdown in 2022, the latest statistics from Innovate Finance show worldwide fintech investment declined by 30 per cent from a record breaking 2021, whereas UK fintech investment only declined by 8 per cent.[20]

Fintech is a phenomenon worldwide. Markets such as Europe, Middle East, Australia, Asia and the US all have an incredible focus on the growth of fintech and innovation. The size of the fintech market is estimated to grow to $16 billion in 2028. Driving this growth is the convenient and transparent value propositions that new firms are bringing to the market, the fact that incumbent and large organizations are implementing new technologies, technology companies are entering financial services and the fact that there is increased collaboration between regulators and industry to solve problems such as cost of living and financial inclusion which fintech is seen as being able to do.

We have seen so many organizations in both the private and public sector embrace fintech. Large incumbent organizations that have been offering financial services since the days of book ledgers are now using technology and are developing transformation programmes to digitize. With this explosion of initiatives in fintech, we must not lose sight of where the risks are and how they may, if not managed well, cause significant disruption, harm and loss of confidence. The foundations by which a sector builds innovative new solutions must be strong. These foundations must ensure the healthy functioning of the market where all parties play their role.

Regulators play a part in encouraging innovation. Open banking has been largely driven by regulators and policymakers and has been adopted worldwide. In Europe the first and second Payments Services Directive, and now a third on its way, have been a catalyst for lowering barriers to entry for payments firms. The Bank of England and many other central banks have allowed non-bank payments institutions to directly link to their Real Time Gross Settlement infrastructure.

It is also recognized by global organizations such as the World Bank that fintech development and adoption is positively correlated with a strong policy and supervisory environment. While not a driver on its own, regulation that fuels fintech growth to promote competition, ensuring consumer protection and the healthy functioning of the market undoubtedly gives confidence for investors to invest and consumers to consume.

The possibilities are endless and across the entire chain. When we think of fintech our mind often goes to consumer services and propositions that are visible to each person. After all, it was estimated in 2020 that 96 per cent of consumers globally are aware of at least one fintech product.[21] But we know that the propositions aren't only about services being offered to consumers. Innovation and financial technology can play a part in the entire chain; AI to fight financial crime, confirmation of payee for secure payments, technologies for the protection from fraud and scams are all innovations that can transform the industry.

We must get it right

The benefit, if we get it right, can have a spillover effect. Innovation creates more innovation. New ideas build on each other. Open finance can build on the success and benefit of open banking. Propositions that are initially targeted for one group can find multiple use cases and benefits. Think about how a payment wallet that was designed for educating young people on how to manage money was soon adopted for vulnerable consumers who needed the support of a guardian, a carer or a power of attorney. Biometrics, such as fingerprints and facial recognition were designed for pure identification purposes. Now other biometrics, such as the typing syle of teh user, can be used as a tool to verify payments and detect unusual shoppintg activity.

The damage if we get it wrong could be harmful and disruptive – catastrophic even. So while we have covered how regulators and policymakers have designed policy to fuel innovation and the fintech market, they also have the task of ensuring that the standards are high, the risks are identified and the development of new technologies impacting financial services will serve to benefit the economy as a whole and move it forward.

In this book, we will explore the need to regulate fintech, and discuss how fintech is regulated with a focus on the UK primarily, comparing it with other jurisdictions on key regulatory developments. We will also look at the principles a fintech can adopt and how they apply to many markets across the world. We will cover why it is practical for fintechs to embrace regulation across the multiple stages of their growth to ensure balanced and sustainable growth.

Summary and takeaways

Financial services play a critical role in the economy. Fintech is a phenomenon worldwide that has captured the attention of innovators, incumbents, investors and policymakers. The recognition that technology is here to stay, that we are moving to a digital economy and the proven benefit of creating the right ecosystem for fintech to thrive have been the key drivers for this attention.

Fintech is a driver of economic growth, creates more jobs and supports strong competition. Supporting a thriving fintech ecosystem will undoubtedly deliver better value for consumers. The definition of fintech is broad and there isn't a particular point at which it started. Rather than insisting on a definition, it is important to think about the ecosystem and the various applications of technology in financial services, the benefits, the risks and how propositions, product and services can be developed in a way that's going to add value to consumers and business. How might fintechs solve some of the key issues that central banks and other policymakers are grappling with?

Regulators have played an important role in fuelling innovation and competition with policy initiatives that open up avenues previously closed to innovators. This has been an effective way of driving innovation in a way that is sustainable and considers the risks in advance.

Today, fintech is centred on technologies that have been adopted and gaining momentum in the last 10 years such as digital wallets, peer-to-peer lending and 'buy now pay later'. New fintechs are emerging in areas such as AI, open banking and crypto. These will continue to develop and evolve with potential growth of the metaverse, quantum computing and other technologies that may emerge. Strong regulation is a foundation by which fintech can start and grow a business with confidence.

The entire industry sees the benefit of fintech and innovation. However, it is important to ensure that we talk about some of the pitfalls and challenges this sector goes through. It is important to recognize the impact these challenges can have on the industry if not managed properly. There will be different challenges across the various stages of a fintech life cycle. Managing the risks in each of those stages will ensure a healthy and strong financial services sector where consumers have confidence consuming and investors continue to be attracted to invest.

Notes

1 HM Treasury. New basic fee-free bank accounts to help millions manage their money. HM Treasury, London 2015. www.gov.uk/government/news/new-basic-fee-free-bank-accounts-to-help-millions-manage-their-money (archived at https://perma.cc/T547-S59T).

2 S Dawson. Why does M-PESA lift Kenyans out of poverty?, CGAP, 2017. www.cgap.org/blog/why-does-m-pesa-lift-kenyans-out-of-poverty (archived at https://perma.cc/GP5B-S4L2).

3 G Hutton. Financial services: contribution to the UK economy. House of Commons Library, London, 2022. researchbriefings.files.parliament.uk/documents/SN06193/SN06193.pdf (archived at https://perma.cc/MRU9-LJJV).

4 Science Museum. How perseverance laid the first transatlantic telegraph cable. Science Museum, London, 2018. www.sciencemuseum.org.uk/objects-and-stories/how-perseverance-laid-first-transatlantic-telegraph-cable (archived at https://perma.cc/L7TM-B9KQ).

5 E Zimmerman. The evolution of Fintech. *The New York Times*, 6 April 2016. www.nytimes.com/2016/04/07/business/dealbook/the-evolution-of-fintech.html (archived at https://perma.cc/TXA3-P6P7).

6 Telegraph Obituaries. Alastair Hanton, former Unilever executive who invented the Direct Debit – obituary. *The Telegraph*. 9 June 2021. www.telegraph.co.uk/obituaries/2021/06/09/alastair-hanton-former-unilever-executive-invented-direct-debit (archived at https://perma.cc/S7FM-A3AK).

7 V Eleonora Bruttomesso. When technology improves the lives of refugees. UNHCR Blogs, 8 March 2019. www.unhcr.org/blogs/new-technology-improves-lives-refugees/ (archived at https://perma.cc/54YZ-XEFW).

8 Crunchbase. Bottomline technologies. Crunchbase, 2022. www.crunchbase.com/organization/bottomline-technologies (archived at https://perma.cc/Y4HD-E43Z).

9 Statista. Online banking usage in Great Britain from 2007 to 2022, 2023. www.statista.com/statistics/286273/internet-banking-penetration-in-great-britain/ (archived at https://perma.cc/H9PN-937F).

10 Open Banking Limited. Outputs (Availability) – The Open Banking Impact Report, June 2022. openbanking.foleon.com/live-publications/the-open-banking-impact-report-june-2022/outputs-availability (archived at https://perma.cc/4JBX-2C4F).

11 Competition and Markets Authority. CMA paves the way for Open Banking revolution. GOV.UK, 2016. www.gov.uk/government/news/cma-paves-the-way-for-open-banking-revolution (archived at https://perma.cc/QR48-F47X).

12 World Economic Forum. Crypto, What Is It Good For? An Overview of Cryptocurrency Use Cases. Economic Forum, Cologny, Switzerland: World, 2020. www3.weforum.org/docs/WEF_Cryptocurrency_Uses_Cases_2020.pdf (archived at https://perma.cc/5XZF-L6JF).

13 Financial Stability Board. G20 Roadmap for enhancing cross-border payments: First consolidated progress report. Financial Stability Board, Basel, Switzerland, 2021. www.fsb.org/wp-content/uploads/P131021-1.pdf (archived at https://perma.cc/SJF2-KPC2).

14 Deutsche Bank. Deutsche Bank and Singapore fintech STACS complete 'bond in a box' proof of concept on the use of DLT for digital assets and sustainability-linked bonds. Deutsche Bank, 2021. www.db.com/news/detail/20210518 -deutsche-bank-and-singapore-fintech-stacs-complete-bond-in-a-box-proof-of-concept-on-the-use-of-dlt-for-digital-assets-and-sustainability-linked-bonds (archived at https://perma.cc/U6AK-EHAY).

15 PayPal Newsroom. PayPal users can now transfer, send, and receive Bitcoin, Ethereum, Bitcoin Cash, and Litecoin, 7 June 2022. newsroom.paypal-corp. com/2022-06-07-PayPal-Users-Can-Now-Transfer-Send-and-Receive-Bitcoin-Ethereum-Bitcoin-Cash-and-Litecoin (archived at https://perma.cc/ RL2P-SLUB).

16 D Ashmore. What is PayPal USD? Forbes Advisor, 2022. www.forbes.com/ advisor/investing/cryptocurrency/what-is-paypal-usd/ (archived at https:// perma.cc/WQW3-PTBE).

17 F Ostmann and C Dorobantu. AI in financial services, The Alan Turing Institute, 11 June 2021. doi.org/10.5281/zenodo.4916041 (archived at https:// perma.cc/J9W6-HJAW).

18 R Kalifa (2021). *The Kalifa Review of UK FinTech*. London: HM Treasury. www.gov.uk/government/publications/the-kalifa-review-of-uk-fintech (archived at https://perma.cc/HLZ9-9BSQ).

19 The Global City. The UK: Innovation hub for fintech, *The Global City*, 2022. www.theglobalcity.uk/PositiveWebsite/media/research-downloads/Col_ Fintech_Final-with-updated-icon.pdf (archived at https://perma.cc/ RUM4-H3M5).

20 Innovate Finance – The voice of Global FinTech. Fintech Investment Landscape 2022, 2022. www.innovatefinance.com/capital/fintech-investment-landscape-2022/ (archived at https://perma.cc/R8B9-4CVH).

21 G Hwa. Eight ways FinTech adoption remains on the rise. EY, 2019. www. ey.com/en_uk/financial-services/eight-ways-fintech-adoption-remains-on-the-rise (archived at https://perma.cc/E3DB-TEQK).

2

The role of regulation

CHAPTER SUMMARY

- The description and theory of regulation
- Market-wide risks and the struggle to balance risk and innovation
- Standard setting: rules and principles
- The link between regulation and good risk management and why it matters to your business

To allow us to understand how to apply regulation to a business like fintech, it's important to understand why regulation exists and how it serves to help you, while achieving economy-wide objectives that governments and policymakers hold at the heart of their activities. A widely accepted definition of regulation is 'the intentional use of authority to affect behaviour of a different party according to a set of standards, involving instruments of information gathering and behaviour modifications'.[1]

This is a fairly intuitive description of regulation as regulation impacts all parts of our lives. There is regulation to keep us safe when travelling (transport regulators), regulation that keeps energy prices reasonable (energy caps), and regulation that protects consumers when interacting with merchants (consumer protection laws). We can also see that with social media and access to information becoming more immediate and widely shared than ever before, the expectation of what regulation does for society is changing. There is a better understanding of how it helps consumers and an expectation that regulators will help when things go wrong. There is a heightened awareness of what is regulated and why. And there are new expectations from governments and from consumers to provide further protections on food safety, availability of electricity and gas supply, education standards, safety of medicines and clean air and water. These are simple but important examples of the changing nature of regulation. In financial services, regulators' expectation is that products are fair, clear, of good value and offer choice to consumers. In this book, I aim to highlight the regulation of financial services and particularly those that impact fintech to give an explanation as to why regulation is here, and a balanced account of how to interact with and implement regulation within a fintech's business.

Regulation theory

Four broad areas of regulation have emerged which impact the way in which regulators consider their duties.

Economic regulation came into its own with the deregulation of infrastructure industries such as water, gas, railway and financial market infrastructure such as payment systems. Large infrastructures such as these are not subject to competition in the same way as other market participants due to barriers to entry being quite high. The cost of setting such infrastructures is prohibitive. Therefore, economic regulation deals with pricing, structure, investment and output. In many countries some of these infrastructures can be quite old and the lack of incentive for modernizing and innovating has become evident. Therefore, more recently, there is an expectation in many countries with ageing infrastructures that embedding innovation and new ideas into the strategy of the infrastructure provider (being private of public sector providers) is necessary. An example of this in financial services is the need to upgrade payments infrastructure. We see the efforts to modernize payments infrastructure and ensure it remains current in all countries around the world.

Competition and Merger Laws are regulations that provide a framework for laws around cartels, collusion, monopolies, mergers and joint ventures that give the new entities excessive market power. Countries around the world typically have a competition authority that looks at these issues. In the UK, this is the Competition and Markets Authority (CMA), in Australia it is the Australian Competition and Consumer Commission (ACCC) and in the US it is Federal Trade Commission (FTC).

The **legal system** is the basis within which regulation exists: the rules, standards and structures that exist to ensure regulation is adhered to. It includes a legislative framework under which all regulation must be followed from competition laws mentioned above, to consumer protection laws and implementing regulatory expectations within the business. It also offers a framework for enforcement when rules are not followed or unfavourable outcomes occur. Understanding regulation through the legal system, requires understanding how laws and structures apply and how effective they are in delivering the outcome intended.

Social regulation is there to tackle social issues such as health and safety, environmental issues, discrimination, equality and equity issues. This is not a new area of regulation; however, social regulation is becoming a lot more prominent due to the public interest in issues of equality, the environment, cost of living, socio-economic factors and more. There is pressure on regulators that have not previously considered social regulation as part of their remit, to do so.[2]

From economic and competition to social

Financial services and indeed many regulators in various industries are seeing pressure to consider areas such as vulnerability, financial inclusion, environmental issues and social responsibility which they may not have considered before. In the UK, financial regulators do consider financial inclusion a government policy matter. Ofwat, the UK's water regulator, which previously looked at pure economic regulation, now places obligations on the conduct of water suppliers to ensure good outcomes for consumers. A full end-to-end view of the service and where the points of vulnerability are across the entire value chain is the approach utility regulators such as Ofwat must consider. Consumer protection has become at the forefront of the regulatory agenda in the UK.

For example, the Financial Conduct Authority (FCA), the UK's financial services regulator, issues a periodic financial lives survey that assesses the concerns of the UK adult population when it comes to financial services.[3] It focuses on areas of vulnerability, affordability and financial health. It considers the level of anxiety among consumers to meet their financial obligations and forms a barometer for consumer and SME financial health in the UK. The survey allows the FCA to add or track questions that are important for them to consider in a changing environment with changing expectations on how they regulate. Environmental issues, green financing, diversity and inclusion are also areas of focus for regulators across the UK and many countries around the world. With financial services, and related to the discussion I've outlined so far, the basis for regulation is ensuring markets are efficient and market failure is addressed.

The key reasons for market failure are:

a. Market power such as monopolies, cartels or oligopolies.[4]

b. Externalities where the operations of one entity impose losses (or benefits) onto another. For example, a production company disposing its waste in waterways is an externality that, if not regulated, can cause consumer health harms and market failure to other entities.

c. Free riding. Usually in relation to public goods. If public goods (such as a financial market infrastructure), cannot be paid for by all users, this leads to the concept of free riding by those using the service but not paying for it. If the provider of the public good is not collecting full and due payments, they won't have the ability to provide the optimal outcomes.

d. Asymmetry of information where both parties to the transaction don't have the same information therefore decisions are not made with equal information on both sides. This is a typical case in insurance where asymmetry of information gives rise to moral hazard thus risky behaviour, knowing that one is insured, cannot be priced or measured. In recent years, push payment fraud compensation has suggested that a default compensation can give rise to moral hazard, where consumers may not take the same due care if they know they will be compensated in each case.

In the last few years an additional focus of wealth distribution, fairness, equity and justice has started to emerge. Public interest in these matters has grown driven by issues such as cost of living, income inequality, financial inclusion, and racial and gender equality. Financial regulators consider everything we have discussed so far and their objectives are centred on market stability, consumer protection, competition and systemic risk management. The last point, risk management, is a key focus for this book.

The topic of risk is quite fluid. For example, if we consider asymmetry of information in the mortgage market, this can lead to unfair pricing which in turn offers worse outcomes for consumers and can cause harm in times of difficulty. Financial regulators talk about mitigating the risk of unfair pricing practices, or lower choice to consumers. The language used and the interpretation of the role of regulation is an important consideration here because public opinion matters.

Regulators look at risks in the market. All the various theories outlined so far of why regulations exist are, arguably, due to risks. The risk of anti-competitive behaviour, asymmetry of information, lack of innovation in public infrastructure or a weak legal system all lead to worse consumer outcomes and markets that don't function properly. Regulators look at how to mitigate these risks and what standards, rules and approaches they must take to mitigate the risk or deal with it when it crystallizes. As mentioned above, risk and how it manifests itself in society, how government, industry and consumers perceive risks, interpret them and their attitude towards them all play an important role in how regulators organize themselves.

Market risk and regulation

Risk, on its own, has its own set of literature and we will only touch the surface to allow us to understand that when regulators look to mitigate some of these risks, the tools available to them are setting standards, actively supervising in some cases and enforcement in most cases. Therefore, the role the regulator plays is immediately connected to the attitude of firms to their obligations to comply and adhere to these standards.

Society's perception of risk here is an important consideration. Think about how the world dealt with Covid and the various decisions made by governments around the world. There was an imminent threat. The majority of the population agreed it was a risk that must be dealt with and looked to governments and policymakers to do what was needed. I am deliberately ignoring the nuance of the circumstances, the public discourse and outcomes from those decisions. I'm merely illustrating an obvious threat and the public's attitude towards it. The public by and large agreed to lockdowns and adhered to them. Contrast that with drownings at the beach. While fatal, the public would not agree with a decision to fence off all beaches! and this will not be an acceptable policy choice.

How much risk should we allow while innovating?

In the context of innovation and fintech, regulation focuses on mitigating risks that arise from technologies developing in a way that will give rise to many of the market failures above or harms to consumers. They also focus on the traditional financial services risks that apply.

Let me take a small detour here. The balance of how much regulation is a wide discussion. Obviously, there are two sides to the debate particularly around the role of regulation in nascent innovations and technologies. On one hand, it could be seen as red tape and bureaucracy particularly considering the cost of regulation or the regulatory burden. Those on this side of the debate argue that regulation can stifle innovation where novel ideas are being tested. At the same time, they face the expectation that they must adhere to regulation that has been in place for decades and is suitable for older technologies and the traditional market set up of financial services. They also argue that the cost to simply assess their compliance with current rules for small start-ups and entrepreneurs is prohibitive when the business needs to spend its very limited resources elsewhere.

The other side of the debate argues that regulators can be an enabler of innovation. Where regulators and policymakers identify markets not functioning well, they can intervene with rules and directives to address the market weakness and in turn encourage firms to find innovative new ideas to serve the market. An example has been the growth of open banking, which is giving rise to the concept of open data around the world. It started in the UK with a competition remedy brought on by a regulator. The Competition and Markets Authority identified that consumers in the UK were not getting the best deal on their savings yet were still not switching between providers.[5] This gave rise to the open banking initiative which allowed third-party providers to access various sets of account data held with the largest banks in the UK to allow these third-party providers to identify better deals and offer new products and services to consumers. We will discuss open banking in this book in greater detail as we go along, as it has been an initiative that governments and regulators around the world are adopting. It is also interesting that firms can see the value in this and in some markets such as the US, open banking has been a market-led initiative.

The challenge of an ecosystem is always to get right the balance of new innovations and managing the risks they pose. Visa highlights this as an important area to consider for the regulators and industry to come together to solve. Chapter 10 highlights more of Visa's fintech perspective. It is not an easy task, and it is one that needs all participants to engage to get the right outcomes. This book is not about proving one theory over the other. Instead, it is designed to help you navigate some of these dynamics that sometimes seem contradictory.

Risks in financial services

Financial services risks are much more nuanced than physical risks. When harm occurs, it can be damaging to the individual and if that harm is widespread, it can impact market integrity and confidence. In the past some of these harms were not always visible. The rise of social media and the ability for consumers to instantly receive information has meant that our perception of risks that cause consumer harm has significantly changed.

As an example, fraudulent activity is a harm to society, not only from the obvious angle of an individual losing their life savings and having their livelihoods taken away which then leads to all manner of physical and mental harm. Often fraudulent activity involves illicit activity, drug smuggling, human trafficking and terrorist financing. There has always been a focus on making the financial systems in the UK and indeed many countries around the world a hostile environment for scammers and financial criminals. A reasonable duty of care placed on consumers is also expected which is why raising awareness has been an important part of how to combat fraud. This involves equipping consumers with the knowledge to take the right precautions, follow all the processes their bank has asked of them and take care when making transactions. Often, on the basis of these questions, consumers will have a degree of protection and will be offered compensation or recourse.

In the last few years there has been a debate about push payment fraud in the UK. Regulators have encouraged a solution where those who have been victims of push payment fraud receive compensation. In the past no compensation would have been offered.[6] Naturally, this attracted a lot of differing views from commercial organizations, consumer groups, the government and regulators. Fintech firms also had an important role to play in this debate. As smaller entities with more nimble and technology-based processes, often with limited resources, the provisioning for such compensation has been a concern.

I've included this example so as to come back to it at later stage to discuss how the assessment and mitigation of industry-wide risks must be understood by individual fintech firms. I will explain how this has an impact on the fintech and its decisions, recourse allocation and strategic planning. I also don't want to give a perception that risks are only selected and assessed on the basis of public opinion. Scientific research, empirical evidence, market studies are all key inputs but there is no doubt that public opinion and perceptions of risks are important. This landscape is dynamic and changing.

In a general sense, regulators will consider whether a precautionary approach is required, whether there is enough resilience in the system to deal with the risk and what the cost benefit analysis of mitigating the risk is. In risk management terms, what is the residual risk? And how do regulators judge what is enough safety for the market and consumers? This is an incredibly difficult dilemma for regulators, and it is often the subject of debate. It links directly to the question of whether regulators are helping the market or stifling it.

How to identify harm

As we said previously, regulators test where there are risks and where those risks lead to harm. This is a very broad term and while not an exhaustive list, some of the key categories of harm include meeting consumer needs, the quality and pricing of the product, the customer journey and the service standards offered through the customer life cycle, the impact on market integrity and consumer confidence and more broadly wider effects on society as shown in Table 2.1.[7]

TABLE 2.1 Categories of harm

Key categories of harm	Examples
Meeting customer needs	The design of the product excludes consumers inappropriately, and aggressive growth targets neglect consumer needs over profitability.
Quality and price	Fees are excessive and the quality of product not commensurate with its price.
Sales and service standards	Sales approach is not appropriate (pressure selling). Services standards drop once the customer is onboard.
Market integrity and confidence	Market-wide outages cause loses of confidence in the financial system.
Wider effects on society	Financial crime and money laundering controls occur.

Of course, once regulators have identified and assessed a risk, they will look to set standards, change behaviour and collect information for monitoring purposes.[8] These tend to be the activities that are familiar to us and that regulators take to affect the outcomes they wish to see.

Standards, behaviour and data

Setting standards is about giving direction to the market on what the expectations are and the reason behind them. Standard setting, at a crude level, takes the form of rules or principles. This is a key concept that we will return to when we discuss the new Consumer Duty in the UK.[9]

Standard setting, in the case of financial services, gives firms an idea of how the regulator wants to see firm behaviours change to achieve the outcome desired. Firms must show their intention to follow the rules with evidence at the point of seeking their licence, and then during their operations as they are supervised. Of course, then there might be enforcement, which is a deterrent and comes into effect when it is proven that a firm has not shown the behaviour desired by the standard.

Information gathering is important for the regulators to assess that the standard is being implemented and has the desired outcome. Information gathering at its most basic is the regulatory returns that most firms need to submit on a regular basis. It can be regular periodic pieces of data or can be ad hoc or project specific information.

In the UK, the Financial Services and Markets Act 2000 (FSMA) is the basis for the standards that are set by regulators and govern how a firm must operate. Compliance with the Act, as it relates to a firm's type of business, is an obligation and non-compliance can lead to enforcement. Firms under the Act are required to deal with the regulator in an honest, open and transparent way and submit regular information via 'regulatory returns' on time and at high quality. Even at this very basic level of expectation, submitting returns on time and with high quality, can have a positive impact on a firm's business and its relationship with the regulator. Most fintech firms fall under FSMA. Payments firms fall under the Payments Services Regulations and e-money firms under the UK's e-money regulations. Both have strong links and similarities with FSMA.

A similar approach is taken in almost every country, with regulatory regimes looking to mitigate the risks that these business models bring with them. The UK has been looked at as a strong example of quality regulation and many of its regulations have been used as a basis or guide in other countries. This a key reason this book uses the UK as an anchor, but we will reference nuances in other countries where applicable.

It is worth noting that some firms may not be directly regulated but conduct business via a sponsored relationship with a regulated entity. This is very common in payments firms with firms acting as agents or distributors. While the obligations fall on the regulated firm to oversee it's sponsored agents or distributors, it is important that these agents understand these requirements and the spirit in which they are intended to ensure a healthy ecosystem.

Minimum standards or Threshold Conditions in the UK

At a very basic level, to simply enter the financial service industry and be able to operate, firms must meet what are called Threshold Conditions. For payment firms and e-money firms, these are called Conditions for Authorization.

Threshold Conditions are standards. They are the minimum and most basic standards that a firm must meet to obtain an authorization and to continue to operate. Meeting Threshold Conditions will grant the fintech a licence to trade as a financial services firm. The fintech must continue to meet Threshold Conditions throughout the life of the organization to retain its licence to operate and regulators will continue to assess that the firm meets these conditions. So at a basic level, financial regulators in the UK assess market-wide risks, select the areas of minimum standards that they need to set for firms to operate in the sector, obtain information to assess if firms are adhering to these standards and use regulatory tools in the case of breaches or near breaches.

Below are the Threshold Conditions that apply in the UK. You will find that each regulator in financial services will have a similar set of standards. There will be some variation and the focus may slightly vary, but in the main, these are the conditions that are key for all financials services to meet.

The Prudential Regulation Authority's (the UK's prudential regulator for banks, large insurers and large investment companies) Statutory Threshold Conditions for banks are:

- Legal status: Deposit-takers must be a body corporate or partnership.
- Location of offices: A UK incorporated corporate body must maintain its head offices and, if one exists, its registered office in the United Kingdom.
- Prudent conduct of business: The applicant must conduct its business in a prudent matter, which includes having appropriate financial and non-financial resources.
- Suitability: The applicant must satisfy the PRA that it is a 'fit and proper' person with regard to all circumstances to conduct a regulated activity.
- Effective supervision: The applicant must be capable of being effectively supervised by the PRA.

The FCA's Threshold Conditions for banks are:

- Appropriate non-financial resources: The firm's non-financial resources must be appropriate in relation to the regulated activities it seeks to carry on and keeping in mind the FCA's operational objectives.
- Suitability: The firm must be a fit and proper person. The applicant firm's management must have adequate skills and experience and act with integrity (fitness and propriety). The firm must have appropriate policies and procedures in place and the firm appropriately manages conflicts of interest.
- Business model: The firm's strategy for doing business is suitable for a person carrying on the regulated activities it undertakes or seeks to carry on and does not pose a risk to the FCA's objectives.
- Effective supervision: The firm must be capable of being effectively supervised by the FCA.

In addition, in the UK most firms regulated under FSMA are subject to the Senior Managers and Certification Regime (SM&CR). This falls broadly under 'Suitability'.

For completeness, the Conditions for Authorization which are solely assessed by the FCA are:

- Corporate and activity requirements: These are of similar nature to the legal status and location of offices requirements under the Threshold Conditions above.

- Governance, risk management and internal controls: This is a critical area of assessment in the case of payment and e-money firms given their business model holds and moves customer funds but is not subject to the same requirements of a 'Bank'. (We are using the regulatory technocratic definition of Bank in this case given they are subject to higher thresholds of capital, liquidity, operational and senior management requirements.) It covers financial resources such as capital, liquidity and financial management requirements and non-financial resources such as systems and controls, governance frameworks and wind-down plans.

- Personnel requirements: These are similar to the fit and proper test above and ensure that persons involved are qualified and are of good repute.

- Close links: This relates to a situation where the firm is part of a larger group. The firm must make sure there are no conditions that will hinder the regulator's ability to supervise the firm and is closely related to effective supervision.

- Business plan: This requirement requires the firm to have a sound business plan in place that describes its activities and business model. It must demonstrate the provision of its own funds to operate in a sound and safe way. This is particularly important to demonstrate given that most payments firms will deal with and move customer funds.

- Safeguarding: This has been an important topic in recent years where firms must safeguard customer funds appropriate in separate accounts without co-mingling with their own funds and demonstrate that the systems of keeping, moving and reconciling funds is sound and effective.

- Anti-money laundering: These requirements mean that firms must comply with the money laundering regulations. This is explicitly called out due to the nature of a payments business model and its impact in a payments chain.

On closer inspection we can see that many of these areas overlap and the outcomes these rules and standards are looking to achieve are all the same. If we inspect many other requirements by regulators around the world, we will see that they are very similar, only differing with some of the nuances or the exemptions that may be granted from time to time. Table 2.2 summarizes the similarities between the UK's Threshold Conditions and Conditions for Authorization.

We can see similarities across the regimes but we can also see similarities in overall regulation of financial services round the world. In fact, in Chapter 9 we will explore those similarities and the drive of

TABLE 2.2 Threshold Conditions and Conditions for Authorization

FSMA dual regulated (PRA and FCA)	FSMA solo regulated (FCA)	Payments and e-Money firm (FCA)
• Legal Status		
• Location of office	• Location of office	• Corporate and activity (location)
• Prudent conduct of business	• Appropriate financial and non-financial resources	• Governance, risk management and internal controls.
• Appropriate non-financial resources		• Capital requirements
• Suitability	• Suitability	• Personnel requirements
• Effective supervision	• Effective supervision	• Close links
• Business model	• Business model	• Business plan requirements
		• MLR requirements
		• Safeguarding of customer funds
		• Professional Indemnity Insurance for Payment Initiation Service or Account Initiation Service providers

global regulator bodies for consistency across topics and emerging technologies that are cross-border in nature.

Regulation requirements overlap with risk management

In this book, we demonstrate how there is a lot of overlap between the fintech's regulatory obligations, its strategy and an enterprise-wide risk management framework.

Let's start with **the business model** requirement. This condition will assess how an organization develops and delivers its products. Does it offer good outcomes to the target market and how does it add value? The assessment necessarily looks at the product description and how the product has been developed, sales incentives, revenue model, the target market it is designed for, growth plan and end-to-end customer life cycle.

The firm will have to describe how it has thought of the value it is bringing to the market. Does its competitive advantage offer a unique selling point that meets a need for consumers? Is it priced fairly? Are third parties used and how are they incentivized? What are the marketing tools and selling techniques and are they fair and not putting pressure consumers?

The **suitability** condition requires firms to be fit and proper. This includes the people it hires in key roles across the organization being qualified and of good repute, that its links and connections with other organizations including parent and affiliates are clear and transparent, and that it is able to deliver on its commitment to its customers, suppliers and regulators.

This lends itself to a good strategy and risk management framework. Attracting talent, appropriate skills and qualifications in key roles is good people management. Managing relationships with parent and affiliates mitigates any legal and regulatory risks. In order to operate effectively, firms must manage strategic and reputational risks.

Appropriate resources: This is probably one of the most confusing and debatable areas of the standards set by regulators. It asks firms to decide appropriate financial and non-financial resources and think about their risk and how they mitigate these risks in a proportionate manner. Under this category, there are rules that are prescriptive and set minimum standards, such as capital requirements and those that are less prescriptive such as appropriate systems and controls.

This category naturally changes as the firms goes through its various life cycles. As a start-up with very limited customers, they may be able to run Know Your Customer (KYC) processes via a spreadsheet. As the business grows, they must think of how the KYC system and process needs to change to ensure that they are meeting anti-money laundering requirements effectively.

This is also an area that firms tend to neglect as they go through their stages of growth. It is often the case that firms work hard to obtain their licence, then focus their time and resources on launching in the marketplace and gaining market share. Similarly, as firms start to see exponential growth, the focus is on client onboarding and there is a danger that the infrastructure that keeps the business safe, such as anti-money laundering controls get neglected. We will spend some time in the next chapters referring to what this might look like in those stages from start-up to maturity.

A word on culture

Since the financial crisis in 2008, there has been a focus on the culture of organizations in financial services and a drive to transform cultures. Culture has been widely considered as the root cause of many issues and failings by financial services firms. The FCA defines culture as '… the habitual behaviours and mindsets that characterize an organization.'[10]

If culture is a set of behaviours, it clearly has an impact on people's actions and decisions which can deliver good or bad outcomes. Therefore, driving right behaviours that will contribute to a healthy conduct culture is key to ensuring the right outcome for markets and avoid the mistakes of the last financial crisis. In the UK, standards have been set around culture and individual accountability in the organization with the FCA's five conduct rules and the senior manager and certification regime.

The five conduct rules are intuitive: acting with integrity, acting with due care and diligence, being open and cooperative with the regulator, paying due regard to the interest of customers and treating them fairly and observing proper standards of market conduct.[11]

But is culture the role of the regulator to set standards and enforce? It is an area that cannot be measured, but plays an important part of the strategy of the organization. If an organization's culture is to delight consumers, then this drives a particular behaviour. If it is to maximize profits only, it drives another. One particular fintech that became a credible challenger organization describes how being a digital bank means that they have a human-based customer service centre. They argue that the reason a customer phones in is because the technology has failed. They want to understand why and want to fix it to make the digital journey better. That is living their culture.

It doesn't matter what stage a fintech is in the growth cycle. Culture matters. As a fintech, from start-up to scale-up stages, the culture may change. A fintech may have a very nimble, 'everyone mucks in', long hours to get things done culture in the early stages. As they expand, bring on more staff and grow their client base, behaviours that served them well in a start-up stage may no longer give the same results. We will talk about culture at length and some of the challenges firms and CEOs of fintechs go through as they journey through the growth stages.

Culture isn't tackled on an organization level alone. Industry-wide cultures exist and each participant plays a role. Fintechs are entrepreneurial organizations by nature and there is a perception that the culture of a fintech is one of testing new ideas within a loose control framework. This was not helped with large tech giants, of whom fintechs in many ways looked up to, boldly encouraging staff to 'move fast and break things'.

There is something about industrial culture that usually is connected to its reputation. A move fast, break-things industry, which has been largely associated with innovative fintechs, may not have the same level of trust as others. Banks, clunky and old, are trusted to hold our money. This is an area that new innovative fintech firms will have to respond to as they set up and grow their operations.

The principles of culture are the same no matter the size and nature of the organization. The four key drivers of culture are purpose, leadership, approach to rewarding and managing people and governance. We can already see the links of these drivers to the Threshold Conditions described above.

Rules, principles and outcomes

Now let's return to the concept of rules vs principles and how they affect outcomes. In its most simplistic form, rules are prescriptive and describe what needs to be done. An example is a firm must hold a specific amount of capital for the type of financial services it offers. An e-money firm must hold 2 per cent of safeguarded funds in capital or a firm must have certain key functions in the UK.[12]

A principle is much broader in description and allows for some interpretation. For example, firms must have appropriate governance frameworks in place, appropriate systems and controls or good risk management frameworks. What we have seen from the FCA recently is the move towards outcomes-based regulation with the Consumer Duty.[13] This is a new and significant piece of legislation that is a fundamental shift in how the UK regulator will assess risks, assessing them based on outcomes.

The Consumer Duty sets higher standards for firms to meet the objective of consumer protection in financial services. It requires firms to consider the needs of their customers, the target market, price and value, how consumers engage with the product or service in the various stages of their interactions and what support they enjoy when things go wrong. It is largely outcomes-based and requires firms to ensure that they are delivering good outcomes for consumers.

The outcomes are:

Market need: Products and services are designed to meet the needs of the target market. Firms must assess that this continues to be the case over time. Are there unintended consequences where the service has been consumed by a different target market and does it remain suitable?

Customer support: Are customers supported throughout the relationship with the firm? Is the support when selling better than onboarding or dealing with issues? Are there practices such as sludge and nudge that will influence how customers meet their financials needs across the life of the relationship?

> The concept of sludge and nudge comes from behavioural science and focuses on how humans respond differently if friction is introduced (sludge) or friction is removed (nudge). Depending on the situation, each can have a positive or negative outcome. For example, introducing some friction when offering a risky product to allow the customer to think about their decision is positive. Introducing friction when the customer no longer believes the product is suitable and wants to terminate it is harmful.

Consumer understanding: Does the consumer have clear information that they understand easily to make an informed decision? Is it timely and updated when things change?

Price and value: Can the firm satisfy itself that they are not charging excessively and believe that what they offer is fair value for the price? This requires the firm to look at the overall product life cycle and make an assessment on value vs price.

This may offer another layer of regulation that can be confusing. Again, we can see quite a lot of overlap with standards and rules already in place. If we consider a conduct culture at the heart of the firm's strategy and operations, we will find that when looking to adhere to one, a fintech will satisfy the other.

Firms may consider the standards as a box ticking exercise and the Consumer Duty moves the firm away from this approach. It is a judgement call and not always a straightforward one for firms. However, there are ways in which a firm can consider where it is important to decide to set higher standards rather than simply the bare minimum. This is why it is important that the spirit of regulation is embedded into the risk management framework of the organization.

Risk management and how it links to conduct regulation

Risk management is one of the key functions of an organization that should not be ignored. It is sometimes seen as a boring topic. It shouldn't be.

Risk management keeps the business and its customers safe. Risk exists everywhere around us. Good risk management means that a fintech is able to assess the environment and make strategic decisions with confidence. It supports the decision-making of an organization at its highest level. Risk taxonomies (the set of risks that apply to an organization) vary depending on the organization and the key impact areas that are important for its survival and operation. In the case of a fintech, a risk taxonomy that they may wish to consider could include the following.

Financial risk management means that a firm can continue to operate as a viable entity, and it has adequate financial resources. This a familiar requirement for a regulated entity. It is a fundamental component of any risk management strategy for obvious reasons. No firm can operate without financial resources. Understanding the key financial metrics from capital and liquidity to various financial ratios applicable to the business and a strong cash flow forecasting and budgeting framework all supported by an accurate and frequent reporting cycle are crucial components to good financial management.

Operational risk management is about ensuring firms continue to offer their services within what it considered to be an acceptable level with minimal disruption. Examples of operational risk management include minimal outages and disruption to services, having the right systems and controls, a framework for escalation and a business continuity plan. This is another requirement under the adequate non-financial resources as shown in Table 2.2.

The FCA and the PRA outline expectations of regulated entities in relation to operational resilience.[14] The framework they set out focuses on key services that if disrupted, will disrupt the functioning of the business. It requires firms to map out those business services and decide the minimum resource and focus needed to keep it operating. It asks firms how they identify breaches and what the communication strategy is until resolved (internally and externally). This sits together with how an organization ensures that its disaster recovery is working well and within tolerance levels.

These rules are applicable to payments firms, insurance firms, banks and building societies, investment firms designated by the PRA and recognized investment exchanges.

Cybersecurity is key for any risk taxonomy, although we may consider that it sits under operational risk management. Every organization may treat it differently, but the importance of cybersecurity and data protection is coming to the fore in a digital economy like never before. We have already spoken about cybercrime topping the list of risks globally for a number of years.

In the UK, there are a number of key regulations under which cybersecurity falls. Primarily the general data protection regulation, otherwise known as GDPR, the Data Protection Act and the Security of Network and Information Systems Directive which are all market-wide. We will focus on the PRA and FCA requirements placed on financial services firms in relation to cybersecurity.[15]

It is recognized that cyber threat is increasing and dynamic, and firms must be on alert at all times. Some basic areas of focus include the following.

- **Identity and access management:** Having strong and unique password hygiene across systems and staff accounts at the very basic level is a requirement. Ensuring that policies are effective in protecting the organization from hackers gaining access to vital systems and causing significant disruption and harm to the organization, its staff and its customers is also needed.

- Encryption and spotting anomalies in the fintech's environment should be a focus by having the right level of monitoring and detection. Spotting phishing and strong password hygiene can support the fintech from ransomware attacks. Monitoring and detection tools can also support against data loss and data breaches internally and externally. Inappropriate access rights or weak controls on the storage and exchange of data can cause data breaches that can be costly to the organization.

- Having an overall strong grasp of the risks across the entire supply chain is key. How do third parties and outsourcing partners play their role in ensuring a chain is resilient to cyber-attacks? If you are a fintech providing these outsourcing solutions, how do you ensure that you are not creating a weak link or an area of vulnerability in the chain.

Closely linked to managing cyber threats is to test back up and recovery processes on a regular basis to ensure that they work quickly and securely when they are needed. Fundamentally, having a culture that keeps the organization safe is essential. Strong policies around data and cybersecurity are important, but more crucially, the entire organization should recognize of the importance of these policies. It only takes one weak link for an attack to take hold.

It is worth noting that there are various credentials and certifications that firms can seek to support their cybersecurity practices. A fintech in start-up or scale-up stage can make a decision to become accredited; however, larger financial institutions will be expected to gain certification and demonstrate a reliable and strong operational and cyber-resilience environment. We will go through these as we follow the life cycle stages of a fintech in this book.

People risk: Is about having the right skillset in the right places commensurate with the business need. Shortage of talent has been a topic of conversation in the fintech space recently and is seen as a global phenomenon. We also see that fintechs don't automatically think of risk management or compliance skills as necessary ones. The reality is that a fintech will need different types of skills and talent as they go through their life cycle and we will cover some of these later in the book. This also connects with the suitability requirements we outlined above.

Reputational risk: This bites when firms don't deliver the service promised to customers, when customer needs aren't being met or there are sludge and nudge practices that are harmful. When outages occur or when their systems and controls have not prevented financial crime and money laundering, there is also a serious reputational risk.

Legal and Regulatory risk: Legal risk is about ensuring that a firm conducts itself according to the law. Regulatory and legal risks are connected and observing rules and regulations is a legal requirement in many cases. There are many grey areas within regulation where guidance and outcomes-based regulation may give more scope for interpretation. Some taxonomies separate these two.

Credit risk: This is one of the more familiar risks and generally, financial services firms are well versed in it. It is about the credit worthiness of the customers and partners the fintech serves or works with. Credit risk generally relates to all parties connected with the fintech and their financial viability and ability to allow the fintech to continue its operations.

In all cases when we look at regulatory requirements, the expectations placed on firms fall within the risk management taxonomy outlined here. I want to make that point again as we will see time and time again how risk management will lend itself to meeting regulatory obligations and vice versa. How firms deal with regulatory requirements will change depending on the stage of their life cycle, a point we will make in the various chapters of this book.

Environmental, Social and Governance: There has been much attention on ESG, rightly, in the past few years. Environmental issues are taking centre stage and financial services is seen as an important partner in supporting the economy and society to move to a more sustainable future. Social issues around diversity and inclusion are also gaining momentum. There is a lot written on this matter and much of the expectations are around creating transparency and trust in labelling and reporting green investments, or declaring an organization's own sustainability goals, as well as diversity and inclusion programmes, for the most senior levels across the organization. It is an emerging topic and we will cover some of it as it relates to the various life cycle of a fintech later in the book.

Governance is a fundamental function in an organization and getting governance right ensures the fintech is steering itself in the right direction.

The Chartered Governance Institute, UK and Ireland defines governance as *'a system that provides a framework for managing organisations. It identifies who can make decisions, who has the authority to act on behalf of the organisation and who is accountable for how an organisation and its people behave and perform.*[16]

Governance frameworks, when implemented well, keep the organization safe, ensure it operates legally and responsibly for effective outcomes for its consumers, staff and other stakeholders. It also ensures the right oversight and controls are in place and the right decisions are made at the right levels. It provides a framework for accountability not too disconnected from the senior manager and certification regime.

The overlap is real

The point here is that there is a lot of overlap between good risk management practices and meeting the regulatory obligations. I intended to draw on these overlaps to demonstrate how a strong risk management culture that serves the business well also lends itself to a good conduct culture. We call financial services an ecosystem for a reason. Each participant has a role to play and if it is played the right way, we get the outcome that supports a strong sector and in turn a strong economy. One weak party to the chain can cause quite a lot of damage in a small space of time.

An example we have seen recently is the failure of some of US banks. Silicon Valley Bank was what was considered a fintech-friendly digital bank. It had a large customer base of fintech and entrepreneurial businesses. It played an important role in the ecosystem. When the parent entity faced liquidity issues and declared itself insolvent, there was an ability to contain the effect in the UK market. A few points were at play here. One is that the UK entity was subject to the regulation in the UK as a standalone entity under the expectations some of which have been described in this chapter. It was considered well capitalized and well liquidated as a standalone subsidiary in the UK. The second is that the bank was the banker of many fintechs and this group of firms together with trade bodies, investors and other representatives understood the significant downstream impact that the UK subsidiary failure could have had on UK fintechs. Fintechs often find it difficult to establish banking relationships and many only had a relationship with Silicon Valley Bank UK. With no alternative options to access their bank accounts and conduct regular day-to-day activity, the risk was quite severe. At the very least, this meant firms might not be able to access working capital to pay their bills. In the end, SVB UK was acquired by HSBC following swift and intense involvement from UK regulators which guaranteed minimal disruption to its clients.

This is significant because a systemic market integrity matter might have unfolded, stemming from the many individual firms potentially being technically insolvent simply due to their inability to access their working capital. The ecosystem including regulators, government and legislators were able to avert the issue, but there are many lessons to learn.

This is a great example of how individual resilience and risk management and market-wide resilience and risk management are not mutually exclusive. Good organizations should always think of the interplay of these two things not just to meet regulatory requirements, but to ensure that they play a part in a strong and resilient sector where the benefits can be enjoyed by all.

Summary and takeaways

Regulation plays a crucial role in the economy to ensure that markets function well, market integrity is maintained and confidence in financials systems is high. A strong and resilient sector is one where all participants in the market, service providers, investors and consumers will thrive. In an increasing digital economy, the lines are blurred, and regulators are looking to ensure effective ways of maintaining consumer and investor confidence as well as market integrity and stability. At the same time, they need to allow space for fintechs to thrive.

Risk plays a crucial role in how regulators organize themselves and deliver their objectives, focusing on the biggest risks of harm and how to mitigate these. While the focus is on market risk, regulators look to change firm behaviour which collectively will deliver the right outcomes. Therefore, it falls to firms to ensure that they are engaging positively in what role they can play to manage these harms.

In thinking of the firm's obligation to meeting regulatory objectives, it is helpful to consider it in the context of its culture and risk management framework. Often these are similar and overlap.

With the spotlight on fintech increasing, and the ambition for what it can achieve, getting it wrong is not an option. An understanding of the benefit of risk management and regulation to support the fintech ecosystem is fundamental to a sector that is a strong, thriving, sets high standards and promotes confidence. While at face value this is agreed, the practical implementation of this philosophy is a subject of debate and, simply, the debate needs to be had. Key questions include who is a fintech, how does regulation apply to a fintech in the various stages of its life cycle, how do we apply proportionate regulation and what does it mean for other partners in the fintech space that are crucial to its success.

Areas of financial and operational resilience, cybersecurity and fighting financial crime, anti-money laundering best practices, information security, privacy and the concept of embedded finance are areas that need to be addressed at a firm level and a wider market level. The cost of getting it wrong is not just one firm closing its doors. Disruptive failure, financial crime and cyber threats, money laundering and privacy breaches not only harm the firm, they have a spillover effect to the market and loss of consumer and investor confidence. A thriving market is one where opportunities are there to be grasped and gained, but it is incumbent on all parties in the ecosystem to ensure its strength and stability. Everyone can benefit when the market is thriving but equally, when things go wrong, everyone loses.

The types of regulation and regulators are wide and varied. In financial services alone, we have competition regulators, conduct regulators, prudential regulators, financial stability regulators and of course, information and data protection regulators. However, when considering the reasons regulation exists, the key objectives are market stability and integrity, good competition, consumer protection and market integrity. All good reasons for regulation and the need for industry to embrace it in a way that is going to benefit a fintech's business.

Fintech is no longer confined to small entrepreneurial start-ups and founders who are innovating to disrupt the market. Fintech is becoming a mainstream phenomenon with organizations growing in size and scale, incumbents transforming to compete with these disruptors, the role of big tech entering financial services and those partnering with each other, together make up a thriving fintech ecosystem, which means innovation, transformation, new ideas and experimentation. With innovation and transformation comes risk. Enter the role of regulation and risk management.

Notes

1 J Black, N Hashimzade and G Myles (2012). *A Dictionary of Economics*. Oxford University Press.

2 HM Treasury. *Financial Inclusion Report 2021–22*. HM Treasury, London, 2022. assets.publishing.service.gov.uk/media/639c91f4d3bf7f37618b5c5d/ Financial_Inclusion_Report__002_.pdf (archived at https://perma.cc/GJ37- 5TYW).

3 Financial Conduct Authority. Financial Lives 2022 survey, Financial Conduct Authority, 2023. www.fca.org.uk/financial-lives/financial-lives-2022-survey (archived at https://perma.cc/6QNL-G6BQ).

4 J Black, N Hashimzade and G Myles (2012). *A Dictionary of Economics*. Oxford University Press.

5 Competition and Markets Authority (2016). *Retail Banking Market Investigation*. Competition and Markets Authority, London, 2016. assets. publishing.service.gov.uk/media/57ac9667e5274a0f6c00007a/retail-banking- market-investigation-full-final-report.pdf (archived at https://perma.cc/ B4N9-P6LF).

6 Payment Systems Regulator. App scams, 2023. www.psr.org.uk/our-work/ app-scams/ (archived at https://perma.cc/GF9D-4Y7Y).

7 Financial Conduct Authority. Our Strategy: 2022 to 2025, Financial Conduct Authority, London, 2022. www.fca.org.uk/publication/corporate/our- strategy-2022-25.pdf (archived at https://perma.cc/678V-M3WL).

8 M Lodge and K Wegrich (2012). *Managing Regulation: Regulatory Analysis, Politics and Policy*. Palgrave Macmillan.

9 Lodge and Wegrich. *Managing Regulation: Regulatory Analysis, Politics and Policy*.

10 Financial Conduct Authority. *Transforming Culture in Financial Services*. Financial Conduct Authority, London, 2018. www.fca.org.uk/publication/discussion/dp18-02.pdf (archived at https://perma.cc/AB24-RUSE).

11 Financial Conduct Authority. *Transforming Culture in Financial Services*. Financial Conduct Authority, London, 2018. www.fca.org.uk/publication/discussion/dp18-02.pdf (archived at https://perma.cc/6ZFA-HP3U).

12 Lodge and Wegrich. *Managing Regulation: Regulatory Analysis, Politics and Policy*.

13 Financial Conduct Authority. *A New Consumer Duty: Feedback to CP21/36 and final rules*. Financial Conduct Authority, London, 2022. www.fca.org.uk/publication/policy/ps22-9.pdf (archived at https://perma.cc/SS3Y-KTQU).

14 Financial Conduct Authority. Operational Resilience. Financial Conduct Authority, 2024. www.fca.org.uk/firms/operational-resilience (archived at https://perma.cc/P5JG-CJNN).

15 Financial Conduct Authority. *Cyber Security – industry insights*. Financial Conduct Authority, London, 2023. www.fca.org.uk/publication/research/cyber-security-industry-insights.pdf (archived at https://perma.cc/6REF-3HDU).

16 Chartered Governance Institute UK and Ireland. *Discover Governance – What is governance?* Chartered Governance Institute UK and Ireland, 2021. www.cgi.org.uk/professional-development/discover-governance/looking-to-start-a-career-in-governance/what-is-governance (archived at https://perma.cc/9MHH-HDBR).

3

Old regulation, new technologies

CHAPTER SUMMARY

- How regulators are adapting to new technologies

- How open banking has evolved, regulated and what's next

- Crypto currencies: the debate and new regulation

- Artificial intelligence, the debate and the horizon for regulation

- Regtech and suptech: technologies in the ecosystem supporting financial services

---

We have already touched on the role of regulation and some of the theory and approaches behind it. Regulation has been around for a long time. It is fair to say that absent other theories or approaches, the current approach to regulation is here to stay. However, there has been a recognition by regulators around the world that new technologies are posing challenges to how regulation works today. The general view of the regulator community, as we've discussed, is that regulation is technology agnostic. Regulation is activity-based and while it has a set of rules and principles, they tend to focus on ensuring the right outcome.

But this idea is being challenged. In fact, there are voices suggesting regulation is old and archaic, slow to adapt, backward looking. Technology is moving fast they argue, and regulators can't keep up. I tend to think this is a debate that will attract various views on both ends of the spectrum. Arguably, this is needed to drive the right action. Take crypto assets for example. Depending on the point of view, you may suggest that regulating crypto has come too late, whereas others believe that regulators have been engaging with the debate in proactive way to identify the uses, benefits and risks of the rise of digital assets.

How soon regulators need to act is an important question here. In a hypothetical world where there are unlimited resources, one would expect regulators to assess and act on emerging risks as early as they appear, even if it's simply a fad. However, we don't live in a world of unlimited resources and regulators need to make a call on where they spend their effort. The approach that many regulators around the world have been taking is to acknowledge the rise of new technologies in financial services and to understand them more via various forums including 'techsprints', research papers and partnership forums, after which they decide what action to take.

A digital economy

As we discussed in Chapter 1, technology has entered our lives on all levels. We are living in a digital economy. Governments around the world talk about new technologies and innovation impacting our lives and the need for them to grow and develop but in a safe way. The recent UK government's policy paper on digital regulation in October 2023 makes this precise point.[1] It talks about how technology and innovation are key to the prosperity of the UK, but its development must be done in a 'responsible' way that keeps in line with citizens' rights and protects society. This is an important move by the UK government. It signals the need to set an ambitious strategy for a growing digital economy but also highlight how regulation is key to its success. The paper states that quality regulation will support trust in the system, which gives companies and investors certainty and encourages consumer uptake of new products and services.

There are real and practical implications of the development of a digital economy that mean the current structure and responses to risks in the market may not be appropriate. I'll illustrate this with a few examples. The digital economy has meant that we have access to information instantly and on a wide scale. We not only get access to the news itself, we also get access to the vast array of opinions and attitudes of the general public commenting on social media platforms.

When there is a particular scam that has hits a relatively small number of consumers the focus on it in the various media outlets we have access to is greater than what we have seen before. This influences policymakers' and regulators' responses as we've seen in Chapter 2. The public attitude towards risk is one factor in the assessment of market risks.

We've illustrated the Silicon Valley Bank example in Chapter 2. It is an example of how quickly there can be a run on the bank (i.e. withdrawals happen in large amounts and at a fast pace) in an online environment given that you do not need to queue up to withdraw your money. In this scenario, the bank in question and the regulators will have hardly any time to deal with the matter before it has happened.

We've also seen lower barriers to entry due to technology and the ability to scale at speed. Many of the fintech start-ups rely on very few resources for their idea. Technology means that they can do a lot without the large infrastructure cost that traditional banks had to contend with. Data centres are housed in the cloud, services are delivered via a mobile phone and there is no need for physical premises or face to face contact with customers. A *concept* grows from a small idea to a large-scale operation in a shorter period of time using social media and online channels. Word of mouth has taken on a new meaning with the way in which many communicate in a digital world. Unicorn (a predominantly privately owned company worth at least $1bn) status is seen to be achieved within seven years, but this time can be dramatically shortened due to technology. [2] [3]

Characteristics of a digital economy

A very obvious characteristic of the digital economy is that we are creating a vast number of data sets every day. It is estimated that in 2025 we will have created 181 zetabytes of data worldwide.[4] We create them across all areas of our lives, and we see them interacting and influencing each other. That connectivity is creating more convenience, but also creates ambiguity of where accountability lies when things go wrong. How safe is our information and do consumers truly understand how their data is being used?

Of course, linked to the vast amount of data we create every day is how it's used. We have seen artificial intelligence gaining momentum at an incredible speed with very little widely understood knowledge of how it's being used and what the implications may be.

A study by a maths-loving executive at a company, Canadian Tire, that sold various automotive products alongside tyres, concluded that if you purchased felt pads, the stick-on pads that stop your furniture from scratching the floors, you will never miss a payment. Those who bought chrome skull car accessories almost certainly will eventually miss a payment. The study was covered by *The New York Times* and identifies the riskiest drinking venue in Canada and what the safest product that indicates a strong credit score is. This study was done back in 2002.[5] Today the variations to this story and the various data sets that feed into each other to seem to create trends or correlations are far greater and therefore more far reaching in impact, positive or negative.

As we create more data, the threat of cybersecurity increases. The World Economic Forum calls out digital dependencies and cyber vulnerabilities in its 2022 risk report.[6] Cyber risk has featured as a global risk for a number of years now and will likely continue to do so in the future. Given the vast quantity of data in financial services, the sensitivity of the information and the increased reliance on digital in all aspects of the sector, maintaining cybersecurity in financial services is paramount. These are only a few examples of the impact of digitization on financial services and how it has forced a different debate and approach to respond to the emerging market dynamics and risks. We will cover these in more detail in the coming chapters.

Financial services in a digital economy

What characterizes financial services in a digital economy is that all types of data sets start to interact with each other. Where does financial services stop and start? How far do the obligations on the firm go when we look at regulated and unregulated activity? There are a number of dimensions to consider here.

In financial services, activities are regulated, not whole firms. A firm may perform a number of activities, some which are defined as regulated or within the regulatory perimeter and some which are not. Firms must only provide products and services for which they have a licence, authorization or permission to do so. In addition, some firms are sponsored by a regulated entity to perform financial services on a limited basis. These, as we described previously, are agents or distributors of the product or service the regulated entity is licenced to offer.

> Note: A licence to provide products and services requires an authorization process from the financial services regulator. This is also referred to as seeking the right permissions to conduct financial services. The phrases licence, authorization and permissions, for the purposes of this book, mean the same and will be used interchangeably.

A payment institution (a type of fintech, i.e. a paytech company) is not a deposit-taking institution, therefore they should not hold our deposits. Payment institutions, however, can hold transaction funds for a reasonable period to affect transactions. E-money institutions can hold funds for customers as they relate to payments rather than savings.

An e-money firm is not a bank, therefore they are not protected by deposit insurance or the UK's financial services compensation scheme (FSCS).[7] In practice this means that if the e-money institution becomes insolvent and winds down, customers will not be able to claim funds using the national deposit insurance scheme available to those who hold funds with a bank. (A bank is any entity with banking licence which effectively allows them to take deposits and give out loans.)

There are many more examples across all parts of financial services from credit and lending to insurance and wholesale markets where this applies. There are also many exemptions, exclusions and various licences and permissions to navigate, which would need a number of volumes to cover in detail.

You can already see how existing regulation applicable to fintech today can be confusing enough for the average person. It is no doubt confusing for the fintech to navigate. However, it is important to do so to ensure that there is clarity of message to its customers on what is regulated and what is not, what they are allowed to do and what their can customers expect. Financial promotions plays a very important role here, an area we will explore further in this book.

We've covered areas of existing regulation that are applicable and arguably have been designed for fintechs that have been in operation for 10 or more years. The challenge is similar for new technologies. Crypto asset firms across the spectrum of crypto are by and large not regulated; however, many regulated entities have started to offer crypto trading alongside other regulated financial services.

The incredibly large amount of data created by humans is another important development in the direction of financial services. When open banking and PSD2 were introduced in the UK (note this was before the UK left the EU), it meant that third-party providers (TPPs) were able to access customer payment information held with banks and non-bank financial institutions in order for them to offer products and services that could help consumers from credit scoring to budget management or getting the best deal on financial products and services.[8] What we didn't anticipate is companies looking to access payment information to calculate our carbon footprint and suggest ways in which we can reduce it!

More practically, you can see how access to health data could offer an insurer the ability to price health or life insurance with less uncertainty. At the same time, it could also lock out a number of people from the insurance market. It can provide more cash flow data to your energy provider for bill management or provide data on your shopping behaviour that may create assumptions on your credit worthiness. These are new examples of regulated vs unregulated services (not always by design) where customers need to have a full understanding of what they are getting into, what the risks are and what recourse or protection, if any exists for them.

Regulation is responding

Regulators recognize the greater availability of data. The need to learn, adapt and collaborate is becoming greater. Regulators are reacting positively towards these new technologies. We may argue the speed, the governance processes, the understanding could be greater, but in the UK and many countries around the world we are not seeing a 'bury our head in the sand' attitude.

A recent theme from regulators is setting up and running tech-sprints. The UK's FCA, sometimes in partnerships with other regulators, has run numerous techsprints on open banking, open finance, crypto assets, fraud and money laundering prevention and more. The idea of a techsprint run by regulators is to help inform policy thinking and subsequent standard setting in a way that collaborates with industry.

There have also been public/private forums to inform policy thinking. The recent artificial intelligence public/private forum led by the Bank of England and the Financial Conduct Authority is an example of this.[9] It gave regulators the view that AI has benefits and risks to society and decided regulation of AI was not immediate. Since that forum, ChatGPT and the very rapid development of AI has changed the rhetoric and public view which shows the difficulty of keeping up with fast-paced technologies.

Regulators are finding that collaborating with each other is now necessary in a digital world. The way we live our lives is so interconnected that there are no longer boundaries among financial services, information security, data protection, competition and financial crime activity and this will continue to evolve. Recognizing this and to help industry players navigate the regulatory landscape, a direct response to the industry's concerns about the complexity of regulation is published by the FCA in the form of a regulatory grid. The regulatory grid outlining the various initiatives in any one year and the lead regulator for each.[10]

Digital Regulatory Cooperation Forum

A new, first of its kind, forum in the UK was also established for this same purpose. The Digital Regulatory Cooperation Forum (DRCF) was set up in 2020 by the Competition and Markets Authority (CMA), the Information Commissioner's Office (ICO), and the Office of Communication (Ofcom).[11] In 2021 the Financial Conduct Authority (FCA) joined and these four regulators look at topics that span across areas of competition, data privacy and information security, the use of online communication tools and platforms underpinning the digital world and conduct matters around these. More specifically, Ofcom was tasked to oversee the implementation of the online harms bill and a new Digital Markets Unit was established in the CMA. The forum was established to increase cooperation but crucially to coordinate and ensure a cohesive response to regulating the digital economy. It set out its key priorities of a strategic response to technology developments in industry with a focus on a joined-up approach to responding to these and finding a way to build 'shared skills and capabilities'. It also is clear on its work plan and publishes updates.

Its 2022/2023 plan of work focused on issues such as protecting children online, transparency in the use of algorithms, privacy and competition in online advertising and promoting safe and responsible innovation. How the forum develops and the impact of its work will evolve over time but there is no doubt that the interest of regulators and government to coordinate on topics where there is natural overlap in the digital world is increasing. This has been welcomed by the industry as a response to the digital economy and the need for a bigger picture approach to managing economy-wide risks. Other countries are looking to replicate the DRCF in their own jurisdictions.

Open banking, open finance, open data

In the UK, open banking is defined by Open Banking Limited as a '*simple, secure way to help you move, manage and make more of your money*'. It started as a retail banking market investigation that was launched by the Competition and Markets Authority. It is now considered a prominent catalyst for innovation and fintech.

The aim of this particular market investigation was to identify if there are any adverse effects on competition in retail markets with a focus on personal current accounts, business current accounts, overdrafts, deposits and lending including SME lending. The study resulted in observing a number of adverse effects on competition for which the CMA developed a package of remedies. In 2017, this came to be known as the 'CMA Order' or 'the Order' in the fintech circles, particularly 'Part 2 Open API Standards and Data Sharing' or open banking for short.

The order mandated the nine largest banks in the UK (known as 'the CMA 9') to allow third-party providers to access payment data for the purposes of fintechs developing more transparency, quality and variety in services to consumers to help them manage their financial affairs. The measures were developed to affect outcomes around increased engagement and participation from consumers and small businesses, making comparison of services easier and more transparent and making switching between providers easier. It also looked at overdrafts and services targeted at SMEs to improve provision for them in the UK.

An entity known as the Open Banking Implementation Entity or the 'OBIE' was established to develop the standards that will ensure the implementation of open banking will deliver the outcomes expected. There has been a lot of excitement by the remedy and in the main industry was supportive, but it was divided on detail and timing. It is a market-wide remedy and very diverse parts of the ecosystem had to find a way forward. There was a divide between the banks mandated and third parties on speed and willingness to collaborate. The cost of the implementation from funding the OBIE to changes to internal systems and developing the API common standards was a contentious point.

Things have moved on since 2017. Six of the 'CMA 9' banks have completed the implementation of the original order and the remaining three continue to do so. There are also mixed results on the effectiveness of open banking and speed at which consumer engagement or behaviour change has occurred. For example, it is not clear if bank account switching has not increased due to limited effectiveness or increased competition means that providers are matching and improving deals enticing consumers to remain.

Open banking created a new set of fintechs that needed to be regulated: Account Information Service Providers and Payment Initiation Service Providers. The most obvious benefit at the beginning were solutions offered by Account Information Service Providers or AISPs. Being able to collect payment data from multiple sources and present them to a consumer in one simple dashboard was the start of a radical transformation. TrueLayer is one of the first fintechs to develop an open banking proposition and features as a case study in Chapter 10.

Today there are an estimated 8 million users of open banking and the applications are wide and varied. Obvious applications are budget management. Apps study payment behaviour and suggest how to smooth cash flow or the best deals that can save money for consumers. Other applications include bill management apps where an alert is sent to avoid late payments thus late payment fees. There are also savings apps that look at how small amounts can be saved to reach a goal.

Payment Initiation (the other new type of fintech to emerge from open banking) started slow but has also gained traction. To complete propositions on open banking, payments need to be developed and be part of the solution. This will allow a smooth customer journey. If, for example, account analysis shows a need to switch or move money, the actual movement of money is part of the proposition and needs to be done quickly.

What's next for open banking?

There is now an effort in the UK to ensure open banking continues to develop. Its natural expansion is to move from open banking to open finance and beyond. Access to more financial information will allow for a fuller picture of our financial lives and propositions that can be more helpful for how we manage and move money.

Once the order was largely implemented, the conversation turned to the next stage of open banking. The regulators again collaborated to drive the right outcomes on the basis that industry has not driven that development without regulatory intervention. As a result, the Joint Regulatory Oversight Committee or JROC was established with the Financial Conduct Authority and the Payment Systems Regulator as co-chairs and HM Treasury and the Competition and Markets Authority, as members.

In collaboration with an industry advisory board and working groups, JROC reviewed how far open banking has come and what the requirements to unlock the next stages are. Their vision focused on three key priorities.

- Unlocking open banking payments propositions and functionality.
- Creating a sustainable footing for open banking to continue to develop.
- Creating a sustainable model that is the basis for future data sharing.

In their 2023 report, JROC specifically focus on developing Variable Recurring Payments and the design of the future entity that will take the vision of JROC forward.[12] It also outlines five themes that must be progressed in the next two years: 'Levelling up availability and performance, mitigating the risks of financial crime, ensuring effective consumer protection if something goes wrong, improving information flows to TPPs and end users, promoting additional services, using non-sweeping variable recurring payments (VRP) as a pilot'.

So how is it regulated?

Open banking is here to stay and many fintechs will develop propositions off the back of the infrastructure and access available due to this initiative which has been replicated around the world. Open banking is not only about moving money. It's about accessing data, moving it, storing it, processing it and this activity comes with risks if we have not thought carefully about how to mitigate those risks. It's important to note that some of the practical implementation created issues that were not foreseen, but UK regulators listened and tried to pivot and show a reasonable approach where it made sense. One example is the requirement around the electronic Identification, Authentication and Trust Services (eIDAS) certificate where to avoid disruption in open banking services post-Brexit, the FCA allowed other forms of acceptable identification between third-party providers and Account Service and Payment Services Providers (ASPSPs which are in most cases the banks who hold the majority of our current accounts).

Most third-party providers offering open banking solutions are authorized due to a payment activity they undertake already. No further authorization is needed for them to perform activity under open banking as long as they follow the technical, performance, security and conduct standards. In all cases, you will need to get suitable permissions from your national competent authority which in the UK is the Financial Conduct Authority.[13]

Standards are at the heart of the open banking ecosystem. Standards around the technical specifications, security and performance of the open banking Application Programming Interfaces (APIs), standards around identification and authentication of third parties looking to access information via banks, and standards around consent to allow third parties to access payment data are essential. Standards are needed to ensure consumers know when to switch access to their data on and off, understand how their data is being used, the value they receive and how data is being utilized for identity verification or transaction authentication. These are all key to mitigating the risk of new innovations in open banking. The ecosystem also looks at how to build trust in open banking and the level that will unlock consumer engagement and access to many of the services that are being developed in this space.

This is an area that will continue to grow with the UK government's focus on open finance and unlocking data sets. It might help consumers and SMEs unlock their financial potential and make their money work better for them. Open banking has been a global phenomenon and we will look further into in its international development in Chapter 9 of this book.

Crypto currencies and digital assets

The Financial Services Markets Act 2023 defines crypto assets as *'any cryptographically secured digital representation of value or contractual rights that: a. can be transferred, stored or traded electronically and b. that uses technology supporting the recording or storage of data (which may include digital ledger technology'.*[14]

Note that the Act talks about digital representation of value or contractual rights. Therefore, the focus is on digital assets not on the underlying technology. This technology is not a financial instrument and can have multiple uses, not all of them in financial services. There has been a rapid evolution of crypto in short space of time. Currencies, assets, stablecoin, non-fungible tokens (NFTs) or simply the underlying technology of blockchain offering applications such as smart contracts have all developed rapidly.

This is one of the key themes that dominate when we speak about the world of new fintech. It started on a small scale. A limited number of individuals with a server started to 'mine' Bitcoin and trade it. Currencies started to emerge such as Ethereum, Solana, Dogecoin and many others. We also saw the emergence of stablecoin which is a crypto currency is backed by a stabled asset such as fiat currency or other financial assets. We now have exchanges, trading venues, intermediaries, lending platforms and custody. It has become a very complex landscape with an extremely active market.

How did crypto in financial services start?

Crypto currencies started the defi revolution or decentralized finance. This is the idea that you don't need a central body to govern and regulate money via a centralized ledger, and that the nodes in a blockchain all hold the same ledger that gets updated simultaneously to reflect the transactions. It also claims that transactions are immutable, therefore traceable and that everyone can be a member. Exciting propositions have been suggested that can tackle things such as cross-border payments and financial inclusion to name a couple.

I don't intend to go over the history and technical details of crypto assets and digital currencies. I am keen, however, to highlight how this innovation has rocked the financial ecosystem and the various cycles it has gone through which no doubt has not yet reached stability relative to other financial products and services.

The emergence of crypto saw strong enthusiasm behind the idea for philosophical as well as practical reasons. The idea of decentralized finance was seen as rewriting the financial market infrastructure and ecosystem as we know it today, as well as creating practical solutions to practical problems. We started to see the technology develop where crypto exchanges emerged and you no longer needed an expensive server using a lot of power and technical knowledge to crack a code and mine crypto. Anyone can sign up and trade a crypto currency via a crypto exchange platform. The promotional activity and advertisements stepped up, where many people told stories of getting rich, celebrities marketed the coin and the average citizen started to use their savings to buy cryptocurrency.

Regulators and market responses

Regulators were weary and observed the emergence of this. They also warned against the volatility of the emerging coins, the fairness and transparency of the promotional activity, the complexity of the product, the anonymity of the platform users and the fact that consumers have no protection whatsoever when things go wrong. At the start of the defi revolution, there was a very divided set of views where regulators were seen as stifling innovation and not understanding this new world technology. You were either on the side of crypto or you weren't. Not many considered what the market risks were or what might happen if the market failed.

Then came the 'crypto winter' in 2022. The LUNA coin started with a value of less than $1 in 2021 and reached $116 in early 2022. It was seen as a superstar coin. A complicated structure with the US Terra coin or UST backed by LUNA on the same platform, with both pegged to the USD via a complicated algorithm, was supposed to keep it stable. An event occurred where the UST suffered a large liquidation in a short period of time. It is not clear what precisely caused this, but it resulted in LUNA flooding the market and being devalued. This wiped out an estimated $60 billion of value from the crypto market.[15]

Now, as we mentioned before, most stablecoins are backed to fiat currency, hence the word stablecoin. Even those backed by other valid financial assets may have different levels of stability depending on the risk and volatility of the asset and it is something that has to be considered.

Another high-profile collapse was FTX, a crypto trading platform that was highly leveraged and faced liquidity and solvency concerns. Having been valued at a peak of $32 billion in January 2022 and having raised $400 million from investors, it filed for Chapter 11 bankruptcy in the US in November 2022.[16] Market integrity of crypto assets came into question. This is when a more balanced view of crypto and the need to regulate it started to emerge, supported by the voices of many in the market.

Crypto regulation – where is it now?

In the UK, the government has approached regulation of cryptoasset activity on an incremental level. After an amendment to the Money Laundering Regulations (MLR) the FCA become the supervisory body for crypto exchanges and custodian wallet providers for the MLRs. In 2022, the FCA consulted on bringing cryptoasset promotions under the financial promotions regime. This was to address misleading information and cryptoasset promotions. Stablecoin backed by fiat currencies for the purposes of payments has been brought into regulation as of June 2023 when the Financial Services Market Act 2023 received royal assent. A broader cryptoasset regime is in the process of consultation by HM Treasury as covered in Table 3.1. Is it worth saying that things are moving quickly as this has now progressed since writing?

In February 2023, the UK government put out a consultation on the future regulation of crypto.[17] The approach to regulation was based on some core principles which as we mentioned previously. It is activity-based in order to consider what is a financial product and must come within the 'perimeter' of financial regulation. It also considers that the same risk should have the same regulatory outcome. I underscore the word outcome vs regulatory instrument or tool.

TABLE 3.1 HM Treasury's future financial services regulatory regime for cryptoassets (2023)

	Security tokens and other specified investments	Fiat-backed stablecoins	All other investments
Issuance	Already Regulated[1] (e.g. prospectus rules apply to security tokens)	Stablecoin legislation	Cryptoasset legislation[3] (specifically addressing admission of cryptoassets to a cryptoasset trading venue or a public offer of cryptoassets)
Payments	Already Regulated[1] (e.g. Payment Services Regulations apply to e-Money)	Stablecoin legislation (+ regulated as systemic DSA if meets criteria)[2]	Not applicable (could theoretically be regulated as systemic DSA if meets criteria)[2]
Exchange Trading	Already Regulated[1] (e.g. MTF / OTF rules apply to security tokens)	Cryptoasset legislation[3]	
Custody	Already regulated[1] (e.g. CASS rules apply to security tokens)	Stablecoin legislation	Cryptoasset legislation[3]

1. Unless specific exceptions / exemptions apply.
2. Any systemic Digital Settlement Asset payment system or service provider would be subject to regulation by the Bank of England and Payment Services Regulator (PSR).
3. HM Treasury Consultation. Future Financial Services Regulatory Regime for Cryptoassets February 2023.
SOURCE: HM Treasury 2023.

TABLE 3.2 HM Treasury's categorization of crypto activity (2023)

Activity category	Sub activity (list is not exhaustive)
Assurance activities	• Issuance and redemption of a fiat-backed stablecoin. • Admitting a cryptoasset to a cryptoasset trading venue. • Making a public offer of a cryptoasset
Payment activities	• e.g. execution of payment transactions or remittances involving fiat-backed stablecoins

(continued)

TABLE 3.2 (Continued)

Activity category	Sub activity (list is not exhaustive)
Exchange activities	• Operating a cryptoasset trading venue which supports: (i) the exchange of cryptoassets for other cryptoassets (ii) the exchange of cryptoassets for fiat currency (iii) the exchange of cryptoassets for other assets (e.g. commodities) • Post-trade activities in cryptoassets (to the extent not already covered)
Investment and risk management activities	• Dealing in cryptoassets as principal or agent • Arranging (bringing about) deals in cryptoassets • Making arrangements with a view to transactions in cryptoassets • Advising (to the extent not already covered) on cryptoassets • Managing (to the extent not already covered) cryptoassets
Lending, borrowing and leverage activities	• Operating a cryptoasset lending platform
Safeguarding and /or administration (custody) activities	• Safeguarding or safeguarding and administering (or arranging the same) a fiat-backed stablecoin and/or means of access to the fiat-backed stablecoin18 (custody) • Safeguarding or safeguarding and administering (or arranging the same) a cryptoasset other than a fiat-backed stablecoin and/or means of access to the cryptoasset19 (custody)
Validation and governance activities	• Mining or validating transactions, or operating a node on a blockchain • Using cryptoassets to run a validator node infrastructure on a proof-of-stake (PoS) network (layer 1 staking)

Regulation should be focused and proportionate and the regime must be agile and flexible.

The consultation focuses on a variety of different crypto activities as shown in Table 3.2.

It also calls for evidence on several other items which includes decentralized finance, advice and portfolio management and mining and validation and considers sustainability aspects. Of note, and given the LUNA example above, the government has deemed 'so-called algorithmic stablecoins' not the same as stablecoins backed by fiat currencies. These should be subject to the same regulation applicable to unbacked cryptoassets.

Throughout the consultation, the UK government has focused on areas where they see risk arising in a traditional sense such as money laundering concerns, financial promotions, market abuse and stablecoins when used as a medium of payments. It also identifies that any firm providing services to a UK customer is in scope, whether the firm is incorporated inside or outside the UK.

An important question is the authorization the firms need. Authorization applies to all the four activities outlined in the paper. The firm must outline the business model and proposition, details of how they plan to operate, describe governance arrangements, risk management frameworks, operational resilience including cybersecurity and outsourcing arrangements.

The regulation also focuses on prudential requirements, consumer protection, data reporting and resolution in the case of insolvency. What will become evident over time is how this regulation will interact with the Consumer Duty. In all cases, a principle- and outcomes-based approach that will deliver good consumer outcomes will be expected. Holding the Consumer Duty at the centre of product design and delivery will be key in all cases.

These aren't new and form part of strong risk management in any organization. Financial and operational resilience as we mentioned earlier are key components of good risk management practices that ensure longevity and sustainability of the business. Good consumer outcomes build confidence in the brand and collectively the market which ensures market activity for the benefit of all, firms included.

Artificial Intelligence (AI)

Artificial intelligence is a rapidly developing emerging technology. AI is not new. We discussed the data analysis of customers' buying behaviour in a tyre store in Canada earlier in the chapter, but it has progressed to unimaginable levels today. It's another example of innovation that can bring exciting new opportunities for society yet if developed without checks and balances, will no doubt create significant harms.

The opportunities of AI

Let's start with the opportunities, noting that we may need a whole volume for the potential of what AI can offer. AI has the ability to increase productivity, a much-needed issue to be tackled in the UK and many other countries. A study in April 2023 by the National Bureau of Economic Research suggested that in the US, if over 5,000 customer support agents used an AI conversational tool, a rise in productivity of approximately 14 per cent could be achieved.[18]

In the health-care industry, there is wide belief that AI can move health care from the traditional treatment of diseases and illnesses to predicting and treating causes, thus focusing on preventative and well-being approaches. This predictive technology is what makes AI such an exciting prospect.

In financial services, the use of AI for robo advice was one of the first propositions to emerge. Many of these propositions were tested for example through the FCA Sandbox. In 2023, an FCA study of the financial advice market found that access to financial planning and advice has become prohibitive for many people due to cost.[19] AI has the potential to offer solutions at a much lower rate thus opening this market to many who have previously been locked out of it. Asset management, credit and mortgage advice and in fact any other financial product can benefit from the same. The benefits to consumers are real and tangible.

The application of predictive analysis on a large scale can have significant benefits in tackling fraud and financial crime, cyber-crime and other harms in financial markets. In fact, regulators are now considering how to use AI in their supervisory work, being able to predict and act on potential firm failure, weak systems and controls, or weak governance structures that can lead to consumer harm.

Threats of AI

Unchecked AI can have significant harms. Just as we are trying to use it for good, illicit activity, financial crime and scams are using AI in earnest and have no regard for law and regulation. Martin Lewis, a respectable financial commentator in the UK, was seen in what seemed to be a credible video promoting a financial product which turned out to be a deep fake. Many of these are popping up and the average person won't necessarily be able to spot them.[20] ChatGPT has emerged and caused a stir in a way not seen before. Generative AI has so much potential but when it relies on data that could be fake, or false, it will produce results that, while they look credible, are untrue. The danger with generative AI is that it has the ability to create new content and data that if it is based on false facts creates a vicious cycle. We have a name for it. 'Hallucination bias'.

What must we do about it

There is a live debate on how to ensure AI will develop in a way that will support and benefit society. The approach the UK has taken is to observe the development of AI. Regulators are offering various ways in which AI innovation in financial services can be tested. The FCA offers this via the innovation pathways. In the main, financial services firms are expected to observe the regulation which applies to their activity. For those firms offering robo advice or assessing applications using AI tools, they must ensure that regulation set by the data regulator is also observed. For example, if an application is assessed without human intervention, the firm must offer the option for the outcome to be appealed and reviewed by a human. Of course, there are arguments on this matter that suggest that human decisions have been and continue to be biased.

The Consumer Duty requires firms to ensure good consumer outcomes, that products and services meet consumer outcomes, and the product design life cycle can show that the firm has thought of how they have considered the right consumer outcomes. Therefore, if using AI models, you must be able to explain how the results have delivered the objectives of the Consumer Duty.

In terms of accountability for regulated fintechs, many fall within the UK financial regulator's Senior Manager and Certification Regime (SM&CR) which again is another angle in which there is clear accountability for decisions made by the firm. This regime and other similar regimes around the world places accountability on key senior positions in an organization to ensure the functions that oversee the risk management, compliance and governance are effectively protecting the organization, its customer and market integrity. Penalties and sanctions can be placed on individuals who do not perform their duties effectively. We will discuss the senior manager regime in the following chapters of this book.

AI models

AI is a space where there is an asymmetry of information. Technical knowledge is concentrated with a small group of people and much of what actually goes on is unseen. There are a number of issues that can create concerns with the unchecked development of AI.

AI models analyse large amounts of data, learn from trends and patterns and make decision or solve problems. The complexities of the models means that it can produce false results and we won't even know. The expertise and data held with a small group of firms can create concentration of power and less effective competition. The quality and integrity of data is essential. If data is not accurate or has inherent bias which we know it does, results will no doubt be false and biased.

AI can potentially automate simple tasks, but this also leads to ethical issues. How far do we go with AI and how to we instil ethical and moral values in the models? How do we know they work? And as we mentioned earlier, it can fall into the wrong hands, where significant damage can be done to markets and societies. Cybersecurity becomes even more pressing globally the more data we create and the more our lives rely on AI.

Where does the liability sit?

Where the liability sits is an important question that needs to be resolved along with how to regulate AI. Who is responsible for the damage when things go wrong? We mentioned earlier in financial services, those regulated firms must adhere to the Consumer Duty and the SM&CR in the UK. There is an ambition from regulators in the UK to control what are deemed as 'critical third-party providers' in financial services. Some of this regulatory oversight already exists in other markets such as the US.

UK regulators see that these are technology companies that have grown in size and market share in their provision of services that power financial services (such as cloud services or fraud prevention analysis) and that their failure, operational disruption or a cyber-attack can have a systemic negative impact on the market. Often AI is a large component of their operations.

There is also a discussion regarding big tech companies and the role they play in harvesting so much of our data, AI techniques that are used, often effectively, and what that means in terms of competition, consumer harm and good market outcomes. These are difficult questions that need to be worked through. In the UK there is an effort to work with industry and various stakeholders to get this right as mentioned earlier.

Regtech

It's difficult to discuss fintech without talking about regtech. Regtech is short for regulatory technology and it is the use of technology and automation, software as a service and cloud computing to enhance compliance and risk management processes in an organization. It is active in highly regulated sectors such as financial services.

Regulation as we discussed in the first chapter must be proportionate and the 'burden' of regulation must always be considered. Many firms are also looking at how to reduce the cost of regulation and compliance. Regtech has emerged to solve that issue.

Some of the key services they provide are anti-money-laundering monitoring, spotting irregular transactions and automation of compliance processes using large amounts of data, usually housed on the cloud. They partner with financial institutions to deliver solutions cost effectively.

Currently, regulated entities working with regtech providers must satisfy themselves that they are meeting their regulatory obligations. It is the responsibility of the regulated entity, not the third-party regtech. In fact, regtech is not a regulated activity despite its core proposition of helping financial institutions manage their regulatory compliance processes efficiently. In the event of compliance failures, the regulated firm can suffer serious legal, regulatory and reputation damage. It is critical for regtechs to truly understand the regulatory obligations of their financial services clients to ensure the services are delivered will guarantee a well-functioning ecosystem and enhance the role of regtechs in providing value in financial services compliance. We will come back to this point of service providers not being regulated themselves but providing critical services to financial institutions who are.

Regtech and suptech – two sides to one coin

Alongside regtech, regulators are looking at how to use technology to allow them to supervise more effectively, hence the term suptech. The nature of data supplied to regulators on a regular and often ad hoc basis is a cause of grumbling by firms. This is not a lack of willingness to provide the information, but in the different systems, formats and frequencies in which it needs to be offered. Firms are not always clear why they need to supply the data they do or what is being done with it.

Where regtech helps with streamlining compliance processes including supplying the required data and reports to the regulator, suptech helps with taking in the data and processing it for effective oversight and supervision. Regulators are considering how to use data, AI and technologies themselves to make the receiving of data from forms and the ability to use it effectively for supervisory purposes.

Summary and takeaways

Regulation has been around for a long time. It has been generally viewed as technology agnostic. With the rise of the digital economy, this view has been tested. Regulators are now responding to new technologies by first understanding them, how they are developing and what the possible scenarios in which they will impact competition, market integrity and consumer confidence are.

Working with various stakeholders including firms in the market, regulators are looking at solutions to how we regulate new technologies. The overarching expectations around authorization for regulated activity, observing and implementing the Consumer Duty and understanding requirements under the senior manager and certification regime (or equivalent) will underpin many of the responses to new technologies.

Notes

1 Department for Science, Innovation and Technology. *Digital Regulation: driving growth and unlocking innovation.* Department for Science, Innovation and Technology, London, 2023. www.gov.uk/government/publications/digital-regulation-driving-growth-and-unlocking-innovation/digital-regulation-driving-growth-and-unlocking-innovation (archived at https://perma.cc/2LMP-USJN).
2 D Walbanke. Tech unicorns UK – complete guide to the billion-dollar club. Growth Business, 2022. growthbusiness.co.uk/tech-unicorns-uk-complete-guide-to-the-billion-dollar-club-20057 (archived at https://perma.cc/9JVN-B2WT).
3 Business Cloud. How long does it take to become a unicorn? Business Cloud, 2018. businesscloud.co.uk/news/the-fastest-road-to-becoming-a-unicorn/ (archived at https://perma.cc/3BKF-YEAS).
4 Statista. Volume of data/information created, captured, copied, and consumed worldwide from 2010 to 2020, with forecasts from 2021 to 2025. Statista, 2023. www.statista.com/statistics/871513/worldwide-data-created/ (archived at https://perma.cc/WLC5-GTZ3).
5 C Duhigg. What does your credit-card company know about you? *The New York Times.* 12 May 2009. www.nytimes.com/2009/05/17/magazine/17credit-t.html (archived at https://perma.cc/WBP6-2HCK).

6 World Economic Forum. Global Risks Report 2022. World Economic Forum, Cologny, Switzerland, 2022. www.weforum.org/publications/global-risks-report-2022/ (archived at https://perma.cc/F3R7-6KRQ).

7 Financial Conduct Authority. Ensure your customers understand how their money is protected. Financial Conduct Authority, London, 2021. www.fca.org.uk/publication/correspondence/dear-ceo-letter-e-money-firms.pdf (archived at https://perma.cc/K3BU-C9TQ).

8 European Central Bank. The revised Payment Services Directive (PSD2). European Central Bank, 2019. www.ecb.europa.eu/paym/intro/mip-online/2018/html/1803_revisedpsd.en.html (archived at https://perma.cc/ZPJ6-XUV8).

9 Bank of England. *DP5/22* – Artificial Intelligence and Machine Learning. Bank of England, London, 2022. www.bankofengland.co.uk/prudential-regulation/publication/2022/october/artificial-intelligence (archived at https://perma.cc/W8S3-GRG7).

10 Financial Conduct Authority. Regulatory Initiatives Grid. Financial Conduct Authority, London, 2023. www.fca.org.uk/publication/corporate/regulatory-initiatives-grid-nov-2023.pdf (archived at https://perma.cc/HAU6-RQGM).

11 Competition and Markets Authority, Information Commissioner's Office, Ofcom, and Financial Conduct Authority. The Digital Regulation Cooperation Forum, GOV.UK, 2023. www.gov.uk/government/collections/the-digital-regulation-cooperation-forum (archived at https://perma.cc/2ZFG-N6MX).

12 Financial Conduct Authority. The future of open banking and the Joint Regulatory Oversight Committee, Financial Conduct Authority, London, 2024. www.fca.org.uk/firms/future-open-banking-joint-regulatory-oversight-committee (archived at https://perma.cc/H2TQ-E4BZ).

13 Financial Conduct Authority. Account information services (AIS) and payment initiation services (PIS). Financial Conduct Authority, London, 2023. www.fca.org.uk/firms/account-information-services-payment-initiation-services (archived at https://perma.cc/4RTX-S5BY).

14 HM Government. Financial Services and Markets Act 2023. www.legislation.gov.uk/ukpga/2023/29/enacted (archived at https://perma.cc/M4LG-RUYC).

15 Q.ai. What really happened to LUNA Crypto? Forbes, 20 September 2022. www.forbes.com/sites/qai/2022/09/20/what-really-happened-to-luna-crypto (archived at https://perma.cc/63N2-PN9Y).

16 N Reiff. *The Collapse of FTX: What Went Wrong with the Crypto Exchange?* Investopedia, 2023. www.investopedia.com/what-went-wrong-with-ftx-6828447 (archived at https://perma.cc/CTF4-JQ6V).

17 HM Treasury. Future financial services regulatory regime for cryptoassets Consultation and call for evidence. London: HM Treasury, London 2023. assets.publishing.service.gov.uk/media/63d94ea68fa8f51881c99eb4/TR_Privacy_edits_Future_financial_services_regulatory_regime_for_cryptoassets_vP.pdf (archived at https://perma.cc/7NSE-Z3EM).

18 E Brynjolfsson, D Li and L R Raymond (2023). *Generative AI at Work.* National Bureau of Economic Research, Cambridge, MA. www.nber.org/papers/w31161 (archived at https://perma.cc/6VPG-M947).

19 Financial Conduct Authority. Cash Savings Market Review. Financial Conduct Authority, London, 2023. www.fca.org.uk/publication/multi-firm-reviews/cash-savings-market-review-2023.pdf (archived at https://perma.cc/3XXY-MABN).

20 ITV News. 'Absolutely terrifying': Martin Lewis issues warning after deep fake video of him appears online. ITV News, 7 July 2023. www.itv.com/news/2023-07-07/martin-lewis-issues-warning-not-to-fall-victim-to-deepfake-scam-video (archived at https://perma.cc/TQ6B-36YR).

4

The start-up stage

CHAPTER SUMMARY

- Understand how to navigate the risk taxonomy at the early start-up stage
- Navigating the risk taxonomy in the first years after launch and what to look out for
- The services available from regulators in the UK to help with testing new technologies and business models
- What the benefit of these services is and how to think about them in the contexts of the limited resources the fintech has at those early stages
- Why there is no substitute for understanding risk management and embedding a conduct culture early on

The start-up stage

One definition I use of a start-up is a business that has been in operation for up to five years. However, within that time there are various stages that a fintech goes through from funding requirements, talent and experience, structure and set up, the value proposition and the regulatory considerations. Here we will look at the start-up stage as pre-market launch and post-market launch.

Pre-market launch are the very early stages of a fintech's life. It is an exciting time for an individual or a small group of people coming together with an idea that will close a gap in the market, will add value to consumers or they might be simply experimenting with a new technology. Founders go through a validation of the idea from problem/solution fit to creating a proof of concept, the working prototype, identifying the target market and looking at funding options.

These stages require true entrepreneurial qualities: agility of mind and approach, a culture of openness and willingness to experiment, and a higher tolerance to risk. That mindset and approach is very different from what is expected in larger more established organizations but must not be confused with a lack of discipline and a carefree approach.

The difficulty of start-up stage is misunderstood at times. The resources are limited and the demands of the business often outstrip the available resources. The founders must be very focused on prioritization which will have to be agile as priorities may change every day. Often risk management is not at the forefront of their priority list which is not unreasonable. However, understanding the fundamentals of risk and implementing the right risk management techniques at the right stages is important. An awareness of what is needed at every stage of the life cycle can help the business pre-empt and plan for their requirements as part of their operations and growth cycle.

As an example, at a start-up stage, some form of financial support is needed. The business is not profitable or bringing in revenue so looking at the funding sources and ensuring that financial resources are available for the business to survive is vital. Having a sound plan that will see the business through to the next stage of client acquisition is tied into the funding requirements. The funding requirement is often directly tied to the ability for the business to move to the next phase of launching which requires obtaining a licence from the regulator to operate. From very early stages, the fintech must ensure that it is adhering to the regulatory requirements within which it falls.

It can be a minefield. There is so much to think about and so few resources, human and financial, to get to a point where an idea is gaining traction, winning customers and investors alike. Markets that see the benefit of fintech start-up and innovation will take action to develop programmes that support fintechs in those early stages. Accelerator programmes are available in earnest and via large organizations or trade bodies. There is a wealth of support and expertise fintechs can access in most developed and many developing markets.

Many of these accelerators, however, support the founders in what to think about, where to get funding, how to develop business plans or run good financial management. They don't typically talk about risk management as a concept to be embedded in the business early on and while they mention regulation and the need to be regulated, they don't typically go through the depth required.

There is a case for linking these together and many trade bodies in the UK (such as Fintech Scotland, the Payments Association and Innovate Finance) are trying to do just that. In the meantime, there are a number of initiatives and services offered by regulators to think about the business proposition and consider how they may sit within a regulatory framework. The UK has led globally on offering initiatives to innovative start-ups to test their ideas within a safe regulatory framework. These initiatives have been replicated around the world and we will discuss some of these in this chapter.

In these early stages, a business must often consider whether there are other similar business models out there and how these businesses navigated their way through their development. They need to think about whether they are testing something that is truly innovative and what might be the considerations they need to think about to ensure that they are developing a solution that will satisfy areas of consumer protection, market integrity and general good risk management.

How should start-ups think of risk and regulation?

In this chapter we are looking at the start-up stage of a fintech. This includes the period from the idea creation, various testing and validation stages to a post-authorization stage two to three years later. This chapter will not cover the authorization process as there will be more detail in the following chapter on this topic. However, we will cover how to consider regulation in the start-up stage before and after obtaining a full regulatory licence to launch and operate a business.

So how does a start-up embed risk management and regulation into its culture in those early stages? The general view is that very little consideration is given to risk management or regulation requirements other than getting a licence at that early stage. I beg to differ. If we look more closely at organizations that have gone from start-up to growth and maturity, that is not the case.

Perhaps the image of neglecting risk management comes from the entrepreneurial approach that is needed for a start-up which requires a higher degree of risk taking. But risk management isn't by definition a low tolerance to risks. It is, at a strategic level, a conscious and informed decision of what the risk tolerance of the organization is to ensure that it will fulfil its strategic objectives safely and sustainably. What are the frameworks that keep the organization within that risk tolerance and what is their fall back or mitigating actions if they fall outside? (We will link this to regulatory obligations shortly.)

There is no reason a fintech start-up should not consider risk management as an ally to the ambitious plans it has for launch and growth. It also demonstrates that the fintech understands these issues and has carefully thought through how they apply and why. This is important to demonstrate to a regulator if the fintech requires a regulatory licence to operate, or to their regulated partners if they offer services to other regulated firms. Or indeed to their sponsor if they are delivering services as an agent or distributor of a regulated firm.

Of course, the level of risk to think about is different for fintechs in start-up stage to fintechs in other parts of the life cycle. If we use the same taxonomy introduced in Chapter 2, we can look at the various risks at this early stage and how a fintech might think about them.

Enterprise-wide risk management

The concept of enterprise-wide risk management (ERM) is the recognition that risks don't operate on their own. Taking an end-to-end business-wide view of the operations of the business, thinking what the key impact areas are and what might be the risks that need to be managed but crucially how they change relative to each other is an important strategic approach to risk management.[1]

Impact areas relate to the risk taxonomy. A business usually considers its top risks relative to the most important areas of the business. Every fintech at a very early stage should consider the areas that will keep the business going and an end-to-end approach to managing the risks is important. Think of a simple event that may lead to a chain of events where multiple risks are being compromised. For example, a data loss incident may lead to reputational damage, a regulatory breach and fine, and loss of clients which in turn will impact financial resilience.[2, 3]

Even more basic, a lack of strategic direction may lead to lower than projected financial results which in turn leads to financial resilience concerns. Financial resilience concerns lead to behaviour, conduct or decisions that may create other areas of concern and the cycle continues. Enterprise risk management does not have to concern large organizations only. It's about applying the concept rather than the rules. Understanding why this helps allows a fintech to apply it in a proportionate way to their operations at every stage of their growth. It's about developing the right mindset not about ticking the right boxes.

Front office runs away from back office

There is a classic pattern when a fintech starts to grow revenue and market share. Client acquisition and growth are, naturally, a key objective of any fintech. Experiencing client acquisition and growth is generally a good sign that the fintech is covering a market need. As we go over the risks, it is important to understand how and where to invest in infrastructure that will support that growth. This tends to be the area that is missed the most. Anecdotally, revenue growth and back-office functions to support that growth do not tend to scale at the same pace and I refer to this as front office running away from back office.

The risk management and compliance systems and structures a fintech has put in place must be commensurate with the size of the business. Ensuring the right planning around that end-to-end enterprise-wide risk management is key and as I have been pointing out in this book, getting the right back-office tools, infrastructure and operations in line with the business size and scale is an area the regulators care about as they see it as sound risk management. It is one for fintechs to look out for in the start-up post-launch stage but will really be key for the stage at which they see serious growth which we will cover in Chapter 7.

Risks management for start-ups

Here are some of the risk areas that a fintech can and should think about in the start-up stage.

Strategic risk   Strategic risk at this early stage links to everything the organization is doing. It is the appeal of the business model in its response to a market need, its response to external factors, the competitive landscape and the belief that the idea will give them a unique selling point. Thinking very carefully about the proposition, the environment, the business model and business case, the legal structure and regulatory requirements are all part of the business strategy. The risk is if any of these are missed, things may go wrong.

To bring this to life, the strategy must ensure the product appeals to investors. As a source of its funding, investors being convinced in the value proposition is tied to the viability and financial resource availability of the fintech. The strategy will also consider legal structures and what regulation applies, which then cuts across the legal and regulatory obligations the fintech must observe. The strategic decisions of a fintech effectively impact other risks within its taxonomy. In the case of the early stages of a start-up, strategy has a significant impact on financial risks and the viability of the business.

Financial risk   At pre-launch, it will be very important to manage financial risk. I will caution that this will be important at every stage, and we will cover the reasons as we go along. In this case, it ties directly to the survival of the fintech. At this early stage, there is no revenue coming in, only costs. Post-launch, the fintech starts to acquire customers but the costs will still outstrip the revenues. The fintech is not profitable and client acquisition is the primary objective.

Founders need to understand very clearly what their cost base is, have strong budgets, and clear and accurate monthly financial management tools (a spreadsheet is fine in the early stages) that will allow them to track acutal costs vs budget. They must understand their runway (how much time they have before they run out of money). These are all important components to satisfy investors and know when a funding round is needed or in some cases understand when it is the right time to wind down and close up. Regulators want to see that the business is being financially managed in a sound and prudent manner, that accounting is done according to standards and financial resources are used in a legal manner.

Part of financial risk is funding and inadequate financial resources. The fintech must also consider the scenario where they cannot launch or they do not survive. Winding down is an emotive topic. No entrepreneur believes their idea will fail. That is why they do what they do. It's a mindset and we wouldn't want that to change. However, under a risk management framework, building in indicators of where financial stress is appearing, means spotting problems early on and dealing with them to ensure the survival of the fintech. Equally, where no solution is found, a sound and solvent closure so that customers are not impacted and left exposed is essential. This is an important component for consumer protection and market integrity which most financial regulators around the world, including the UK, care about.

When regulators ask about a fintech's financial resilience, or financial risk management, it is not from the angle of ensuring each business must survive. That is not a regulator's role. In fact, it is widely believed that the sign of a competitive market is that businesses enter and exit. Regulators want to ensure consumer protection and limited market disruption. It is also believed that when there is financial stress in an organization, certain behaviours may follow.

This causal chain is of interest. For example, in Early and High Growth Oversight, a department I set up for the Financial Conduct Authority to work with start-ups in setting and testing higher standards, we found that where a firm is tracking below its financial projections, there is a great risk of financial promotions that can be seen to be misleading.[4]

Operational risk   Operational risk will be fluid in pre-launch stage. As described in Chapter 2, operational risk is not just about the technology working. It is all the processes, policies and systems that keep the lights on and the business functioning. At pre-launch stage, there is a lot of validation to test how the solution fits the gap and how the product design and delivery will fill the gap from a practical real-life lens. Many technology firms in these stages are testing the stability of the solution and iterate as they find bugs and issues. This is a reasonable characteristic of this stage and fintechs should be allowed to do this.

> It is worth referring to the operational resilience framework set out by the UK's FCA and PRA we mentioned in Chapter 2 which requires a fintech to look at business services that if they fail will disrupt the functioning of the business. Naturally, the business services in question will change as the fintech goes through the various stages of its growth.

These early stages usually have minimal IT requirements, a very small number of staff, limited need for real estate and associated services and a huge reliance on the founders to be all things to all people while working remotely and in an agile way. It doesn't necessarily mean that a fintech focuses less on operational resilience at this stage. There are broadly two considerations here. The first is the fintech starts to see high growth, as is the case for most fintechs, therefore operational resilience is inevitably an important area to manage well. The second is the fintech's business model must have operational resilience at its heart regardless of its size, as is the case with Insignis

Cash Solutions where they identified at the very first stages that operational resilience would be a core prerequisite to attract any partner (large financial institutions). Insignis is a case study featured in Chapter 10.

When the fintech starts to see high growth, the founders need to ensure the operational resilience is maintained. Starting to look at platforms and solutions that can offer scale while maintaining the same level of product quality and service is required. Often when this is overlooked, the company will start to see complaints. This is a sign they should look out for and a sign at which the regulator certainly looks.

In distinguishing between a start-up that is acquiring customers to one that is looking to work with large incumbents, operational resilience will take another angle. If a fintech is looking to become an outsourcing partner of a large organization, ensuring operational resilience will be key. Large organizations in financial services have heavy expectations to ensure their services are delivered with minimal disruption. Operational resilience is high on their risk management focus and the regulatory expectations of them. When a fintech is no longer a standalone service provider, but is rather part of a service delivery chain, although they may not be regulated, the expectation is they must fulfil their role to the standard of the service expected by their client – the regulated financial institution in this case.

Cybersecurity, financial crime and money laundering   Cybersecurity very much follows the discussion outlined under operational resilience. It is about proportionality and ensuring the right data protection and cybersecurity tools available for the size and scale. Most regulators have outlined their expectations around cybersecurity as we discussed in Chapter 2. For a fintech in pre-launch stage, understanding who might target the business and why is a good starting point to allow them to design a framework that is suitable. This must be kept up to date as the business changes and grows and the threat to the fintech therefore changes.

Fintechs must understand where the data, technology and operational vulnerabilities are that can lead to cybersecurity breaches and prioritize what gaps they want to cover. At the very least they should have the right protective software that is suitable for them, the right encryption, identity and access management tools and policies and a suitable framework for detection. They may not be considering accreditation at this stage, but living the culture of data security policies driven from the top will go a long way in the future.

Financial crime and money laundering is an industry-wide topic that not only regulators, but all parties in the ecosystem are concerned about. Financial crime is an operational resilience and cybersecurity matter as much as it is a regulatory compliance matter. In many cases it is also a reputational risk and financial risk matter. While the pre-launch start-up may not have financial crime at the top of their priority, thinking about how financial crime might happen in the business and ensuring the right expertise, systems and investment is committed to this area will serve the fintech well in their licence acquisition stage as well as post-launch stage.

Post-launch is where the practical elements of embedding systems and controls that monitor and manage financial crime and money laundering will support the fintech. Regulators want to ensure that fintechs demonstrate that understanding as part of the design of their product, not as an afterthought.

People risk   The focus of people risk in the fintech space is lack of talent and ensuring that the fintech has the right skills at the right stage. At pre-launch stage, the fintech has a very small staff, usually the founders and depending on the skills the founders bring (they are often technologists) they may add one or two other skilled staff with legal or security expertise. It is very different from one fintech to the next but what is common is that firms bring on product and data experts. Post-launch and as the fintech acquires customers, a fintech may bring in product implementation and sales teams, for example. They may think of boosting their onboarding team, add a team of compliance officers, risk managers or policy experts.

A general characteristic is fintechs look to technology to deliver some of the customer service or compliance functions. A fintech should be very careful about ensuring they can demonstrate that this works. For example, the Know Your Customer (KYC) process for pay tech firms is much more streamlined and tends to be a digital experience. This, in the main, has been accepted by regulators although there is still debate around how this process can be strengthened. Contrast that with a customer service chat bot experience which has generally been hit and miss. It's mainly missed the mark as fintechs have grown in size and scale. Customers have increased in numbers and complexity but the systems that support that growth have not scaled at the same pace. It's a classic case of front office running away from back office. Something we will come back to across the book.

Fintech brings the benefit of automating various activities and making the process simple and streamlined for customers. What is automated matters and how the end-to-end process aligns with the proposition and the strategy is an important consideration. Therefore, what human talent is needed to fulfil some of these functions needs to be considered carefully.

> AI is an emerging area where there is a shortage of talent. The interaction of AI and human is an important balance. If a proposition relies on AI, how are the results scrutinized? Is there a need for human intervention at some point? What skillset is needed for those particular individuals? A report by the Alan Turing Institute talks about 'humans in the loop' and 'humans on the loop'.[5] Humans in the loop is the scenario where a staff member will confirm the output or decision of the activity as being appropriate and humans on the loop allows the staff member to override the activity.

If a fintech has used technology to deliver compliance and monitoring obligations, at what point do they think of the regulatory expertise that is needed? Some expertise around compliance and risk management will be required for regulated entities from a very early stage. These fall under the UK's senior management and certification regime. In the UK, significant influence functions (or SIFs), may be required upon applying for a licence. Head of risk, head of compliance and money laundering reporting officer are some examples that apply to some business models. There are organizations that offer these services to fintechs. They are referred to as 'rent a SIF'. It may well be a reasonable option in these early stages, but it is crucial that the directors and founders understand what their obligations are as they are ultimately responsible for the regulatory requirements and the sound operating of the company.

Reputational risk   Every organization must always think about reputational risk. The tolerance to reputation risk changes depending on the stage the organization is in and the message it has put out on what it stands for and what it will deliver.

At pre-launch, a fintech is experimenting, testing and validating new ideas. It is usual to expect a high overall risk tolerance to things not going to plan. The proposition is not fully defined therefore it is reasonable to expect that with a high risk tolerance defined at a strategic level, the amount of reputation risk must be considered proportionally. Reputational risk can be as simple as when a product doesn't match the commitment a fintech has put out to investors, the regulators and consumers.

At post-launch, those promises made and how consumers rate the service are crucial. Word of mouth travels far and wide and has an impact. It is important that a fintech gets this right early on. There may be a few opportunities where the reputation gets a hit and the fintech is forgiven if it acts quickly but it won't get too many chances for too long. The various rating platforms, reviews, social media forums and the speed at which all this travels means that a fintech shouldn't dismiss reputation risk when they are launching. Ensuring that they set the right level of risk tolerances across the organization will ensure the reputational risk tolerance is maintained. This is another example of enterprise risk management in play. Reputation risk isn't considered in isolation. In fact, it is only impacted if other parts of the organization have breached their tolerance levels in areas such as operations (customer service), legal or regulatory compliance. Regulators look at the reputation of the organization as an indicator to its culture. Does it ensure consumer protections? Is it responsive when things go wrong? Does it contribute to high standards in the market?

It is equally important if a fintech is providing services to large organizations. Their reputation for delivery, responsiveness and a quality resilient product goes a long way. Reputational risk tolerance at these early stages is very personal to the founders. As the fintech grows its client base, tolerance to accepting this risk declines as it directly ties to trust in the brand.

Legal and regulatory risks   We discussed in Chapter 2 how these legal and regulatory risks are linked. When starting a new enterprise and particularly as the fintech is innovating, understanding where legal and regulatory obligations lie is an important component to how they are able to design their product and deliver services to their customers. It is worth being familiar with Threshold Conditions outlined in Chapter 2, or Conditions for Authorization if you are a payments and e-money fintech. It is also worth considering the Consumer Duty, and operational and financial resilience components discussed here in a general sense. As fintechs are pioneering new technologies and innovations, we have already outlined areas where there are specific requirements for consideration. Some are still emerging. We will outline in this chapter some resources fintech can access to help with this process.

Regulation for a fintech will vary from one subsector of financial services to another. Given the vast spectrum of business models, it won't be possible to cover them in this chapter. One helpful way in which the UK's Financial Conduct Regulator (FCA) communicates its priorities for each subsector is by statements called 'Dear CEO' letters. These are letters that outline their latest assessments of risks and harms in each subsector and the actions or focus areas for the firms in that subsector to consider. These are published and can be found on the FCA's website.[6]

THE CONSUMER DUTY – A UK APPROACH TO OUTCOMES-BASED REGULATION

The FCA's Consumer Duty which launched in July 2023 is an important consideration for fintechs at all stages.[7] At the early design stages, fintechs in the UK should consider the Consumer Duty requirements. It is an outcome-based approach to regulation and requires that firms think about the design, development and implementation of products and services with a particular focus on how customers interact with the product throughout its life cycle.

At pre-launch, while developing the proposition and testing its validity, the Consumer Duty requires that a product or service meets the needs of the target market and asks if these have been tested. The testing environment is ideal to give an indication of the requirements of the duty and setting the baseline for the continued assessment of good consumer outcomes.

Some of the areas of the Consumer Duty that are interesting for fintechs to consider are designs that can be seen as deceptive digital practices such as sludge and nudge. In thinking about the Consumer Duty, fintechs should consider how technology can result in positive or negative outcomes for consumers. Sludge is adding friction to a customer experience that will result in a different outcome should it not be there. Sludge practices can be used to deliver positive or negative customer outcomes depending on how they are implemented. For example, a good practice is to add friction to the sign up of a risky product allowing the customer to think about the suitability of that product. Contrast that with building in friction when a customer wants to cancel a product or service and they are paying more than needed as a result. This is particularly unhelpful if the sign up is streamlined but the cancellation is not.

Nudge is a similar concept using the opposite method, using tools to 'nudge' a customer in a particular direction that may or may not work for the customer. Gamification is another area of interest. With app-based products and services this is particularly in focus. Building in gamification, which drives behaviour in a certain way for immediate satisfaction may not be the best long-term outcome for a customer and must be considered carefully.

Another deceptive practice which has been a topic of much interest is greenwashing thus allowing consumers to invest in what on the surface are green investment assets but in fact they are not. Behavioural science has been an interesting area of study for a few years in all areas of the economy including financial services. Giving due consideration for how financial products and services support positive outcomes to customers will be help meet fintech's obligation to under the Consumer Duty.

Other countries, and other industries in the UK, are looking closely at the Consumer Duty. The fundamentals behind the Consumer Duty can apply to any business in any market. Fintechs can look at how the Consumer Duty supports the development of their business and may use it as a differentiator in building trust in their brand that sets them apart from their competitors.

Environmental, social and governance   ESG might feel like a new area of focus although governance has always been there. We will talk about governance in detail in this book as it is an important component of risk management and regulatory requirements. Environmental and social at very early stages of the fintech's life is ensuring there is consideration for these in the planning and growth of the fintech. This is also something that will depend greatly on the founders.

Governance is about the oversight and the systems and frameworks allowing effective decision-making up and down the organization. Pre-launch, the fintech is run by the founders and they have full oversight across all areas of the organization with decision-making primarily sitting with them. That is reasonable given the limited resources available, no customers at that point and the focused activity.

Post-launch and as the fintech grows, the spans of control become too large for the founders so they should consider the right senior team and frameworks to delegate decision-making and allow for an effective running of the business. It is common that founders continue to be heavily involved in the operational decisions. Inevitably, this can create risks in areas such as group think, a lack of challenge and bottlenecks for decisions to go through. The founders need to find a way to be focused on the strategic direction of the organization while allowing senior staff to get on with the operational work.

When we talk about sound governance frameworks, it needs to be proportionate. We mentioned the regulatory need for some senior roles, but it also makes sense to have the right roles on the board and on the executive team with specific expertise. It is still reasonable that the firm has three to four members on its board which comprises the founders and investors. Proportionality is the key theme and ensuring that the fintech continues to meet its regulatory obligations.

Returning to the Consumer Duty and how it interacts with governance, there is an expectation that adherence to the Consumer Duty has to be overseen from the top of the organization and a board member is assigned as champion for the implementation of and continued adherence to the Consumer Duty. The assigned board member here must be a non-executive director to ensure independence of views and oversight. In the initial stages of most fintechs, they don't have a non-executive director, therefore the fintech must ensure that the requirements of the duty have been met and embedded in the organization. There is a large amount of responsibility on the shoulders of the founders in those early stages and making sure that they focus on the areas that are priority for their stage in the life cycle will be key.

There is a lot to navigate here but there are resources the fintech can access. Start-up fintechs with new and novel ideas can take advantage of the innovation services offered by regulators, notably regulatory sandboxes. This is concept pioneered by the UK's Financial Conduct Authority and replicated in many jurisdictions around the world. The FCA has also launched the Digital Sandbox and Innovation Pathways which we will cover in this chapter.

The Regulatory Sandbox

The FCA launched the Regulatory Sandbox in June 2016 and this has now been replicated around the world.[8] A report by the World Bank stated that in 2020 there were 73 regulatory sandboxes across 57 jurisdictions.[9] The FCA's Regulatory Sandbox specifically focused on new and innovative ideas that firms brought to market. Innovation is less about a new technology that has not been created before and more about creative ways in which a firm is finding a solution to a gap in the market, or a business model structure that has not been thought of before.

As a result, when launched there were many applications and they were varied in nature and proposition. In the early days, approximately a third of firms were payments firms looking at various ideas to make payments, cross-border payments in particular, quicker, cheaper and more traceable. Then with the launch of open banking and PSD2 the Sandbox saw many applications leveraging what open banking can offer. In 2022 and 2023 many of the propositions still focus on open banking as well as on digital assets, artificial intelligence and robo advice. They are spread across payments, consumer credit and wholesale markets.[10]

How and when to apply

The idea of the Sandbox is to test a new idea that a business wants to launch from the purview of risks. How is the fintech building its proposition in a way that will deliver value and not cause harm?[11] To apply for the Sandbox, a fintech will need to have developed an idea and business model. They should be clear on what value this offers and who the target market is. It is also worth knowing who the consumer group will be when entering the Sandbox. For many founders this is family and friends. It can also be in partnership with a larger organization where they can have access to their client base. Knowing and mapping out the customer journey in those early stages helps in providing clarity for the proposition and gives the regulator an idea of how the fintech is testing the business model in the Sandbox.

One of the areas considered when applying for entry to the Sandbox is value for money while balancing a reasonable level of profitability. For example, is the fintech considering delivering a proposition where the charge is a fixed fee rather than a percentage of the value of the transaction. If so, will that disadvantage a client base that transact in low amounts?

Another thing to think about is the target market. Is the fintech marketing to vulnerable consumers? Will vulnerable consumers be disadvantaged by the product? How are the financial promotions being written? What happens when things go wrong?

The FCA Regulatory Sandbox allows the firm to test its idea in a live environment with a defined number of customers. The fintech is operating in the real world for all intents and purposes. If accepted in the Sandbox they will be required to obtain the right permissions or licence to allow them to operate.

So before applying, the fintech will have to be ready. Which means:

- Having the proposition ready. They are able to clearly articulate what it is, what technology is being used, what client base this will help, and the financial model that sits behind it.

- Demonstrating clear value it will bring to consumers, how it will be value for money.

- Having the customers ready and available to test the product in the Sandbox.

- Having the right resources, human and financial to carry out the testing in the Sandbox.

- Ensuring that they have researched what regulations might apply. That they have made the effort to understand what their obligations may be.

- Having done pre-live testing.

An additional point is if successful in the Sandbox, they can go on to obtain full authorization and fully launch their product or service in the market.

There has been a huge benefit of this service to fintechs that have gone through it. The FCA assessed that 92 per cent of firms that go through the Sandbox achieve full authorization and that they receive an estimated 15 per cent more funding compared to non-innovative firms.[12] It also helps them navigate the complexity of regulation. Fintechs will get a dedicated case officer who might signpost what type of regulatory permission is required. They may explain how the rules can be interpreted in the context of the proposition being tested and in some cases can offer an informal steer where the case officer may discuss some of the outcomes of the business model and what that might mean. The Regulatory Sandbox in the UK has been successful and replicated around the world. It is worth noting, though, that the various regulatory sandboxes around the world differ in the expectation and experience.

Innovation Pathways

The FCA's innovation initiatives started with its sandbox. However, there are limitations to the number of fintechs that can enter the Sandbox. There will be some that may not meet the eligibility criterion. This is where a broader service was established that addresses those limitations. The FCA's Innovation Pathways recognize that the Sandbox is not always the best service for a fintech looking at a new idea. Effectively, the idea behind Innovation Pathways is that not all firms will necessarily need a sandbox.[13]

In many cases, what a fintech needs is to understand how their idea works within current regulation and to get help to navigate regulation early on. The criteria for innovation pathways is similar to the Sandbox in that the fintech will need to be able to articulate a business model, how is it different, how it really brings value to consumers and differentiates the fintech from other propositions. It will also be helpful to know what questions the business would like answered. The more specific and precise, the more value they will get from services such as Innovation Pathways.

This applies to all interactions with the regulator. It is important to demonstrate that there has been a level of research and effort to understand what regulation the fintech falls within and what their obligations are. The questions then become about the specific proposition and how the outcomes produced deliver effectively on that proposition. In a similar manner to the sandbox, a fintech can have access for one-to-one discussions with experts who can offer some guidance, an informal steer or they may signpost what licence or permission the fintech may need.

Innovation Pathways may also help put the fintech in touch with the FCA's authorizations team for a pre-application conversation. This is very helpful if they are at a stage close to obtaining a financial services licence.

TESTING AN AUTOMATED ADVICE MODEL

A big benefit for the FCA in offering these services is to observe and learn from the innovations that are emerging in the market. From time to time, some specific areas of focus appear and one of the innovation services can support in building knowledge of the risks while fintechs are experimenting. One such area is automated or robo financial advice. The FCA's Innovation Pathways specifically calls out support for firms looking to offer automated financial advice models.

There have been multiple reviews since 2016 on the effectiveness of competition in the financial advice market showing that many retail clients do not invest effectively and many keep cash deposits rather than other higher yielding investments.[14] Robo and automated advice was considered as an alternative to offer simple retail investment advice. Another review in 2020 showed slow progress but similar results and very slow uptake of robo and fully automated advice by retail customers. This continues to be an area of focus for regulators, particularly in developed markets, and there is a role innovation can play in closing the gap.

Digital Sandbox

Firms in the UK can access the FCA's Digital Sandbox.[15] This is a novel idea initially tested in 2020 that allows firms to access synthetic datasets, compliant with data laws, to test new ideas or create proof of concepts on particular topics that are important to the financial services sector such as financial crime, diversity, equity and inclusion, and green financing and reporting.

One of the biggest challenges fintechs face when developing new propositions that rely on large datasets is getting access to such data sets in a compliant manner that allows them to test and validate their

THE START-UP STAGE   99

idea. Creating the Digital Sandbox, although not explicitly described in that way has the potential to support smaller firms competing with the big tech companies who naturally have access to large data sets by virtue of their large client base.

In addition to offering a development environment for fintechs, it offers opportunity for collaboration with other organizations, not only other fintechs with complimentary solutions but also incumbents, academia or even investor groups and government bodies. In addition it offers a platform for showcasing solutions as they are being developed and tested live. Business models based on AI and open banking or ideas around open finance can be tested in the Digital Sandbox but it is not limited to that. Any proposition that relies on data can use the Digital Sandbox as a testing environment.

Should everyone apply to these services?

Thinking carefully about what these services will offer a fintech and how they can truly add value is important. The fintech will need to ensure that they have the right resources to access these platforms so they need to be clear on the benefit they will get from enrolling in such a programme.

For genuinely unique and new propositions, the anecdotal evidence is that these services are of benefit. Particularly if the fintech is considering the Regulatory Sandbox or Innovation Pathways where they can get direct support. Most of the organizations looking to use these services are considering new technologies within existing regulatory frameworks. The benefit of these services is to get a good understanding of regulation and how it applies today, what the questions that a fintech should ask itself in relation to inherent risks that could arise from the business model they are proposing and how to do they plan to address those risks.

When considering the Digital Sandbox, the platform offers opportunities to showcase proof of concepts and partner with other organizations and academia. A fintech must again consider the targeted and focused need for applying to the Digital Sandbox and be clear on the outcome it wishes to achieve to ensure that it is dedicating its limited resources effectively.

None of these services replace the need for a fintech to consider what it means to have a conduct risk culture and to manage the risks that will give rise to harms to consumers or to market integrity. This continues to be the responsibility of the fintech and ensuring that they have done the work on understanding what this means for their organization will serve them in the long term.

Summary and takeaways

This chapter looks at how to embed regulation and risk management in the start-up stage, part of which starts before a financial services licence is obtained and part is after authorization. It serves a fintech to start thinking about embedding the culture from the start. This will allow them to apply risk management and be compliant with the requirements of regulation.

While a start-up, the requirements in a pre-launch stage where the firm proposition is developing and being testing can be slightly different from the authorization process and launching as a fully regulated entity. Creating a framework that will allow the fintech to review and assess its risk management will help it evolve its frameworks as it grows.

We also consider the various services available to fintechs to ensure an understanding of their regulatory obligations before they apply for a licence and launch. These services are particularly designed for fintechs that are developing new ideas and using new technologies. The various platforms available to them ensure that they can test how they can implement a business model that is new under an existing regulatory framework. It also supports the regulators in understanding what new innovations and business models are emerging so they can consider policy responses that will be suitable for technological advancements that will deliver systemic future changes to how we interact with financial services in a digital world. We will cover the authorization process in detail in the following chapter.

Notes

1 Institute of Risk Management (nd). What is Enterprise Risk Management? Institute of Risk Management. www.theirm.org/what-we-do/what-is-enterprise-risk-management/ (archived at https://perma.cc/K6Q4-33M6).

2 B Boultwood. How to Develop an Enterprise Risk Taxonomy. Global Association of Risk Professionals, 2021. www.garp.org/risk-intelligence/culture-governance/how-to-develop-an-enterprise-risk-taxonomy (archived at https://perma.cc/EH5T-ARKV).

3 A Kruizinga. The taxonomy's role in transforming risk management. PwC, 2021. www.pwc.nl/en/topics/blogs/reshaping-the-risk-taxonomy.html (archived at https://perma.cc/RS53-DH59).

4 Financial Conduct Authority. Early and High Growth Oversight. Financial Conduct Authority, London 2023. www.fca.org.uk/firms/authorisation/early-high-growth-oversight (archived at https://perma.cc/U4AK-6UJ8).

5 F Ostmann and C Dorobantu. AI in Financial Services. The Alan Turing Institute, 2021. doi.org/10.5281/zenodo.4916041 (archived at https://perma.cc/UT3M-GG7R).

6 Financial Conduct Authority. Supervisory correspondence, Financial Conduct Authority, London, 2023. www.fca.org.uk/about/how-we-regulate/supervision/supervisory-correspondence (archived at https://perma.cc/2Q7Y-B7JC).

7 Financial Conduct Authority. A New Consumer Duty: Feedback to CP21/36 and final rules. Financial Conduct Authority, London, 2022. www.fca.org.uk/publication/policy/ps22-9.pdf (archived at https://perma.cc/MGY2-ABGW).

8 Financial Conduct Authority. Regulatory Sandbox, Financial Conduct Authority, London, 2023. www.fca.org.uk/firms/innovation/regulatory-sandbox (archived at https://perma.cc/D8L5-UNYX).

9 World Bank. Key Data from Regulatory Sandboxes across the Globe. World Bank, 2020. www.worldbank.org/en/topic/fintech/brief/key-data-from-regulatory-sandboxes-across-the-globe (archived at https://perma.cc/8DVP-Z6LH).

10 Financial Conduct Authority. Regulatory Sandbox accepted firms. Financial Conduct Authority, London, 2023. www.fca.org.uk/firms/innovation/regulatory-sandbox/accepted-firms (archived at https://perma.cc/8SEB-PA95).

11 Financial Conduct Authority. Regulatory Sandbox. Financial Conduct Authority, London, 2023. www.fca.org.uk/firms/innovation/regulatory-sandbox (archived at https://perma.cc/8DHD-W5CH).

12 J Rusu. Innovation and Regulation: Partners in the Success of Financial Services. Financial Conduct Authority, London, 2022. www.fca.org.uk/news/speeches/innovation-regulation-partners-success-financial-services (archived at https://perma.cc/LF48-Z5YM).

13 Financial Conduct Authority. Innovation Pathways, Financial Conduct Authority, London, 2023. www.fca.org.uk/firms/innovation/innovation-pathways (archived at https://perma.cc/Y4WG-DD2G).

14 Financial Conduct Authority. Evaluation of the impact of the Retail Distribution Review and the Financial Advice Market Review. Financial Conduct Authority, London, 2022. www.fca.org.uk/publication/corporate/evaluation-of-the-impact-of-the-rdr-and-famr.pdf (archived at https://perma.cc/T7AS-D2FA).

15 Financial Conduct Authority. Digital Sandbox. Financial Conduct Authority, London, 2024. www.fca.org.uk/firms/innovation/digital-sandbox (archived at https://perma.cc/8V7V-TFLC).

5

Licence to operate

CHAPTER SUMMARY

- An angle on the regulatory life cycle and what is expected at each stage
- An understanding of the various tools the regulators use to authorize and supervise regulated entities
- The key components of an authorization process and how to be prepared
- How a fintech can navigate its way through the authorization process when not all functions of the business are fully in place or operational
- An explanation of the baseline standards expected of the fintech to be authorized

Licence to operate

For most fintechs, the launch stage is about obtaining permissions to operate. In order to do this, they need to go through an authorization process to obtain a licence from the country's financial services regulator. This chapter will focus on the UK as an example of what a fintech needs to think about when obtaining a licence to operate.

> A reminder is that not all fintechs need a licence to operate. That is to say, not all fintechs are offering regulated services and some offer limited services via sponsorship by a regulated entity. For those who are offering direct financial services to consumers or businesses, a licence by the financial services regulator in the relevant country will need to be obtained.
>
> The UK is seen as setting standards in financial services regulations and many of what is discussed here applies to other jurisdictions across the world including Europe, South East Asia and the Gulf countries.

This chapter is not about detailing how to get a licence. There are many support organizations and compliance and management consultancies that can help with the mechanical process of licensing. Instead in this chapter, I attempt to unpack the rationale behind some of the requirements and explore how a fintech is able to engage with the spirit of requirements in a helpful way to its future operations and its future relationship with the regulator.

The regulatory life cycle

The regulatory life cycle from a purely technical perspective starts with authorization. It is often the first real engagement with the regulator and the start of the regulatory journey. Practically, and given what we discussed in the previous chapter, the regulatory journey for some firms starts well before that. For fintechs with innovative and new ideas, it will and frankly should start well before the authorization process while the business is starting to develop its operations. Figure 5.1 shows an overview of the UK's regulatory life cycle. Once the firm is authorized and it becomes a fully operating entity, it is then supervised. The authorization process is not a one-off process. This means that once you are regulated and authorized, you might one day return to authorization.

FIGURE 5.1 An illustration of the regulatory lifecycle

Regulatory innovation services

- New idea, pre-authorization
- Innovative technology or business model to be tested
- Existing or new firm to financial services
- Large or small or a partnership

New innovative idea

Authorization/ licence to operate

- Threshold Conditions are met
- Organization demonstrates that inherent harms in business model are addressed

- Variation in business model may require a variation in permissions or a new authorization

- Newly authorized firms move into supervision

Supervision
Reactive
Proactive
Early and high growth oversight

- Information gathering
- Regulatory relationship
- Remedial action
- Referral to enforcement

Because regulating financial services is activity-based, if you add a service or change how you offer services, you may need to obtain the right licence to conduct that service. Some examples include when:

- You have had a change to your business model that needs a variation to the licence type you obtained.

- You are adding new product lines that require new licences. For example, you are a payment firm that now wants to extend consumer credit.

- You have had a change in control, that is the significant shareholder of the organization has changed.

- You want to return your licence as you no longer operate some or all of the regulated services you did previously.

The list is not exhaustive, but it gives an idea of how a fintech may need to return to the authorization process. We will see how the activity at this stage of regulation ties directly into the expectation of how firms embed regulation and maintain high standards once they are authorized.

> As a regulated entity, you are a supervised financial services firm in the UK. The primary financial services regulator in the UK is the Financial Conduct Authority. Some of the larger banks and building societies, larger insurance companies and investment firms are regulated by the Prudential Regulation Authority (the PRA, an arm of the Bank of England, the UK's central bank) in addition to the FCA. These are referred to as 'dual regulated firms'.
>
> This dual regulation is not common elsewhere. In most jurisdictions, the prudential and conduct regulator will be the same with some exceptions, the extreme one being the US. In the case of the US, there are multiple federal and state-based regulators that are activity and geography based.

Depending on the size of the firm, it may be supervised on a reactive or on a proactive basis.[1] Proactive supervision tends to be the model for mature and systemically important financial services firms. But it may also apply to organizations that have grown to a point that their disruption can cause significant harm to consumers and the market. By and large, reactive supervision is what applies to the majority of firms across the financial services landscape.

Reactive supervision is based on indicators appearing or intelligence received that may prompt the regulator to look further, often into a particular point or angle. Reactive supervision is often after the fact and often remedial action is done when some kind of regulatory intervention is needed. During reactive supervision, firms are expected to continue to meet the conditions upon which they have been authorized, known as the Threshold Conditions. We discussed this in Chapter 2. There are regular reporting intervals and on a reactive basis the regulator can ask for further information or get in touch to test the various component parts of the Threshold Conditions.

Within reactive supervision, a firm may also be invited to take part in a market study or a thematic study. Often these are to test the effectiveness of a new policy or to test the adoption of new ideas by the market.[2]

At any time, a firm may be required to provide additional information and clarifications on various component parts of the Threshold Conditions. These conditions, as explained in earlier chapters, are the requirements the firm will need to continue to meet in order to keep its financial services licence. At this point, it's important to note that any breach of the Threshold Conditions can give rise to action from the regulator and a consequence could be the loss of licence.

Entering the authorization stage, the regulator is assessing the effectiveness of how you embed regulation. Is it sufficient to address the inherent drivers of harm in the firm's business model? Are the systems and controls and governance frameworks working? Do you have the right conduct culture?

The authorization process, as we will see in subsequent chapters sets the standard for how the business must continue to meet its obligations after obtaining its licence. Once authorized, the firm is subject to supervision by the regulator. If under supervision, the regulator spots that a firm is not meetings these standards, the firm may find itself in a position of being asked to implement simple changes, face full remediation or in some cases of clear misconduct, breaches or harms crystallizing, a firm may be referred to enforcement.[3]

We won't cover enforcement in this book. The idea of this book is to ensure the firm has the tools and the mindset to avoid getting to an enforcement stage. We will, however, talk about some of the common tools available to the regulator to ensure that firms are meeting their obligations and continue to set high standards for their conduct.

The regulators can ask for information at any time, and it is expected that the firm will respond promptly and transparently. A reason does not have to be given in every case particularly if it is relying on intelligence that may be sensitive. Ensuring an open and transparent relationship with the regulator is a requirement under the threshold condition 'effective supervision'. If information is requested from the firm, the regulator often assesses the information and may come back with a number of responses.[4] Below is a non-exhaustive list of some of the responses:

- The regulator may point out areas that can be improved for the firm's consideration and leave it to the firm to make those changes.

- They may point out areas of improvement and add a requirement for the firm to respond with confirmation that action has been taken.

- They may request a remediation plan and indicate a further review following the firm confirming that the remediation plan has been put in place.

- They may request a remediation plan and a continuous monitoring of the progress. This is often a multifunction, large improvement plan that may take a number of months to complete.

- They may request that the firm enter into a voluntary requirement to limit its operations in one way or another. For example, they can ask that it limits a particular type of business, or the number of sales it takes on or a type of market it is trying to serve. Of note, the licence remains the same, it's just restricted.

- The regulator may simply decide that a variation or limitation to how the firm operates is required. This is known as 'own initiative' requirement. It often uses this if the firm does not cooperate voluntarily, or the breaches are egregious.

- They may decide to change the nature of the licence. This is known as variation of permission which is effectively a variation to the licence. This can be done on a voluntary basis or directed by the regulator (known as 'own initiative').

- The regulator may request a skilled person report or what is widely called a Section 166 under the Financial Services Markets Act in the UK. There are similar practices in most other jurisdictions and the technical name differs in different markets, but the objective is the same. A skilled person report is a requirement for a 'skilled' third party appointed by the regulator to conduct an independent review into the operations of the organization and report back the findings. It often also requires a remediation plan to be suggested and a further report once the remediation is concluded.

Many of these tools can also be used in combination with each other and the list as mentioned, is not exhaustive. As a firm considers its status as a supervised entity, it needs to consider to what extent it is embedding regulation and adhering to it. Once some of these tools are used, it can be costly for the organization to remediate.

Getting authorization right

The start of a good regulator journey in the UK is to get the authorization process right. The basis is the Threshold Conditions and they will continue to be the basis by which the firm is supervised. The expectation of the regulator is that the fintech understands what is required of them and why, and that they demonstrate that they embed that in their business, not only at the start, but during the life of the fintech.

The majority of regulated fintech firms in the UK are overseen by the FCA. They obtain their permissions and continue to be supervised by the FCA. Certain criteria apply that put the firm in what is called dual regulation. That is the firm is licensed and supervised by the FCA and the PRA as noted above.

There are a number of things that are worth studying and ensuring a fintech gets right before they submit their application. While the focus is the UK, these are likely to apply to other jurisdictions:

- The Threshold Conditions or Conditions for Authorization and how they apply.
- The business model's inherent risks and what mitigations are in place to address them.
- What a conduct culture is and how to embed a strong risk management and high standard conduct culture in the organization.
- The portfolio risks and how the organization is contributing to a strong subsector, or portfolio by its behaviour, the action it takes and the adherence to addressing the portfolio harms set out by the regulator.
- Consideration for other non-regulated activity that may sit alongside regulated activity and how that will impact the delivery of services from the point of view of consumer understanding.

Knowing this before you submit your application will demonstrate that you are '**ready, willing and organized**'.[5] This concept is not a requirement per se, but a way in which the regulator can assess that a fintech understands the obligations on them to meet the standard now and in the future.

You are **ready** when you have a complete application that has addressed all the initial requirements and is of high quality. You have done your research, sought advice where required, and understood the requirements of the application and how it relates to your business model. You understand what the inherent risks are and how you will look to mitigate them.

You are **willing** when you have understood the requirements to become a regulated entity and display the right attitude and mindset as you deal with the regulator. These include being open and transparent, responding in a timely way, proactively offering information that can be relevant and working with the regulator to get the best outcome for all involved.

You are **organized** when you have supporting documents as required throughout the process, have the resources, financial and non-financial, ready and structured effectively to be able to start operations once the application is approved.

While ready, willing and organized is considered and stressed at the application process, it is a requirement for all interactions with the regulator while the fintech is a regulated entity.

There is flexibility – within reason

The authorization process can be seen as rigid and rules based. But there can be some flexibility. Where flexibility is exercised, it is usually with very good reason and good planning.

In certain cases where the fintech does not have all its resources in place or the application may be missing a slight point, but can demonstrate all the other requirements, the application is of high standard and they have a clear plan on how they are closing any gaps, then there is no reason why the firm should hold back from submitting the application. These circumstances tend to be areas that are beyond the firm's control. The key point in this case is to demonstrate that they are ready, willing and organized, they understand exactly what the gap is and they have a plan to close that gap.

The plan should have a high degree of certainty and a valid reason as to why it needs extra time. The list of examples on offer below is not exhaustive of when a fintech should or shouldn't submit its application before it is fully ready, but it will help provide some guidance.

Financial resources. In the case that a fintech has a full application but it has not yet secured the financial resources that will ensure that it will meet its regulatory capital, liquidity and working capital requirements, it is best that they do not submit an application until their funding sources have been secured and there is certainty that the firm will not breach its financial resources' requirements in the near future. This may sound obvious, but there are cases in which the firm is awaiting a funding round to close or negotiations with investors are underway. An application is a time- and resource-consuming process and taking such risks, particularly where there isn't sufficient certainty and the fintech may need to withdraw its application is a waste of its precious resources at that early stage of its life.

I understand that this may be a difficult point. Funding for fintechs often comes through on the basis of a regulatory application being approved, and it is understandable that a fintech may wish to highlight that in the application. If a fintech is to apply without funding being secured, it must provide solid proof that there is a high degree of certainty it won't be left with inadequate financial resources once authorized. This goes to the organized point of the 'ready, willing and organized' guidance.

Senior manager function. It is recognized that senior managers play an important role in the running of the organization and setting its culture. In most cases, a requirement by the regulator is to hire some senior manager roles before the approval is granted. A head of compliance or a money laundering reporting officer are examples for payments and e-money firms.

In the case of the role holder being identified and serving a notice period, or being identified with the majority of the skills then there is a case for submitting the application with a very clear plan of the certainty of the role being fulfilled in very short order following the approval or in the case of a skills gap, the role holder having a very clear and targeted development plan to ensure they are fully qualified for the role in a timeframe that is reasonable.

Often when flexibility is offered and the application is approved, expect that it comes with conditions. This is where there are requirements placed on the firm, voluntary or own initiative as we discussed earlier, to fulfil the requirement as a condition of the authorization.

Equivalents of the Senior Managers and Certification Regime have been considered or implemented in other jurisdictions. Of note are the Yates Memo in the US, the Banking Executive Accountability Regime (BEAR) in Australia, the Manager in Charge (MIC) regime of Hong Kong and guidance offered by Singapore's Monetary Authority.[6]

Threshold Conditions

For solo regulated firms, there are five key Threshold Conditions from the FCA that they must demonstrate they have satisfied:[7]

- Business model
- Location of offices
- Effective supervision
- Appropriate resources
- Suitability

The Threshold Conditions are wide in nature. They apply to the sector as a whole but the detail in which they apply for each subsector of the financial services industry may vary. This is why they tie directly into the sector analysis that the FCA undertakes, as well as portfolio or subsector analysis which outlines the harms inherent in a particular portfolio (a portfolio or subsector is a group of firms that share a similar business model). For example, appropriate resources is a condition for each firm, but depending on the business model that may mean different things to different firms in practice. Payment firms are subject to different capital requirements to banks and mortgage intermediaries have different expectations to a consumer credit organization.

The regulator considers the Threshold Conditions from the point of view of risk. A clear articulation of the business, its purpose, what is does and how it does it is the baseline. The firm must showcase that the risks have been identified and thoughtful risk management frameworks appropriate for the size and scale of the business have been put in place. Below, we'll discuss the Threshold Conditions and how they tie into good risk management.

Business model (strategic, financial, legal and regulatory risk management)

Business model is an important condition and will be looked at closely during the authorization process and beyond. Under the business model, the fintech should explain its products and services, how they offer value to the market and consumers, how they plan to deliver these services, and whether they are appropriate to the target market, how sustainable they are from a financial and operational perspective and whether they are suitable for its regulated activity. A fintech should also be clear on where the inherent risks in the business model are, that they have identified them and have a plan in place on how to mitigate those risks.

Clear positive indicators of a good business model are when the fintech can explain some of the following:

- A business strategy that is clear on what it is setting out to do and why.
- The design and delivery of the product or service has demonstrated that it provides good value to consumers.
- The structure and operations of the fintech are set up to deliver the strategy.
- A sustainable business model. Can the fintech explain the revenue streams and its cost structures? Can it demonstrate stability in its financial position over the period in question? This is often tied to a three-year business plan.
- Realistic growth. Are the growth forecasts reasonable and are the sources of funding plausible?
- Price and quality. Does that revenue model offer fair prices to consumers and an appropriate level of quality for the price?
- Meeting consumer needs. Is the target market suitable for the product or service it is providing? Has anyone been excluded or are their needs not met due to the nature of the business model?
- Sales and customer service model. What are the sales channels and techniques and are these appropriate for the target market? Is there pressure selling, or are consumers sold products that are unsuitable for their needs? How do customers get the support they need and is it appropriate? How are vulnerable consumers being identified and serviced?

- Risk profile and risk mitigation. Has the fintech thought of its risk profile and considered how the risks are mitigated?

- Oversight of outsourcing arrangements. The fintech should consider any outsourcing arrangements and explain how they plan to oversee the value chain such that fair outcomes to consumers are delivered.

- How will the business model guard against wider society harms such as financial crime and money laundering or other such harms? How will it not cause other market failures such as market disruption, reduced market access or price control?

These are some of the areas a fintech should think about when running their business on all accounts. Clarity of vision and how this is connected to the way in which the organization is operationalizing its business and delivering to its target market will ensure a good dialogue between the fintech and the regulator when it comes to the application.

When explaining a business model, there is often confusion on what's in scope and what is not. If you are a regulated entity, you expect that you are covering the regulated activity. That is not strictly the case. If you happen to offer services that are regulated and some that aren't, it is important that the fintech explains the entire business model end-to-end. This is important and will be discussed later in this chapter.

I started with business model because it is the anchor that ties all the other conditions together. Location of offices, suitability, effective supervision and adequate resources are all components of the business model.

Location of offices (legal and regulatory risk management)

This condition in summary under the Financial Services Markets Act 2023 stipulates that the firm needs to have offices in the UK. If it is a body corporate in the UK, then its head office must be located in the UK. If it is not a body corporate in the UK but has its head office in the UK, then it must do business in the UK.[8]

That is the technical requirement. Effectively, it's about ensuring that there is sufficient focus from the management of the company on the UK market. The term used regarding this condition is mind and management of the firm. Where is the mind and management of the firm? In other words, where are key decisions that the firm makes in regard to the UK market being made? It allows for issues to be identified early on and for customers to know who they are dealing with and who to contact when things go wrong. This is also an important condition under the senior manager and certification regime. Overseeing a firm, its operations and senior management is much more difficult if all these were outside the UK. It's even more difficult if UK law does not apply in the jurisdiction in which the firm is incorporated and its senior managers reside. There is a requirement for specific senior manager functions to be located in the UK as a result of this. You can see how this is inadvertently linked to the next condition of effective supervision.

Effective supervision (legal, regulatory, reputational risk management)

Effective supervision in this case relates to the structural set up of the organization. How complex is its corporate structure? How does the UK entity interact with other entities such as the parent company or other subsidiaries and branches? Where does it obtain its various services such as back office, customer service, accounting or IT and who makes the decisions on the number of resources allocated to it?

What other dependencies does the entity have on the parent and how complex are these structures? For example, an entity that is tied to a liquidity structure of a global parent will have additional complexities around the liquidity adequacy for the UK entity. How complex are the products and services and can there be products that are not regulated interacting with those that are regulated and offered in the same package?

All these questions give rise to additional complexities in terms of how the regulator can oversee the organization effectively to ensure that it meets its local obligations. It is of particular importance in times of stress and disruption. Complex structures make it difficult for anyone to understand the options when things go wrong or what to do in the case of the business having to close down.

This does not suggest that the organization must simplify its structure or product offering for the sake of it, but equally it should not overcomplicate it for no reason either. It simply means that it must ensure that it has a clear answer to all these questions which outlines in a transparent way how these structures do not hinder its ability to offer quality services to UK consumers and meet its regulatory obligations. For example, if it is offering regulated and non-regulated activities, how is it ensuring that this is clear to its customers? If it does rely on the parent for liquidity, how does it demonstrate that in times of stress, it will get the right priority and has an acceptable plan to ensure no disruption to its services?

Appropriate resources

Appropriate is the key word in this condition. It is important that the firm can demonstrate that it has the right resources, financial and non-financial for its stage of its development.

At the application process, demonstrating appropriate resources is based on the business plan the fintech submits with its application. The business plan will usually have forecasts for the size and scale of the operation in the first three years and the resources should cater for the growth the organization is expecting in those early years.

Financial resourses (financial risk management)

Financial resources is about the specific rules around what the organization must hold in terms of capital and liquidity. These are referred to as quantified prudential regime. However, adequate financial resources is more than the rules. When submitting your application, it is important that you submit key information including:

- Financial statements including balance sheet, cash flow and income statements.

- If you have been already operating, then providing three years of historical accounts is essential.

- Three years' forward-looking financial projections.

- Notes to the financial statements outlining key assumptions and how they relate to the business plan. The notes are important to explain how your forecasts are reasonable and not over ambitious.

- Complete details that are relevant to the legal entity that is being authorized. You cannot submit partial information so this may involve information from parent entities as it relates to the financial position of the UK entity.

These are the mandatory and minimal requirements. There are other considerations that may assist in adding to your application to give more context and strengthen to the application. Some are outlined below:

- Consider adding the fintech's finance strategy and an outline of your financial risk management, identifying key risks to your financial position and how you mitigate those risks.

- Wind-down plan. Consider whether the fintech should submit one. This has attracted a lot of focus from regulators during Covid and subsequent economic challenges where firms can face financial stress. The regulator sees that the ideal wind-down scenario is a solvent one. Therefore, ensuring that it is triggered at a point at which the firm is no longer a going concern but has provisioned for a solvent wind-down.

- Stress testing and risk management generally. It is a good habit for the business continuity sake to consider what the buffers required in times of stress are. For example, what is the provision for an operational failure or a loss of confidence, or a run on deposits. What contingency liquidity and capital should the fintech hold?

Non- financial resources (operational, cyber, people, governance risk management)

These are people, systems, infrastructure and services that are needed for the effective running of the organization. Describing these and how they complement the business plan and the three-year forecast will give substance to the application. Proving adequacy here is important. A fintech may not need large compliance teams, or the most state of the art software to run a small operation in the initial three years but aligning resources to the biggest impact areas and keeping that under review is important. They also need to demonstrate that they have thought of what the inherent risks of harm to consumers are and how have they resourced the organization to deal with those risks. For example, in our case study in Chapter 10, Insignis Cash solutions identified that cybersecurity is one of its key risks, as the impact of this going wrong for their business model is too great to ignore. They invested heavily at the early stages in ensuring they got this right.

These impact areas and managing the risk around them will be different for each fintech, but outlining how non-financial resources are aligned to deliver the business plan and manage those risks is key.

HUMAN RESOURCES (PEOPLE RISK)
A fintech should explain their people strategy including attracting and retaining talent, training and upskilling tools outlining key roles that need to be fulfilled and that the skills and experience of the staff are of quality and appropriate level. Some of these roles may be required as a senior manager function, but the fintech must think of its key functions in addition to the regulatory functions. In some instances, considering skills gaps and succession planning or key person risk as part of the application may be needed.

Ensuring the right senior roles in the right place such that there is adequate oversight and effective decision-making is also a key consideration that should align to the business plan and will change over time.

An emerging area to consider for digital-based platforms or app-based businesses is how do consumers reach the fintech if they need to. Under the Consumer Duty, consideration to the consumer experience and the consistency of that experience across the life of the relationship between fintech and consumers is important. How do they ensure that the digital only experience that has been smooth at the onboarding stage continues to be so during the customer services or exit experience. And how do they ensure that there is a human back up to support the consumer when things go wrong.

SYSTEMS AND INFRASTRUCTURE (OPERATIONAL AND CYBER RISKS)

These are the things needed to run the business effectively, from emails, computers and printers to real estate to process and structures that keep the business operational.

Often these are considered back-office-type functions, such as IT services, risk and compliance, detection and monitoring software or even as simple as providing software and hardware to allow staff to do their jobs. These may be considered basics but due consideration for the control frameworks that are put in place to keep the organization and its customers safe is important. For example, ensuring data protection and cybersecurity relative to the size and scale of the operation is essential. For a lot of payments firms, thinking about financial crime controls as well as onboarding and KYC processes is necessary.

Running some of the systems on an Excel spreadsheet or not having three lines of defence may be suitable in the initial stages of the fintech's life but a business model that predicts growth in revenue must also consider growth in the back-office functions to ensure that it continues to operate effectively.

> The three lines of defence is a structure that ensures appropriate oversight of the business operations and is seen as best practice particularly in mature organizations. The first line is your front office teams, dealing directly with consumers or building and delivering products and services. The second line is the support functions such as risk, compliance and legal and the third line is internal audit. Most larger organizations have an internal audit function despite having a requirement for periodical auditing, often of their accounts.

GOVERNANCE AND POLICIES

Governance as discussed earlier keeps the organization on course to deliver its strategy.[9] Considering what the decision-making structure is, how that will change, what the roles and responsibilities are across all levels of the organization and how that ensures the effective running of the business is important to highlight. Senior manager functions are usually prescribed for the fintech by the regulator, but it helps if the fintech is already thinking about how to make this work for them. For example, at what point do they start to bring in a non-executive director, or when do they need a chief risk officer as a standalone function. How are they structured and what reporting tools are used to ensure the right level of oversight and accountability is carried out?

Policies support the governance structures. They offer consistency on how everyone must behave, what their responsibilities are towards each other and towards the consumers they serve. Both governance and policies can play a big part in setting the tone of the culture. An example of this is incident management. In the case of a large-scale incident, how is the incident management team formed? Does everybody know their role and how is the incident management process invoked? What is included in an application regarding adequate resources differs from one organization to another. The business model will be a good starting point that can inform other parts of the application.

Suitability (regulatory, reputational risk management)

Suitability is a firm and those who manage it and make key decisions act with probity and integrity ensuring that they offer value to consumers and do not cause harm. Suitability not only relates to the internal operations and decisions of the organization but its connections, relationships and complexity of its activities.

The ability to competently explain the legal structure of the organization, why it is suitable for the nature of products and services it delivers and declare any relationships or conflicts up front will be required during the application process and beyond. The manner of the fintech's interaction with the regulator is an indicator of this condition. Openness, cooperation and transparency are always the best approach.

The Senior Manager and Certification Regime is designed to ensure individuals in influential functions in the organization have the right skills, experience and knowledge to perform their function, that their professional and personal record does not have an impact on their ability to perform the role and they perform the role with high integrity, driving a good conduct culture that rewards doing the right thing. These are a set of tests that deem them fit for the role. We refer to this as the fit and proper test. This should also be backed up by the right policy and procedures designed to ensure that the fintech is acting with probity and puts the consumers at the heart of its decisions, processes and activities.

Demonstrating that the fintech takes a conduct culture seriously through its hiring process, its induction and onboarding of staff, its process and procedures such as whistleblowing and risk reporting are all indicators of a meeting the suitability condition.

This is an important condition to give the regulator comfort that the organization does not run the risk of being a vehicle for financial crime or other activity that may cause harm to consumers. Note that the fit and proper test does not only apply to financial services activities that fall within the senior manager regime. The expectation of fitness and proprietary applies to all regulated financial services.

Payments and e-money firms' additional requirements

As outlined in Chapter 2, payment firms in the UK follow a very similar set of standards as set by the Threshold Conditions, called the Conditions for Authorization. In addition to the five conditions above, payment firms must explain how their safeguarding is compliant and their anti-money laundering systems and controls are effective. These requirements are very similar to other payments licensing regimes across the world.

In addition, payment initiation service providers (PISPs) and account information service providers (AISPs) which are payment firms that have come under regulation since the second Payment Services Directive (PSD2) across Europe and open banking in the UK, must obtain professional indemnity insurance or PII.

Safeguarding of customer funds

Upon submitting an application to be a payments or e-money provider, you must ensure that you comply with the safeguarding requirements. There is tremendous focus on safeguarding and getting this right is important. The payments firm must demonstrate it understands its obligations and has the right policies and systems to ensure sound and effective safeguarding.

Safeguarding of customer funds essentially is segregating client funds from corporate funds. A firm cannot, under any circumstances co-mingle the two. An example of corporate funds are the funds the firm has for working capital which have to be in a separate account. Customer funds are the funds the firm is holding onto for the purposes of transaction activity as instructed by the customer.

The firm then must ensure that it is performing reconciliation of customer funds at least daily. It must demonstrate that the right systems and procedures are in place to perform this task and any anomalies or issues are identified and rectified quickly.

We discussed previously why this is important and it simply comes down to the fact that customer funds held with payments and e-money firms are not subject to protection by the financial services compensation scheme in the UK. Safeguarding is precisely as the name suggests for these funds.

Anti-money laundering controls

At the heart of payments and e-money firms is moving money. Processes for combating money laundering and financial crime is a critical requirement and the fintech must demonstrate that it has the right systems and controls, procedures and conduct culture that will keep the firm and its customers safe. Payments firms will have to demonstrate to the regulators that they have put this at the heart of their business and understand their obligations. They are required to hire a money laundering reporting officer (MLRO) as a key requirement to get the licence.

Open banking

Open banking firms usually require authorization under the payment services regulations. There are two types of open banking firms.

Payment Initiation Services providers

These are firms that conduct payments, and therefore require payment authorization if they don't already have this. In addition, a fintech as a payments initiation service provide must obtain professional indemnity insurance and implement compliant strong customer authentication and common and secure communication.

Account information service providers

These are firms that provide a consolidated view of the payments accounts held by customers across multiple financial institutions in one location, often dashboard style.

If you are only providing account information services, you can become a Registered Account Information Services Provider or RAISP, which requires you to register your business with the FCA rather than obtain authorization. This means that you do not need to commit any capital and the obligations the fintech adheres to are slightly less.[10]

The fintech must also register any individuals responsible for managing the firm or for managing the payment data received. The RAISP deals with sensitive and confidential payments data, therefore there are obligations around how it manages and protects the data.

Generally, the application requires that you submit:

- Business plan with financial information.
- Risk management frameworks, control frameworks and governance arrangements.
- Cyber and information security policy.
- Business continuity process, incident management framework, data protection policy and complaints handling policy.

- Professional indemnity insurance.
- Implement compliant strong customer authentication and common and secure communication.

Non-regulated activities

Non-regulated activities are an important consideration at an application process and beyond. This has been an interesting area to the regulator in the past few years due to some of the overlaps and consumer understanding of financial products, what might be regulated or how they may be protected. You must report unregulated activity as and when your organization conducts it, starting with an explanation of your end-to-end business model for the body corporate that is looking to conduct the regulated activity as well as reporting substantial changes as and when they occur.

However, it is activity that is still within or related to financial services rather than a completely different industry. For example, if your organization offers credit on the products that it sells, you will need to outline the entire business model and how the regulated and unregulated activities interact. This is particularly important when there is clear overlap between services for a number of reasons. An organization must itself understand what is a regulated activity and its obligations under this status, and what is not. How resources are shared, what is the delineation between the two and how the structure, operations, systems and controls and governance frameworks operate to ensure both sets of services are operating efficiently and in a compliant manner is necessary. There is a commercial reason for this. A firm does not need to dedicate more resources than are needed to ensure that it is compliant.

A word of caution on this. While it makes sense to be responsible with sharing or allocation of resources, the firm should ensure they are doing this with the commitment to embed regulatory obligations and a conduct culture. Culture is the key point. If a firm puts a good conduct culture at the heart of its decisions no matter whether the activity is a regulated or unregulated one, together with an under-standing of the obligations at all levels of the organization, it will no doubt meet its regulatory obligations while managing resources effectively. OakNorth, a UK fintech with a banking licence offering a digital platform for fast and efficient loans which we discuss further in Chapter 10, operates a regulated and unregulated business. It considers the balance between the two and in this case has set them up as two different entities.

It is crucial that the senior executives understand these obligations and requirements and where the regulated activity is a side activity or a complementary activity, that it is not neglected. Decisions made that are relevant to one part of the business may negatively impact the regu-lated activity. Customers must understand what a regulated activity is and what it is not. What are their rights if things go wrong and how are they protected? The lines can be blurred, and it may not be intuitive to consumers which will result in consumers making decisions based on false interpretation and not getting good outcomes. Firms offering unregulated crypto services alongside their regulated activity can cause consumers to surmise their money is safe when it's not.

One common example is in payments. Payments firms conducting specific activities must become regulated under the payment services regulation. Often payments firms conduct spot foreign exchange trans-actions. In fact, in a lot of cases, the firm identifies as a foreign exchange service provider, and they do this well with lower rates and a quick online service. Spot FX (which is offering an FX rate on the spot, or at the time of the transaction) is not a regulated activity, even though it is something most of us do when sending money overseas or travelling. However, the instruction to move money from one account to the other is a payment activity and is regulated under the payment services regula-tion. To offer a full foreign exchange service to customers, the organization will offer FX (the rate to swap money from one currency to another) and payments (the ability to move that money between accounts).

You can see how consumers are confused by this. Furthermore, FX firms may hold funds for a very short time for transaction purposes, but they are not deposit-taking institutions and if you leave money with them, it is not protected under the government deposit cover scheme.

All this sounds like it's irrelevant if the customer is getting what they need, and it is good value. But imagine a situation where the firm is in financial difficulty and fails. The only regulated activity is the payment transfer, and if the funds held with the firm are not protected, the consumer loses their money.

Of note, and using the same example of the FX firm, if it holds funds longer than it should, it may appear to be taking deposits. This will be acting outside its permissions and enforcement action of some kind could take place if uncovered. So, in the case of our FX firm example, explaining how the firm is segregating its clients' funds, not holding funds longer than it should and putting in the right triggers for when a solvent wind-down to ensure there is no disruption is required.

Financial promotions

We have discussed regulated and unregulated activity and how they interact and overlap. A key vehicle to addressing the harm this may cause due to consumers' confusion and misinterpretation is via financial promotions. The marketing activity, advertisements or external communications that the firm puts out to market its products are all considered financial promotions. The FCA defines it as 'any invitation of inducement to engage in investment activity, when communicated in the course of business'.[11]

Financial promotions and unregulated activity that can be confused for financial services that are regulated are closely linked. When digital assets started being promoted, sometimes by influencers who didn't adhere to any of the requirements of a financial promotion, there was a drive to bring digital assets into the financial promotions' regime. The regime came into effect in 2023 and was designed to minimize the harm misleading financial promotions may pose to consumers that are seeing and hearing the hype of investing in crypto assets that will appreciate in value over a short period of time without explaining the volatility of the asset and the fact that it can depreciate just as quickly, resulting in many people losing, in some instances, quite a lot of money.

What a firm says on the various marketing mediums signals to consumers what is on offer. Therefore, ensuring that fair value, accurate information presented in a clear and easy to understand way helps. The regulator refers to this as 'clear, fair and not misleading'. What this means in reality is that a firm must think about every sentence it puts on its website, how it is presented, how it is interpreted by the audience, what might be the behaviour it drives and does this overall experience offer good outcomes.

Clear means that you have to be sure that your audience is able to understand the offer you are making, and you are not using jargon and language that nobody understands. Consumers should have all the information they need including how the product operates, what to expect, what its value is, how to sign up and cancel. In addition, the firm must think about sharing information such as how much protection they have, what is the risk profile of this product and whom this might be suitable for. This is not an exhaustive list, and it varies from one firm to the other.

Fair and not misleading ensures that the offer describes accurately what it is and isn't. Offering attractive rates that lock consumers into a plan not suitable for them is an obvious example. Hidden fees or break clauses is another. Suggesting that the firm is authorized by the FCA is an endorsement that can be misleading. This is where some of the concepts we discussed on Consumer Duty come into effect. Nudge and gamification practices that entice consumers to sign up and get rewards to start using a particular product, often popular in trading apps, can be seen as misleading because it is driving a particular behaviour that is not conducive to the consumer stopping and thinking about whether this is the right product for them.

Other considerations are the balance of how to present the benefits of the offer against the risks. The firms must think about how to present the promotion in a balanced way, giving equal prominence to the risks and where there is no back up such as deposit insurance or FSCS. The medium where the promotion is advertised is irrelevant. The expectation applies to any financial promotion, social media included. Using celebrities to promote the product via a tweet doesn't preclude the financial promotions' expectations being met and the firm being held to account if consumers suffer harm.

The same principles apply when a firm is operating regulated and unregulated activity such as our FX firm example. Clear outlining what the FCA authorization relates to, what protections the consumer has or does not have and ensuring visibility and prominence of those balanced with the benefits of the firm's offer is important.

Financial promotions are tested at the authorization stage as much as is practical. The firm hasn't launched its operations yet and the marketing strategy and content is usually an ambition. When the firm obtains its authorization and starts to trade, the advertising effort increases and the material, content and message can change. The firm must always ensure it is thinking of financial promotions being clear, fair and not misleading as well as presenting the benefits against risks in a way that is balanced. This is an ongoing task. Much attention is paid to financial promotions, and it helps if the firm is proactive in this space.

The FCA's Consumer Duty

The Consumer Duty went live in July 2023. The authorization process requires firms to explain how they have considered and embedded the Consumer Duty in their operations.

Ensuring that the fintech has thought of how the Consumer Duty is being observed in their operations will be an important factor in the assessment process. Now that the Consumer Duty is live in the UK, it serves the fintech to think about it in the very early stages of design not just for the application process. Many firms have had to adjust their processes and systems to implement the Consumer Duty. For new firms, this will already be established. Ensuring consumers are able to achieve their financial objectives, avoiding foreseeable harm and acting in good faith are the key cross-cutting rules of the Consumer Duty. These naturally align to the purpose of the fintech.

The application process should outline how the fintech will embed these and how it will deliver on the Consumer Duty outcomes such as:

- Fair value for money.
- Products and services are designed effectively for the target market.
- Consumers understand what they are buying; the communication is in plain language and simple to understand so they make informed choices.
- Consumer support is effective and available; that it is consistent with the buying experience and ensures the consumer can pursue their financial objectives without unnecessary friction.

Summary and takeaways

Authorization is the licence to operate, and being ready, willing and organized are key principles to ensuring that an application will be a successful one. The principle of ready, willing and organized does largely mean that an organization must understand the authorization process, and what the Threshold Conditions are under which they are assessed.

The Threshold Conditions are the basis of the authorization process but as this is the start of the regulatory life cycle, they are the conditions under which the firm continues to be assessed. Meeting them will ensure that they can continue to hold a licence to operate.

The FCA's Threshold Conditions are business model, location of offices, effective supervision, appropriate resources and suitability. Explaining how the business model works, how the firm is profitable, the strategy and operations, legal structure as well as how it organizes its resources in a way that will ensure the effective and efficient meeting of its regulatory obligations is key information to provide the regulator in the authorization process and beyond.

Explaining the end-to-end business model is key. This includes non-regulated activity. It is important to disclose openly activity that sits alongside the regulated products and services. The firm must clearly explain how the two activities interact and what impact one may have on the other in relation to resource allocation or in relation to interpretation by consumers to avoid confusion. Consumers must be clear about the products offered, what is regulated and what the protections available to them are.

Financial promotions matter. Ensuring that they are clear, fair and not misleading and that consideration is given to the balance of content and appearance of messages in all marketing material and communications is crucial. The medium used on the other hand, does not matter. Financial promotions are agnostic to the medium or platform.

Notes

1 Financial Conduct Authority. SUP 1A.3 The FCA's approach to supervision, FCA Handbook, 2023. www.handbook.fca.org.uk/handbook/SUP/1A/3. html?date=2016-03-07#:~:text=The%20overall%20approach%20in%20 the%20FCA%20supervision%20model,lens%20of%20the%20impact%20 on%20consumers%3B%20More%20items (archived at https://perma.cc/ CGF4-H3SA).

2 Financial Conduct Authority. Supervision. Financial Conduct Authority, London, 2023. www.fca.org.uk/about/how-we-regulate/supervision (archived at https://perma.cc/EX5E-FCCL).

3 Financial Conduct Authority. Supervision. Financial Conduct Authority, London, 2023. www.fca.org.uk/about/how-we-regulate/supervision (archived at https://perma.cc/MAU9-VUNS).

4 Financial Conduct Authority. FCA Mission: Approach to Supervision. Financial Conduct Authority, London, 2019. www.fca.org.uk/publication/ corporate/our-approach-supervision-final-report-feedback-statement.pdf (archived at https://perma.cc/Q86N-FN74)

5 Financial Conduct Authority. How to apply for authorisation or registration. Financial Conduct Authority, London, 2023. www.fca.org.uk/firms/ authorisation/apply (archived at https://perma.cc/B4YS-75L9).

6 Linklaters. A global guide to senior management accountability. Linklaters, London, 2018. www.linklaters.com/en/insights/publications/2018/september/ senior-management-accountability-a-global-perspective (archived at https:// perma.cc/EKE7-MZ8L).

7 Financial Conduct Authority. Supervisory Correspondence. Financial Conduct Authority, London, 2024. www.fca.org.uk/about/how-we-regulate/supervision/supervisory-correspondence (archived at https://perma.cc/Q9FE-NPAS).

8 Financial Conduct Authority. COND 2.2 Threshold condition 2: Location of offices. FCA Handbook, 2023. www.handbook.fca.org.uk/handbook/COND/2/2.html?date=2013-03-31 (archived at https://perma.cc/TML7-YE3H).

9 Chartered Institute of Governance UK and Ireland (nd). What is governance? Chartered Institute of Governance UK and Ireland. www.cgi.org.uk/professional-development/discover-governance/looking-to-start-a-career-in-governance/what-is-governance (archived at https://perma.cc/KR48-CJ83).

10 Financial Conduct Authority. Registered account information service provider (RAISP) applicants. Financial Conduct Authority, London, 2023. www.fca.org.uk/firms/apply-emoney-payment-institution/raisp (archived at https://perma.cc/E9LD-JSK7).

11 Financial Conduct Authority. Financial Promotions, FCA Handbook, 2023. www.handbook.fca.org.uk/handbook/glossary/G421.html (archived at https://perma.cc/5EYM-FMJU).

6

Navigating regulation that doesn't exist

CHAPTER SUMMARY

- Regulation that is emerging in the world of fintech
- Open banking to open finance. The considerations when developing open finance solutions
- Digital assets, the upcoming regulation and what organizations should do in the meantime
- Artificial intelligence is not just a fintech game
- Existing regulations can be a base for new technologies. Same risk, same regulator outcome
- Outcomes based regulation can be a good tool in how to navigate regulation that doesn't yet exist

New and emerging regulation

As we've discussed across this book, there are a lot of new technologies making their way into our lives. As technologies develop, financial services will be a beneficiary of these changes. These can be game changers and have the potential to transform how we transact and live our lives.

Of course, some of these new innovative trends are the three areas we have so far covered in this book:

· The movement towards open banking and open finance.

· Crypto assets.

· Artificial intelligence.

Other innovations that are slowly entering the financial services ecosystem now or on the near horizon are:

· Embedded finance.

· Quantum computing.

· The meta and multiverse and virtual reality.

The momentum of these new technologies isn't going to wane any time soon. As we discussed in earlier chapters, regulation doesn't always keep up with new technology. It's a balancing act for regulators to decide how quickly they should respond.

In the meantime, fintechs using new technologies will have to navigate their own way through regulation to ensure that there are no pitfalls now or in the future. Many of these technologies cut across multiple regulators which makes the task for firms even more daunting. Often legal and compliance teams are able to interpret current legislation and legal frameworks to advise on the regulatory and legal risk facing the fintech. However, it becomes a difficult task when there is no regulation covering the innovative way in which technology is being used.

'Buy now pay later' is a current example of embedded finance and an area where understanding the regulatory risk can be complicated. There have been no standards that guide how they must operate. 'Buy now pay later', as the name suggests, offers micro financing on any day-to-day purchase and is embedded in the shopping journey. The characteristics of how 'buy now pay later' works falls outside existing payments and outside consumer credit regulation. In the UK, Australia and Singapore for example, there is now an effort to bring these activities within the scope of regulation, in other words inside the 'regulatory perimeter'. The UK has confirmed its intention to do so via a consultation process.[1] Crypto assets is another development where the volatility and risk associated with these assets have raised concern across the market. The various company collapses that we have mentioned previously in this book have accelerated the need for crypto assets to be regulated. However, the current state of regulations of crypto assets is quite limited.

So how do companies consider regulation when there is no regulation? The approach will be different for each fintech, but we will cover some of the ways in which the fintech can think of embedding the right level of risk management and think about how regulation may emerge in a way that is proportionate to its operations and the nature of its business. The idea here is the fintech can think of how to use risk management and regulation in a way that will help its business. Meeting obligations it may have now or in the future will be a by-product of this approach.

A WORD ON EMBEDDED FINANCE

I introduced 'buy now pay later' in this chapter as an example of embedded finance. Embedded finance is becoming an increasingly popular idea among financial services professionals and there are frequent discussions its applications. However, embedded finance has been part of our lives for a number of years.

A simple search will give you many definitions of embedded finance. They all effectively mean that a traditional non-financial type of activity will have a financial service 'embedded' in the customer journey in a seamless way. For a long time, we have been offered insurance by ticking a box when booking flights. Payment methods have been embedded in our online shopping journeys for a while now without leaving the online shopping site. Modulr, established in 2015 (see case study in Chapter 10) consider their service an embedded payments service.

'Buy now pay later' is the latest popular use case for embedded finance, adding a consumer credit type of product into a shopping experience. The UK's HM Treasury announced its intention to regulate 'buy now pay later' in 2021 following a review by former interim CEO of the FCA, Christopher Woolard which identified that while this is a useful mechanism for households and individuals to manage their finances, there are potential harms which primarily revolve around the individual or household plunging into debt they cannot afford.

The Woolard review called for bringing these services into regulation thus ensuring that the organizations providing these services perform effective affordability checks. It also called for financial promotions that are clear, fair and not misleading.[2] Guidance, rules and standards will be set by the Financial Conduct Authority for the authorization and supervision of these services. These processes often take time. The process will start with a call for a review that offers recommendations, moves to a consultation process, includes a response to the consultation and the commitment to take action or make changes which eventually could impact regulation itself. However, what do fintechs do in the meantime?

Existing regulation as a guide

Naturally, engaging in the debate, talking to government and regulators is important for fintechs to be prepared for any new regulation. In addition, considering existing regulation and how it might apply or be similar helps too. Keeping in mind the principle of same risk, same regulatory outcome, which has been used in crypto regulation, is a good starting guide. Further, considering the outcomes for consumers and designing product that clearly and visibly takes consumer outcomes into consideration throughout the end-to-end experience goes a long way in providing stability to the market for new services. Outcome-based regulation such as the UK's Consumer Duty discussed in Chapters 2 and 5 is also a good guide. Many fintechs want to do the right thing and this is one way of demonstrating the desire to operate a safe and strong market.

The benefit of starting with existing regulation is the fintech can test what works and what doesn't. In general, regulators have tried to create a space in which to experiment with this via tech sprints that can inform policy thinking. However, fintechs are still frequently left wondering what the end outcome might be. It is up to each fintech to tackle this in a way that makes sense to their vision, strategy and the outcomes they want to deliver to the market in which they operate. In this chapter I will point out some of the ways in which they can consider this as part of their overall risk management approach while keeping options open for how regulation will evolve in the future.

Open banking to open finance – the use of data

I introduced open banking and how it is regulated in Chapter 3. The following standards are at its heart:

- The security of sending and receiving information.

- Value to consumers that will help them make better choices or enhance their financial lives.

- The explicit consent needed to ensure customers are informed and understand what they are signing up to.

- A seamless customer journey that doesn't include unnecessary friction.

There are usually three parties to any open banking proposition: a financial institution that holds a person's information, a third-party provider that wants to access the person's information and, of course, the person. When considering the above, simple and intuitive model, we can see how the development of open banking to open finance can emerge. Holding the same principles can support the development of open finance and open data. However, the move from open banking to open finance has not been as easy as anticipated for many reasons. Some of the key areas of difficulty are technical standards, participation, implementation and regulation.

Technical standards

The required technical standards for open banking and open finance have been one of the most difficult areas to get right for any type of protocol. Technical standards often mean that the protocols and specifications are prescribed in detail and are consistent. But who agrees what those specifications are? Who is confident enough to say these are the standards that everyone must adhere to? What would the impact of this be to the competitive dynamics of the market?

The main technical standards question in the development of PSD2 (PSD2 being a European directive as opposed to open banking which was developed in the UK) was what APIs would be used. Under the PSD2, the final specifications of these APIs were left to the various participants as long as they met the regulatory and security standards. Open banking in the UK developed its own technical standards, and the market was encouraged to adopt the open banking APIs or 'open APIs'. Of course, multiple APIs emerged that met the regulatory technical standards.

There were two sides to the argument. One is that competition forces will drive the right outcomes for the market and regulators should be technology agnostic (the approach Europe took under PSD2). The other is that standardizing APIs provides lower barriers to entry for new and innovative fintechs, known as third-party providers or TPPs, to access the open banking market (the approach the UK took). That is, if they develop the APIs once, they can connect to all financial institutions that hold customer data.

The approach the UK has taken is to offer standards and lower barriers to entry.[3] Open Banking Limited offers details of API specifications, security profiles, operational guidelines and customer experience guidelines.

TrueLayer, an open banking fintech, identified the struggle that multiple APIs pose, particularly to smaller third-party providers in open banking. This is why they developed a proposition to offer an aggregated service where the third-party provider can connect to multiple banks and account providers by connecting to TrueLayer just once. This has proven to be a successful business model which they have deployed around the world.

Participation

In the UK, the Competition and Markets Authority (CMA) mandated that the largest banks in the UK develop open banking. Participation was mandatory. Third-party providers also needed to be regulated or at least registered with the Financial Conduct Authority. The question of participation is an important one. There is an implementation cost to open banking and regulators need to ensure that costs don't outweigh the benefit to the economy. These are sometimes the arguments behind allowing the market and any associated standards to develop naturally. Equally, with limited participation, open banking won't be effective in offering optionality and new propositions to consumers.

Implementation

There is no point in developing a framework that is meant to nudge the market and fuel innovation and competition if it isn't going to be implemented. Implementation is always a contentious issue in any organization. Frequently, it doesn't go to plan, there isn't agreement on how it is funded, costs more time and effort and the end result doesn't always match the very first blueprint design. This is often the case even with a well-defined blueprint, a programme team with oversight and governance and resources dedicated to the implementation.

So how can we expect implementation to work across a market? An open banking implementation entity was set up in the UK to oversee this. It had enough specific detail regarding timelines, participants, some technical specifications and expectations for consumers to make it a successful approach. It has not come without its challenges, but it has ensured that the vast majority of financial institutions who need to comply have done so and have now moved to an entity that will deliver a future roadmap set out by the regulator (see our discussion of JROC in Chapter 2).

Regulation

Does regulation lead, or does it follow? Does it oscillate depending on the time, priorities and resources? In the case of open banking in the UK, regulators were certainly in the lead. It was due to competition remedies that open banking was born and is now a concept replicated across the world.

Regulators leading gives a wide degree of comfort to the market in standards being set and the sector developing in a way that is safe and resilient. Standards, participation and implementation discussed above were set by regulation and it allowed the industry to move ahead. The way the UK has approached the next stage of open banking is to set up a set of expectations ensuring that open banking can develop beyond what it is today. It doesn't cover open finance or open data, but it is another stepping stone to its progress. While open banking was developed via regulation, attempts to move to open finance or open data have not progressed so far in the UK.

What can fintechs do in the meantime?

Fintechs who are looking at propositions that go beyond the scope of open banking today will face challenges due to the lack of regulation. If, however, fintechs find partners that are willing to develop these propositions with them, there are some principles that can be used to ensure the right outcomes for consumers and the market.

- The current open banking protocols can be used as a base. These are now tried and tested and there are guidelines for security standards, operational expectations and consumer outcomes.

- Consider cybersecurity and data protection as a high priority risk to be managed. In the case of data sharing, data protection and cybersecurity will be the fundamental concerns that will come up for any regulator, whether the financial regulator, the data protection regulator or any other regulatory body.

- Use the regulatory sandbox services available. Many regulators have set up sandboxes to test some of the new and emerging ideas around unlocking data sets and data sharing.

- Keep the FCA's Consumer Duty (or equivalent) at the heart. The Consumer Duty can be a strong anchor for how propositions are being developed. This is because it puts the consumer at the heart of the product or service and asks the service provider to think about the outcome at every stage. Firms can therefore think carefully about consent, with whom and how they share data, guiderails to ensure safety and security, what redress or protection they may wish to offer in the case of services not being provided as described and other consumer related outcomes.

TrueLayer, one of the first open banking fintechs to be established and now a successful fintech that operates in many locations around the world, has considered how to navigate new and nascent regulations and how to innovate when a new regime can be restrictive. The case study in Chapter 10 gives more details of TrueLayer's experience.

CONSIDER THRESHOLD CONDITIONS

Threshold Conditions can be another baseline that can help when developing new innovative solutions around open banking. Business model is a key condition that a fintech needs to think about carefully given the lack of or lighter regulation they currently face in this area. We began discussing how they might do so in Chapter 5. Below I outline some of the Threshold Conditions and the difficulty they may present for some fintechs:

- Business strategy. The fintech should be able to provide a business strategy that clearly explains what they do and how they intend to provide the service.

- Design and delivery of the product or service. The fintech must be able to explain how the service will be of benefit to the consumer and what value it brings.

- The structure and operations of the fintech must also be explained.

- Sustainable business model. This is an area of important focus for the fintech. A new service that hasn't been launched before and that is using innovative ways of offering value to consumers should be explained in a clear way. It must be clear to the regulators that there is a sustainable business model, and that the projections are realistic and based on assumptions that make sense.

- Realistic growth. The fintech must offer a convincing explanation of the growth forecasts, the assumptions and crucially the risks. How these risks are mitigated will be important to highlight for the credibility of the business proposition.

- Price and quality. The fintech should have plans to review the outcomes as it delivers its service.

- Sales and customer service model. The fintech should focus on vulnerability or unintended consequences. Could the product find its way to a target market for which is it not suitable or could it inadvertently attract parties with ill intentions?
- Risk profile and risk mitigation. The fintech must regularly review risks as it delivers its service into the market.
- Oversight of outsourcing arrangements.
- Financial crime. How the business model guards against wider society harms such as financial crime and scams is particularly important in a new proposition. The fintech should demonstrate that they have thought of market-wide harms, the impact of their product being rolled out and how they are mitigating these risks. Financial crime, combating scams and cyber security are priority areas the fintech must think about.

Other conditions for the fintech to think about remain fairly similar. These are legal status, location of offices, prudent conduct of business, appropriate non-financial resources, suitability and effective supervision. A competitive and innovative market will find ways to deliver new and exciting propositions. Open banking developed in the US, in the early stages, without regulatory intervention and on a bilateral basis. It is not easy to go at it on your own, knowing that there is no certainty of regulation to guide the path, but this is a decision that fintechs can make based on their vision, belief in the product and approach to developing and delivering it. However, it comes with risks and fintechs will have to make a choice on whether they want to approach an unregulated area or not. In general, crypto has done just that, as we have seen in Chapter 2. Now, regulation is following.

Crypto assets

As we've seen in Chapter 3, crypto assets emerged as a technology that entered financial services in a way that wasn't entirely predictable. We also focused on digital assets being a representation of value and the transfer of value. This is of course consistent with financial services instruments. For example, a payment is a transfer of value from A to B. Securities are financial assets that can be transferred from one person to another. As crypto assets emerged, it became clear that they were seen as financial instruments, similar to those traded in financial markets for years. As crypto entered retail markets (which it did quickly and with no guardrails), regulators and government started to look at what could be done to regulate the market and protect consumers.

What is interesting is that many firms in this space are now advocating for strong, quality regulation to be developed for the crypto market. The recognition that this will create a better playing field, better competition and a balanced approach to consumer protection has been the driver behind this. The 'crypto winter' that we discussed to in Chapter 3 has been another key catalyst to this change. Regulators have started to pay more attention to crypto asset activity and are trying to understand the various activities within crypto assets given the speed at which it has developed. Some of the areas concerning the regulators are financial crime and money laundering, scams more generally and wallet theft, co-mingling of funds and lack of safeguarding controls and volatility of price movement.

In the UK, HM Treasury in late 2023 started a consultation on how best to regulate crypto assets. As I have mentioned throughout the book, for regulators to design a regulatory framework, the risks and how they may be mitigated should be at the heart of this design. Same risk, same regulatory tool is essential. In an outcomes-based approach to regulation, mapping out the journey, considering the points at which risk may crystallize and addressing those risks is the best approach known to us at this moment.

What to look out for in preparation for regulation?

With the principle set out by HM Treasury of 'same risk, same regulatory outcome', it makes sense to look at the existing activities that are similar in nature to the crypto assets activities. This is not a small undertaking. Our financial services today have significant obligations around information disclosure, due diligence practices, Know Your Customer, financial crime controls, liability frameworks and minimum expectations, to name a few. Crypto assets with all the emerging activities over the past few years do not have any of these frameworks in place. However, crypto regulation is imminent.

The future crypto regulation set out by the HM Treasury consultation follows a similar approach to risk, i.e. same risk, same regulatory outcome and drawing on existing regulation which is summarized in Table 6.1.[4,5]

Proportionality and agility

While it is helpful to know on what basis the legislation will be developed and that gives a fintech a starting point on what to expect, it is important to note that the regulation will be adapted to

TABLE 6.1 Basis for crypto regulation set out by HM Treasury in the UK

Crypto activity	Basis for regulation
Crypto asset issuance and disclosure	The UK prospectus regime
Crypto asset trading venue	Existing Regulated Activity Order (RAO) that covers trading venues including Multilateral Trading Facilities (MTFs) which are derived from the Markets in Financial Instruments Directive (or MiFID2) This is spread across multiple locations in the FCA sourcebook.[1]
Crypto asset intermediation	These are similar to existing activities around 'arranging deals in investments' and 'making arrangements with a view to transactions in investments' (Reference iv) these are set out in article 25 of the regulated Activity Order and there are multiple locations which offer further detail of the existing regime and obligations.
Crypto assets custody	The existing custody framework. Article 40 of the RAO and the FCA's Client Assets Sourcebook (CASS) regime.
General market abuse	Existing regulation application to market abuse.
Crypto asset lending platform	Existing regulation applicable the lending platforms.

[1]Financial Conduct Authority (2023) The Woolard Review – A review of change and innovation in the unsecured credit market. London: Financial Conduct Authority.

suit the activities of crypto assets. In addition to the first principle of 'same risk, same legal outcome', the second and third principle are just as important and relevant here. Proportionality and agility are key. Whatever regulatory regime that emerges will have to be adapted to the idiosyncrasies of the crypto market.

Fitness and proprietary

Once an activity falls within financial services regulation, there is an expectation of fitness and proprietary. As was featured in Chapter 5 under the UK's senior manager and certification regime, fitness and proprietary applies to firms across the spectrum and there is a high chance that it will apply to firms performing various crypto activities as we outlined in the chapter above.

Financial crime controls

Given that crypto firms who wish to operate in the UK already fall under the Fifth Anti-Money Laundering Directive (5AMLD) (this also applies to firms in the EU), it has been a requirement that they apply to become registered under this regime.[6]

The application is then assessed by the FCA. There are many elements to a good financial crime control framework, and all must be considered when thinking about it for crypto firms. When we refer to financial crime controls, a major part of this is anti-money laundering but it also includes other financial crime such as scams. It is crucial to put in place the policies, technical systems, staff training and responsible officers for a strong anti-money laundering framework in the organization. The principles in how to obtain authorization outlined in Chapter 5 also apply here.[7] The regulator encourages the application to be complete, that information is being shared transparently and not withheld and the fintech is prepared to provide further information and clarification.

Outlined below are some of the key areas that a fintech should consider when looking to register their crypto activity with the FCA.

BUSINESS-WIDE RISK ASSESSMENT

Ensuring there is an understanding of the enterprise-wide risks associated with the organization's model is crucial as a starting point to assess how to establish the financial crime controls framework. This relates to the company structure, business strategy, target market, product development, delivery and service model. The key areas of consideration here are:

- Customer risk
- Jurisdiction risk
- Product or service risk
- Transaction risk
- Delivery channel risk.

CUSTOMER RISK ASSESSMENT

This is the start of the Know Your Customer (or KYC) checks. It is a requirement to understand who you are transacting with and to do this you need to perform the right assessment and due diligence. The target market and characteristics of customers will be a key determinant of the risk profile here. Developing a scorecard that will allow a proportionate approach to the risk assessment model to be applied will be important. Risk in this case is not always about the customer themselves. It is also about the probability of that customer being deliberately or inadvertently involved in money laundering or financial crime. The nature of the customer's business may be an indicator.

CUSTOMER DUE DILIGENCE

This is the task of establishing that the customer is who they are and the transactions they perform are legitimate and in line with their identity and profile.

There is a lot of detail on how to perform customer due diligence but what is important to highlight for crypto firms here is that this is an ongoing process. It doesn't stop at the onboarding stage. When the nature of the business changes, when transactions are out of character or over certain amounts, due diligence must be performed. Refreshing the due diligence is also a requirement depending on the client profile.

ENHANCED DUE DILIGENCE

Depending on the outcomes of the assessment, the fintech may then need to perform an enhanced due diligence. This is needed for politically exposed persons but may apply to any customer that has gone over a certain threshold the crypto firm has established. Often higher risk profiles will require enhanced due diligence.

Enhanced due diligence in practice is asking more questions about the nature of transactions, obtaining further verification of identities and applying a higher degree of monitoring of transactions. The KYC refresh will need to happen more often for this customer set.

SCREENING

The process of checking customer names against sanctioned individuals and countries should be a priority.

TRANSACTION MONITORING

Tracing the flow of transactions from their origin to destination and applying the right level of flags and indicators to intercept unusual or suspicious activity has been a key focus for financial services firms and regulators. While this is not new, it is gaining more focus with the need to combat money laundering, scams and other financial crime more effectively.

How this applies to crypto flow of transactions will have to be thought through and articulated carefully. Part of transaction monitoring is building a risk profile of customers as they do more transactions. Using data analytics tools in this space can be highly beneficial. However, the methodology and effectiveness of these tools must be explained carefully and clearly.

SUSPICIOUS ACTIVITY REPORTING

Another process that forms part of anti-money-laundering regulation is suspicious activity reporting. Embedding the triggers that point to suspicious activity for reporting to the regulator is important to be set up.

PERIODIC REVIEWS

As mentioned earlier, KYC does not stop at the onboarding stage. Refreshing the information held on customers will need to be done on a regular basis. As a rule of thumb, customer risk profiles are categorized into low, medium and high. Based on these categories, due diligence refresh can follow a pattern of:

Low risk – every 24 months
Medium risk – every 12–18 months
High risk – every 6–12 months.

This also is only a guide. Depending on the indicators that present themselves on an ad hoc basis, further review may be needed on a case by case basis.

AML TRAINING

Ensuring that training and awareness is put in place systematically in the organization at any stage of its growth is key for financial crime controls to be effective. This involves ensuring that everyone in the organization understands criminal personas, indicators of illicit activity and the behaviour that is associated with it.

In addition to some of the commonly known stages of money laundering, such as placement, layering and integration, crypto firms need to think about the value chain and where money laundering and financial crime might happen. Examples of these are off-chain transactions of transactions in between blockchains, wallet theft, dark web transactions to name a few.

RECORD KEEPING

An important and self-explanatory point is the importance of record keeping. However, there is a view that crypto transactions are time stamped and immutable, therefore record keeping, in whatever form it takes, is not needed. However, a fintech must ensure that it maintains appropriate records at all times.

TONE FROM THE TOP

Senior management and the leadership team understanding the importance of financial crime controls is important. As we've discussed throughout this book ensuring that the senior leadership of the organization is aware of these risks and the obligations to mitigate them is important.

There is a lot of evidence that suggests financial crime, money laundering and scams are taking place in crypto transactions and senior leaders of the fintech should take these seriously based on a true and honest risk assessment of the business. Appointing a money laundering reporting officer at a senior level is one such option. Ensuring training and awareness is mandatory and refreshed and constantly monitoring the performance of the financial crime systems and controls at the top of the organization are all indicators that the firm is taking this seriously.

Financial promotions

We touched on financial promotions already throughout the book and the regime in the UK has been expanded to include crypto asset activity. This is the regulation where financial promotions must be approved by an authorized entity as set out by the rules under the regulatory regime. For cryptoassets, there are four ways in which financial promotions can be approved and communicated:

i The promotion is communicated by an authorized person.

ii The promotion is made by an unauthorized person but approved by an authorized person.

iii The promotion is communicated by (or on behalf of) a crypto asset business registered with the FCA under the MLRs in reliance on the exemption in Article 73ZA of the Financial Promotion Order (FPO).

iv The promotion is otherwise communicated in compliance with the conditions of an exemption in the FPO. There are requirements for financial promotions to be clear, fair and not misleading.

The latest policy statement outlines those who can approve financial promotions and some of the rules that govern the promotions.[8] It's worth noting again that financial promotions relate to any medium, print or digital.

The rules cover the following areas and are set out in the policy statement in summary and detail:

- Risk warnings and associated risk summaries
- Rules on direct offers
- Cooling-off period
- Client categorization
- Appropriateness
- Record-keeping
- Date and timestamp of when the promotion is approved.

There are some prescriptive examples of what the risk warnings and risk summaries should say as well as cooling-off periods and client categorization. In Chapter 2 we spoke about rules and principles which tend to apply in most cases of regulation and this is no different. You can see that the regime aims to have some prescriptive rules but there are also principles that guide what a fintech should do when the rules are not prescriptive. How to communicate financial promotion is a tool to meet an appropriate degree of consumer protection. A good baseline is again the FCA's Consumer Duty.

HOW THE CONSUMER DUTY WILL APPLY

We can again see how the FCA's Consumer Duty ensures that consumers are at the heart of the decisions made by firms. The initial expectation is that the Consumer Duty will apply to authorized firms approving and communicating promotions and not yet to non-authorized crypto asset firms under the anti-money laundering (MLR) regime. This exemption is seen to be temporary and will likely change when further regulation of crypto comes into force. In taking the spirit of regulation, it is wise to consider what the Consumer Duty might mean to firms that fall within the regime in the future.

Artificial intelligence (AI)

As I've mentioned a number of times throughout the book, there is a debate on artificial intelligence, its impact on the economy and how to regulate it. Artificial intelligence has been used in different guises for a long time in financial services. The more digital we become, the more data we create and the more advanced AI tools become. AI is not new. It is based on statistical analysis which has been the interest of academics and researchers for decades from simple interpretations to finding relationships such as correlations, causation or predictive analytics.

AI is taking that to the next level, with the ability to work on huge data sets at a fraction of the speed. It has the ability to find relationships we weren't looking for and predict the future in a way that we didn't expect. However, the principles fundamentally remain the same. The use cases for AI range from automating various processes to interpretation of data. There are experiments now on how AI could make decisions as well as finding and predicting relationships. More recently AI has been tested on its ability to develop more human-like outcomes. Automating processes, using chat boxes and robo advice and interpretation and visualization of data are not the areas of most controversy. I'll focus primarily on the category of decision-making and predictive analytics as well as mimicking human behaviour because this is where the key concerns lie. However, it is important to note that the same principles apply to any uses of AI where the outcomes should offer value and not create harm.

GENERATIVE AI

There is a lot of attention given to generative AI as ChatGPT has taken the world by storm. As with other platforms available, generative AI is a great example of how input impacts output. Its ability to create text, essays, limericks in different languages is astonishing as long as everyone understands that the data sets it draws on are not monitored for accuracy in any way. Therefore, its output, as much as it can be compelling in many cases, needs to be verified and judgement needs to be applied. Human judgement, a keen eye or digital tools to detect the use of generative AI remain necessary.

There are tremendous use cases for generative AI and many organizations are exploring these possibilities. Of course, this is not limited to financial services. As it goes a step further, its ability to move beyond text into images, videos and voice is still astonishing as long as it is put to good use. Less fun is its potential to be quite damaging. We mentioned deep fakes and false videos of celebrities or high-profile figures being created to entice investment in a particular financial product. Identity theft, scams using voice recognition and facial recognition are real threat. Cybersecurity and cyber crime is another concerning reality.

Asymmetry of information   Despite the fact that we have used AI in various ways in the past, we find ourselves in a world where knowledge in AI is concentrated with a small group of people who truly understand how the models work. Complex data sets come in, algorithms are created, then trained and output is produced.

The sophistication of the models and the speed at which they are developing is creating a view that this is a highly complex area that is only for the data scientist, architects, analysts and programmers. That may be true, but we have a responsibility to find a way out of this. We don't all have to be data scientists to understand the basis of how these models work. Everything can be broken down into logical steps and the governance of an organization must consider the AI life cycle, from inputs to processing to outputs. If the models are being used to solve real problems in the real world, we should be able to explain them.

How do we know these models are giving us accurate information? Too many variables or too few variables could give us different answers. The data that is fed into the model will determine the quality of what comes out. What models we are using and why must be understood by the management and leadership of the organization. How and when we use the outcomes and applying a critical eye on the inputs and outputs of a model will be key to ensure that there is a judgement approach to what is being produced. This is the responsibility of the senior leadership of any organization. Dealing with this is not up to one party. The financial services ecosystem will stand to gain a great deal from collaborating on how AI can be regulated. Addressing systemic concerns that appear market-wide would be to the benefit of all participants and fintechs have a role to play in this area. How they apply AI in their own organizations, how they offer it to partners across the industry or whether they take an advocacy and communication role to elevate the discussion and drive the right outcomes all contribute to the safe development of AI. Eigen Technologies, an AI fintech offering services to a wide spectrum of companies including financial services, have considered these questions carefully (see Chapter 10).

It's not simple, but we have to act   I recognize it's not that simple, not from the point of view of models being developed but from the broad nature of how AI can and will develop. We spoke about the move from open banking to open finance and AI as discrete topics when actually they are not. The overlap among these three areas of new innovations will develop and increase. Open banking moving to open finance is all about data. How we process it and offer solutions back to consumers of all shapes and sizes will evolve. The use of AI will be a key feature in the development of these propositions.

It is, of course, beyond just the new fintech developments. It sits across financial services old and new. Financial resilience and integrity in the financial services sector are key to ensure strength and stability of the economy. So, if we end up in a position of cyber threats, deep fakes stealing identities and fraudulent activity and scams, trust in the markets will erode.

This is why, when we look at using AI in our operations, no matter the purpose, we need to have full understanding of what impact it will have and what the unintended consequences are.

Agency lies with the fintech, not the model   I confess the discussion on AI in this book is a representation of the layperson's view of AI and I don't intend to go into technical teaching of AI. This is deliberate. My aim is to create a way in which we all engage in the debate, find ways to upskill ourselves on what is needed in this new world order and ensure that every party in the ecosystem plays their role. Every party must have agency.

The point here is that if you are looking to use AI tools, you are responsible for the outcomes they produce. In financial services, existing frameworks could be an effective guide to how to develop AI tools safely, but it has to start with moving from fear to agency. If needed, a crash course into what it is, and how to spot issues would be necessary for the organization to develop propositions that will contribute to a positive outcome and a thriving fintech sector. Getting it wrong will have severe implications for the fintech and the market.

Here are some ideas on what a fintech should think about when deploying AI tools:

- Clearly identify the reason you are looking to use AI tools and how that delivers the vision and strategy.

- Map out the expertise needed to perform the outcomes.

- Simplify it. Don't be bamboozled by the buzz words. If your senior executives don't understand the fundamentals of how AI works, then make sure this gap is closed.

- Ensure that someone on the senior leadership team has knowledge of AI – less from a technical coding perspective (although that helps) but more on the ability to apply judgement and scrutiny to the inputs and outputs of a model and how it is going to deliver the right outcomes without causing harm.

- Have an AI sponsor on the executive team and board.

- Ensure the risk and audit teams have expertise in this area. There should be some oversight on the work that is being produced by data scientists.

- Create a governance framework suitable for the AI activities.

- Make sure operational resilience and cybersecurity frameworks are visibly considering the impact of AI.

- If you are hiring an AI firm to do the work for you, this is a form of outsourcing. Understand your obligations under the outsourcing arrangement (usually you are ultimately accountable to the regulator).

- Ensure that quality data is accurate, consistent and clear of bias.

Eigen Technologies has developed a neat four lines of defence framework when implementing any AI model (for more details see the case study in Chapter 10). These are:

- Model risk management
- Set confidence levels
- Automated verifications using rules and exceptions
- A manual review.

Ensure that you have the knowledge as stated above to apply curiosity and critical thinking to the work that is being performed.

The key words here are curiosity and critical thinking. It is easy to simply say, it's too complex and we'll leave it to the experts. Senior leaders in fintechs should ask questions. That is the only way we ensure that AI is developed in a way that will be beneficial to society. Everyone has a role to play, the spirit of regulation and where applicable the Consumer Duty are at the heart of the development of this exciting area.

The spirit of regulation – an outcome-based view We discussed earlier how the opportunities to use AI tools sit across all parts of financial services. Companies large and small, public and private, are all considering using AI tools. Given its wide-ranging reach, and the variety of applications it has across any part of a business operation, when an organization at any stage of its life cycle thinks of the regulation of AI, a principle-based angle will be best until further regulation is developed. As the debate on how to regulate AI continues to develop, what companies can think about in addition to governance, accountability and existing relevant rules, is an outcomes-based approach.

The Consumer Duty is an outcomes-based approach and is an example of how firms can think about the use of AI and how they influence the value chain. The key outcomes of the Consumer Duty and the cross-cutting themes we discussed earlier in the book lend themselves well to how we need to think about the product development and delivery of services that involve AI.

Whether a business markets to retail or wholesale consumers, the concept of designing products that meet a consumer need, fair value, a good service model and ensuring consumer understanding seem common sense. The Financial Conduct Authority provides an opportunity to discuss AI models particularly in the financial advice sector and is interested in learning about other applications. AI will no doubt fuel further innovation across all parts of the financial services ecosystem and can have significant benefits to public and private organizations.

Summary and takeaways

New technologies develop and regulation either leads or lags. In the case of the new innovations in fintech we are seeing, there has been a mixed bag of regulatory interventions. In the case of open banking, this has been led by regulators but open finance, seen as a necessary next step to unlock the full potential of this innovation, is lagging behind.

For digital assets, after a period of speculation and observation mode, there is now an effort to develop regulation that is agile, proportionate and applies a consistent approach to regulatory risks. Artificial intelligence is in the midst of a debate that will potentially go on for a while yet.

So what do fintechs and organizations of all sizes do while regulation is developing? One answer is to limit operations until regulation is clear and provides the rules. Not many are willing to do that and that is completely fair in a competitive marketplace. If you are launching or operating your fintech ensuring that technologies and associated propositions develop in a way that is safe and positive for the economy is key. There will be a number of considerations for the fintech while doing this. One is to look at existing regulation and use that as a baseline for what might be the right outcome. The UK's Senior Manager and Certification Regime ensures accountability sits with the leaders of the organization performing critical roles. This can be adapted to any part of the organization. Governance frameworks are equally effective and can apply to any organization.

Outcomes-based regulation such as the Consumer Duty is another great example that can be used for firms to think of what they need to develop propositions that provide good outcomes to consumers and the risks have been thought through. This is a period of exciting challenges. However, it's up to us to ensure the challenges create excitement and positive outcomes not fear and consumer detriment. The work we put in has to be on an individual and collective level. Each party can play their role individually and equally contribute to the ecosystem. Coming together to work through these new and exciting challenges is a must.

Notes

1 HM Treasury. Regulation of Buy-Now Pay-Later: Response to consultation. HM Treasury, London, 2022. assets.publishing.service.gov.uk/media/ 62ab50d58fa8f535763df206/BNPL_consultation_response__Formatted_.pdf (archived at https://perma.cc/ZP9L-4Q2W) (archived at https://perma. cc/5Z3U-6LFY).

2 Financial Conduct Authority. The Woolard Review – A review of change and innovation in the unsecured credit market. Financial Conduct Authority, London, 2021. www.fca.org.uk/publication/corporate/woolard-review-report. pdf (archived at https://perma.cc/8B9V-WMPE) (archived at https://perma. cc/6QC8-2CNN).

3 A Constantinovici. Interview with the FCA on open banking, PSD2 compliance and the opportunities for banks. The Paypers, 5 November 2019. thepaypers.com/interviews/interview-with-the-fca-on-open-banking-psd2-compliance-and-the-opportunities-for-banks--1239428 (archived at https:// perma.cc/DX2X-LV82) (archived at https://perma.cc/E9WQ-FW6A).

4 HM Treasury. Guidance on the trading venue perimeter. HM Treasury, London, 2022. assets.publishing.service.gov.uk/government/uploads/system/ uploads/attachment_data/file/1133404/TR_Privacy_edits_Future_financial_ services_regulatory_regime_for_cryptoassets_vP.pdf (archived at https://perma. cc/THM3-PV73).

5   Financial Conduct Authority. The Woolard Review – A review of change and innovation in the unsecured credit market. Financial Conduct Authority, London, 2023. www.fca.org.uk/publication/consultation/cp22-18.pdf (archived at https://perma.cc/8PZ9-FL22) (archived at https://perma.cc/Z5B8-3H4Q).

6   G Conheady. Finance, Professional Perspective - EU Regulation of Cryptocurrency Exchanges: 5AMLD ups the ante. Bloomberg Law, July 2018. www.bloomberglaw.com/external/document/X4F752K4000000/finance-professional-perspective-eu-regulation-of-cryptocurrency (archived at https://perma.cc/V4SC-2MYT).

7   Financial Conduct Authority. Cryptoassets: AML / CTF regime - Registering with the FCA. Financial Conduct Authority, London, 2023. www.fca.org.uk/firms/cryptoassets-aml-ctf-regime/registering (archived at https://perma.cc/2QAJ-LD89).

8   Financial Conduct Authority. Financial promotion rules for cryptoassets. Financial Conduct Authority, London, 2023. www.fca.org.uk/publication/policy/ps23-6.pdf (archived at https://perma.cc/RY56-5HCP).

7

A scaling business

CHAPTER SUMMARY

- Understand the sign of a business that is starting to scale
- The characteristics of a scaling business
- How a scaling business can navigate the obligations and responsibilities it has to various key stakeholders

---

All fintechs would like to see their operations start to scale at some point. Businesses begin to scale once they've started to see significant customer acquisition and market growth.

There are many reasons a business starts to scale and understanding these reasons are important for fintechs. This will allow the fintech to be ready for the complications that come from a scaling operation.

What are the signs of a scaling business?

It is difficult to define a business that is in early-stage scaling. Often the descriptions used look at the growth numbers ex-ante rather than predict growth. Investopedia, for example, describes a growth firm as one that generates significant positive cash flow or earnings.[1]

One cannot simply assign a single criterion for a scaling business and I have specifically made a distinction between first stage scaling and second stage scaling. For ease, second stage will be the point at which the organization has reached critical mass. In other words, it is serving a large number of clients in the market (in the millions) and it is at pre-IPO (Initial Public Offering) or IPO stage. We will cover this second stage in the next chapter.

Early-stage scaling may have many definitions. I've attempted to provide a non-exhaustive list and one that hopefully provides some guidance on what an early-stage scaling fintech might look like. This is in the full knowledge that there may be other indicators or combination of indicators that may induce growth, some of which are deliberate actions by the fintech and others which are market conditions beyond their control.

FUNDING ROUNDS

Most fintechs, as they mature through their life cycle, go through funding rounds. In the initial stages, pre-seed and seed funding, when obtained, are used to develop the business model and strategy. These happen well before any authorization to operate a financial service or product is required. Series A is about supporting the business model and there is support from the investors in what it might deliver. The fintech is either going through authorization or has recently been authorized.

It is suggested that Series B is a time at which a business model is proven, there are real prospects for its success and the business is starting to see signs of growth. The firm needs to invest in people, infrastructure to meet those growth targets and give it a scalable platform. Investors in this category are often looking for good growth. Series C suggests that there has been good growth and now it is rapid and becoming a major player in the market. The fintech is moving to critical mass and further investment in its growth prospects, whether it be market share, geographical expansion or product expansion is required to maintain momentum. Of course, other options in this space are Mezzanine, pre-IPO and IPO funding options (this is a broad description of the various funding cycles and can vary from case to case).

We won't go into details of the various series; however, it is a fair expectation that series B is a point at which the firm is indicating it is growing. This may be the stage at which a firm is scaling.

REVENUE GROWTH

This is an obvious category. One would expect that a firm is scaling if its revenue is growing. The question is what is the level and velocity of growth that warrants the firm to start to think about the implications of this growth. A response to fast growth is different from steady growth. In the latter, the firm often has time to build out other capabilities and can focus its attention on all parts of the business.

When speaking to many fintech founders over the years, there has been an agreement that the type of growth they wish for is 'out of control' growth. Amazon termed that the 'flywheel' effect.[2] There is a point at which some market gap is being fulfilled when the fintech is getting business at a speed they didn't necessarily anticipate when launching. There is also a recognition from many fintech founders that this type of growth is not something that can be orchestrated.

If a firm is hoping for exponential growth, then it should be fully prepared for it. Its business operations, back-office functions and IT infrastructure should be designed to scale at the same speed. If a firm gets lucky, and a market condition made it the most attractive company around, how does it quickly get itself in the right order to capitalize on that growth without causing damage? This is what I term the front office running away from back office dilemma which I will discuss later in this section. It is the start of the phase at which the leadership of the fintech can start to think much more strategically, delegate effectively operational matters, consider carefully how to navigate this stage and not be reactive. Many companies such as Modulr in our case study group as well as OakNorth Bank navigated this phase successfully. I discuss these in Chapter 10. Other, more paced growth is fairly standard and is usually controlled and accounted for. But this doesn't mean that a firm isn't scaling.

AGGRESSIVE MARKETING AND ADVERTISING SPEND

We sometimes see a fintech appear everywhere promoting its brand. There clearly is a penned-up drive for targeted growth. It is not only digital platforms, but traditional media such as bus and train adverts and in some cases television about digital wallets, investment platforms and cash saving solutions. The sudden aggressive marketing can indicate the firm's intention to drive high growth and that is a scale-up.

EXTENSIVE JOB ADVERTISEMENTS AND HIRING

Often the tag line for the job advertisements is 'we are growing'. In fact the OECD defines a high growth firm by growth in number of employees of over 20 per cent year on year.[3] Hiring at a high rate can indicate that a fintech is starting to see high growth and it can be argued it is a good sign that it is ensuring it has the right skills and human capacity to manage that growth.

CAPACITY CHALLENGES

This is an interesting category and one that can vary depending on the fintech. The idea here is that if we see that for a while the fintech has been getting good ratings on platforms like Trustpilot and those start to deteriorate, particularly relating to its customer service, this may indicate that it is seeing growth beyond its capacity.

The various categories outlined here are not an exhaustive list and in many cases can appear at the same time. This is interesting to regulators as they have seen that extra attention may be needed to firms that are seeing exponential growth. Often they struggle with systems, controls and governance commensurate with their growth. Identifying leading indicators will allow the firm and the regulator to support or intervene at an earlier stage and prevent harm down the line.

What are the characteristics?

A business that is growing too fast is a nice problem to have and in talking to founders and CEOs of fintechs that are scaling, they often comment, noting how ludicrous it sounds, that they wish the growth will slow down so they have time to stop and think. Time to think is about strategy, about the end-to-end business operations and how to balance what investors expect with what customers expect and what the regulator expects. Sometimes these overlap.

Investors want to see growth, preferably as quickly as possible. They want to see financial management, operational resilience, strong financial returns and a path to profitability. Good investors want to know that the business is fulfilling its legal and regulatory obligations and that customers are happy.

Customers want to receive the service for the fairest price, that the services will always work and that when it doesn't happen they will receive good and consistent customer service. They want to know that they are looked after and protected and that they can trust the brand.

Regulators wants to know that the operation is legal, it meets its Threshold Conditions and legal obligations, not just as it relates to financial services' regulations but the other laws and regulations it must observe. It also wants to know that the business is sustainable, and it will at some reasonable point make it to profitability. The regulator also wants to see that there is fair value for customers who are put at the heart of the decisions at all levels of the organization.

These expectations shouldn't be at odds, but they can be. I've illustrated how that overlap broadly exists in Figure 7.1.

The ideal situation is that there is more overlap between the various groups' expectations. There are many examples where a focus on

FIGURE 7.1 The overlap of stakeholder expectations in scaleup stages

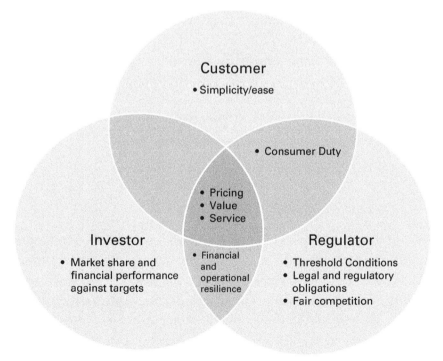

one group's needs without taking into account the others may result in the wrong outcomes for all. Here are some illustrative examples, although this is a non-exhaustive set of examples.

Take investor expectations. What levels of profitability are expected? Are these expectations reasonable? What behaviours do they drive? And will the fintech cut corners to keep their investors happy or will the product be fair value? In other words, would a disproportionate focus on investor expectations drive behaviours that will result in a worse deal for consumers?

If the aim is a focus on the customer and simplifying the customer experience, does the fintech reduce the level of information provided? Will there be some necessary friction that will allow the customer to stop and think whether this product or service is right for them? Is it the appropriate risk level for their needs and will they fulfil their financial ambition by signing up? The regulatory obligations of the Consumer Duty in the UK overlap with customer needs in this particular example and the fintech must find the balance while providing a unique and smooth customer experience.

When looking at the regulator's expectations, how does the fintech implement these in a reasonable and proportionate way to the size of the organization? Do the conditions make sense the way they are today for some of the innovative and emerging business models? And should there be an adjustment, whether it be loosening or expectations?

To find the balance and ensure the overlap of these is as big an area as possible, engaging with and managing these stakeholders is important.

Front office running away from back office

We've introduced this in Chapter 4 and what we discussed so far are, ideally, the types of questions the fintech must ask itself to try to get the balance right. As mentioned earlier, founders do not often have the time to stop and think. The fintech in this stage is experiencing revenue growth with resources that have not grown at the same pace. This is the phenomenon of 'front office running away from back office' and it can be hard to control. Nobody wants to stop the momentum of revenue growth. However, it is important to consider how other business units can catch up.

SYSTEMS CAPACITY AND PROCESS DESIGN

We have seen earlier the indicators of high growth and one of them was capacity. The fintech has simply not anticipated the growth or miscalculated the capacity of their systems. One of my favourite examples I've seen is running a financial crime detection system on an excel spreadsheet. That's fine when you have 100 customers. When the number of customers increases, it can quickly become a problem. An onboarding and Know Your Customer (KYC) system needs to be well equipped for the growth.

A financial management system run from Excel may be fine in the initial stages, but when the fintech grows and its needs become more complex, it needs a system to ensure efficient and effective financial management and budgeting. Generally, the back-end systems and processes can be manual in the initial stages, but as the fintech sees exponential growth, these will no longer be appropriate and will simply lead to errors and potential damage for the fintech and its customers as well as risking regulatory failures.

SERVICE CAPACITY

Service capacity can be front office or back office and it can relate to people or IT systems. In general, it relates to how the customer is experiencing the service. Are there more frequent outages or down time? Has the level of service deteriorated? Are the onboarding teams keeping up with the volume but maintaining the same standards? Is the customer service centre or platform responding within the expected timeframes and are there various poor online reviews and are net promoter scores being maintained?

FINANCIAL EXPECTATIONS

There is often the perception of pressure on founders from investors to deliver revenue growth and market share in a certain period of time. Regulation is seen as a necessary evil. Often the view is that investors want returns in the shortest possible time and the fintech must make decisions on how to use its financial resources in a way that will deliver these expectations. Assuming this is the case, the fintech founders may decide to cut back on manual process, reduce the right level of oversight, and invest much less in the systems and platform upgrades that will keep the organization and its clients safe. System and service capacity that we discussed above will suffer as a result.

I was hesitating in presenting this view as universal. In speaking to many investor groups, more and more investors of regulated entities can see the need for risk management and regulation to be embedded in the organization particularly at this stage. Setting up the fintech with the right mindset of a conduct culture and a risk management and governance framework that is malleable, scalable and suitable for the growth it is experiencing will be an investment worth making.

TALENT AND SKILLS

Starting with the founders themselves. I understand this is a contentious issue. Founders have put their heart and soul into the company and are proud to see that they are starting to see the growth that was dreamt. However, we also often see that they continue to play a very operational role and want to oversee all decisions. They therefore create bottlenecks and decisions are influenced by their own preferences and ideas. This is not an ideal scenario for the fintech if it is looking to grow beyond this stage.

The fintech at this stage needs to consider what skills and experience it needs to grow to maturity and it starts with the skills the founders bring and crucially what skills they don't. In one of our case studies in Chapter 10, the Insignis CEOs recognized very early on that they are 'a fintech company with two fin people running the business', so they hired a great Chief Technology Officer. I would caution that talent acquisition and closing the skills gap has to be a transitional process.

At the early stages of this growth, it is not reasonable that the founders will completely let go of operational matters, rather they should start to consider what senior roles they may hire and how to start a handover process, thus building a diverse executive team with the right skills one set at a time. To be clear, at this stage, I am not advocating that the fintech goes out to hire an expensive senior leadership team across all functions, but it should consider the key roles that need additional support. As an example, most fintechs will have a Chief Information/Technology Officer and a Head of Legal. Adding a senior operations role such as a Chief Operating Officer and a senior risk manager role such as Head of Risk or Chief Risk Officer should be considered.

The founders need to think about how they can free some of their time to be able to carry on the vision and make strategic decisions with the board. Often when looking at talent and skills, the fintech in this stage needs to consider where it is and where it wants to go. With exponential growth, the next stage of the life cycle can come quickly, therefore, a decision on whether it is hiring for today's operations or for the future which may come quite quickly is important.

A final word on skills and talent. This may be a gross generalization, but fintechs often feel that there are two types of skills: those that understand technology and agile ways of working, and those who have grown up in the existing incumbent system of bureaucracy. That is not often the case. There are many who had a career in traditional large financial services organizations and are craving the excitement of the fintech environment and have made a successful transition. One of our case studies, Insignis, is one such example. Equally, I would argue that there is a skills shortage in good risk management and an understanding of how risk management can be used as a strategic tool to help the fast growth of the business in a safe way that meets the expectations of all relevant parties.

In looking at these dynamics at this stage of the fintech life cycle, making the overlap of common interests and outcomes for investors, regulators and customers a much wider area is achievable and ideal for the fintech and its various stakeholders.

Thinking about risk management and regulation as an early-stage of scaling fintech

Risk management remains a strong tool in how to think about balancing the various parts of the business that can be impacted while a fintech experiences high growth. It helps in decision-making and in allocation of resources to support the growth yet continue to satisfy its regulatory obligations.

The fintech at this stage has likely been authorized for a while and is now being supervised by the regulator. We will consider how the fintech continues to meet the obligations we outlined in the previous chapter while linking it to its risk management practices along with the key considerations at this stage in the fintech's life cycle.

In the previous chapter we introduced the Threshold Conditions. Regardless of jurisdiction, meeting the Threshold Conditions will likely continue to be the baseline for maintaining its licence to operate.

In most cases, the firm has to wait for its authorization before it can actually do business. The application should describe the plan that the fintech has to operate a business, even though it has not yet launched. Once it obtains its licence, the reality for the fintech moves from 'theory to practice'. In setting up and running the Early and High Growth Oversight Function at the FCA, I saw first-hand how a regulated entity needs to pivot its business model in the first couple of years to respond to market changes or to tweak the model as it learns from practically being in the market.

So, how does the business ensure that it continues to meet its obligations after being authorized? Some of the categories in the Threshold Conditions are straightforward as long as they don't change, such as 'location of offices'. Others change as the business grows. In the UK, the FCA being the primary conduct regulator will consider the various components of business model and culture.

In Table 7.1, I illustrate how the Threshold Conditions translate into the everyday areas of supervision and their mapping across a risk management framework that are important for the regulated entity to get right:

TABLE 7.1 The overlap of regulatory obligations with the risk management
framework

Threshold Conditions	Daily supervision	Risk management
Business model	Business model: • Vision and strategy • Is it a sustainable business? • What are the inherent risks that may cause harm to consumers and the market and how are they mitigated?	Strategic Financial Legal and regulatory Reputational*
Location of offices	Location of offices. Any changes to this need to be compliant and proactively communicated to the regulator.	Legal and regulatory
Effective supervision	Covered under business model and structure of the organization but also relates to the interactions with the regulator being open and transparent.	Legal, regulatory and reputational
Appropriate resources	A key area that relates to cultural drivers. What are the resources and how are they organized to ensure the right outcomes are achieved? This includes: • Systems and controls • Governance framework and oversight of the business • Financial resources and prudence • People, skills and capabilities.	Financial, operational, cyber, people, governance. Reputational*
Suitability	This has strong links to leadership and the UK's Senior Manager and Certification Regime (SM&CR). It tests that the profile, skills and experience of senior staff are appropriate for setting the right culture, acting with integrity and have the right background, skills and experience to do so.	Regulatory, reputational

(*continued*)

TABLE 7.1 (Continued)

Threshold Conditions	Daily supervision	Risk management
Overlapping areas	Cultural indicators can sit across all the Threshold Conditions. It is easy to think about culture in a business sense. For example, the purpose, vision and mission of the fintech, how is the fintech structured to ensure it delivers its vision, what are the systems and controls, people skills and capabilities, internal policies, leadership behaviors and governance frameworks that model the culture. How does the risk management mindset wrap itself around the operations of the business and how is a conduct culture embedded in all parts of the organization? The way in which the regulated entity is supervised is fluid and all the Threshold Conditions are considered holistically. An important consideration for regulated entities is to study and understand the FCA's 'Dear CEO' letters which outline some of the key areas of interest that the regulator is examining.	Reputational*

*Reputational risk will always be relative to the specific business model and stage of the fintech.
NOTE non-regulated activities will continue to be monitored throughout the life of the fintech.

Supervision and risk management

Now as a regulated entity, we will focus on what is required under a typical supervision regime and what the areas of focus for a business in scale-up stage are. It is important to ensure that we continue the close link with the risk management taxonomy we've introduced previously.

As a fintech in its early stages of scaling, the supervision model will be a portfolio style supervision which means the firm is part of a group of firms where the regulator will respond to indicators of what it might see as drivers of harm or risks.[4] The response may be a specific request for further information from a particular firm or from a group of firms. Indicators may not always be about risks per se, it may be a change in the market dynamics and the regulator would like to understand this further.

When financial services companies started to become more interested in AI, the FCA for example asked a group of firms to share how they planned to use AI in their business.

Purpose, vision and mission

A fintech would have identified its purpose at early stages of set up. When it starts to see scale, the business expands and the ability to communicate its purpose precisely and effectively to all stakeholders is critically important.

Purpose has to be clear and consistent across all its communications. The messages and narrative delivered externally to customers and internally to staff must be consistent and coherent. The way in which the fintech demonstrates this is through its various channels of communication. Crucially, the tone from the top, the behaviours and how the culture is modelled across senior management, the executive team and the board of directors is essential. Consumer outcomes also demonstrate how the firm is delivering on its purpose. A firm may market itself as offering unique solutions to vulnerable consumers as its core purpose. Yet if the evidence demonstrates that the consumer is not getting a fair deal, it is a clear indication that it is at odds with its purpose.

Purpose also must permeate in all its internal policies, practices and values. A test of whether this has been successful is if all staff understand the purpose and how what they do contributes to it. It is a significant component of the culture of the organization.

The regulator will also consider the fintech's dealings with the regulator and whether it has been open and transparent, submitting required information on time and to high standards and whether they self-report and proactively inform the regulator of any incidents or changes that they have an obligation to report.

They must also demonstrate that they are a positive market participant. As a scaling organization, the fintech will need to start considering its place in the market, competition issues, its contribution to ensuring a market of high integrity and whether its strategy and operations are taking into account market integrity issues as it grows at a high rate.

Leadership

Effective leadership supports the firm to deliver its purpose and strategy. It steers it in the right direction and sets the tone for the culture of the organization. As a scaling firm, the fintech should start to consider the effectiveness of its leadership relative to its size and scale as no doubt the regulator will. Performing a gap analysis of the skills and experience needed at this stage of the life cycle could help the fintech identify what are the profile of leaders needed. We have said previously that the founders continuing to perform operational tasks as well as strategic while in a period of rapid growth will only create risks that will materialize down the line.

The assessment of leadership for scaling fintechs focuses on ensuring the key functions are supported by strong leaders that have the right skills and expertise to perform their roles, that they act with integrity and are accountable and responsible for their actions. The minimum standard would be the senior management functions being fulfilled but in addition, the fintech should proactively consider key functions and the appropriate leadership team. The CEO often considers what other 'Chief' roles are necessary.

For many fintechs in this stage, a chief operating officer is a key additional role. The COO tends to have a wide scope and it varies from one organization to the other which allows the fintech to place multiple functions under the COO.[5] But the key leadership or 'C-suite' roles as they are often called may vary depending on the fintech and their value proposition. Some consider the priority is to hire a chief people officer or a chief risk officer or a combination of these. The fintech needs to demonstrate how its risk profile is changing and what it is doing to ensure the right spans of controls and leadership are in place to address this change. This also applies to the composition of the board of directors which we will cover later in this chapter under governance.

The scaling stage does not necessarily mean an expensive senior leadership team, and certain roles can be rolled into others; for example, a chief operating officer can include risk management, facilities and human resources. As mentioned, these individuals should have the right skills, be accountable and act with integrity. They are also responsible for setting the tone for the culture of the organization and overseeing the various strategic and operational functions to ensure that the purpose, vision and strategy are on the right path. Leaders must have a clear understanding of their responsibilities and that they are making decisions and setting expectations within those boundaries. Under the UK's Senior Managers and Certification Regime, developing a statement of responsibilities for senior management is a best practice; however, depending on the size of the scale-up, the firm may decide to implement this now or at a later stage.

Business model and strategy

Business model and strategy looks at the proposition and service the organization is delivering, its structure, its strategy and how the external environment impacts its plans. Regulators are interested in the viability and sustainability and how resources are obtained and organized to support it. These are important considerations for a scaling firm. Identifying the ingredients that have contributed to its growth and how the economic, social, political or legislative environment has helped in the growth they are seeing today are vital. For example, has a foreign exchange payments firm seen growth due to unexpected currency fluctuations, or has a payments firm seen revenue growth due to higher margins?

Understanding the business model, the target market and how variations in external conditions can impact the fintech are key at a growth stage. The fintech also needs to think about whether it can weather the volatility of economic cycles, and how prepared they are for changes in the environment in which they operate.

SCENARIO PLANNING

Scenario planning is a technique that scaling fintechs should start to think about, taking into account what is supporting their growth, and should those conditions change, how would that affect its resources. As the fintech grows further, it can add additional scenario plans that can support its decisions when it starts to see the market conditions shift.

Key areas for scenario planning and stress testing are financial metrics such as capital and liquidity. Fintechs should consider not only the minimum amounts required under the rules but, given that they are still likely not to be profitable, they should also take into account their own assessment of the levels of capital and liquidity required to ensure they can withstand the economic cycle. The fintech should model the scenarios under which they will start to see stress on their financial resources and what plans they have in place to ensure that they manage this. These can be plans to rearrange resources, changes structures, obtain additional funding, review partnerships, review size and scale ambitions to triggering a solvent wind-down and minimizing disruption in the market.

A good end-to-end risk management framework starts to build this out for the organization. This is where risk management is a strategic function of the organization, and it demonstrates to the regulator that the fintech has a level of maturity regarding the benefit of risk management to their business. However, the benefit is primarily for the business, not just to please its regulator.

People

People are an important component of driving a high-conduct culture in an organization. When a regulator is looking at conduct within an organization, their assessment is about ensuring the people, practices and policies are designed and implemented to drive a culture of doing the right thing.

It starts with recruitment, the assessment criteria, the onboarding process and the continuous development and training around the cultural characteristics the fintech wishes to instil. It also relates to remuneration, professional development, career progression and other financial and non-financial incentives. The assessment will also consider appropriate policies that ensure there is a speaking-up culture, a whistleblowing policy and procedure and that these are promoted as part of the culture of risk management and doing the right thing.

If we take a few examples of why this is so crucial in driving the right culture and thus assessed by the regulator, if the individual doesn't have the right skills for the role and is not given professional development, this may lead to errors, which may also lead to intentional or non-intentional cover ups. Incentives drive behaviour. Often incentives are linked with numerical performance rather than risk management or conduct. While staff may be rewarded for meeting numerical performance (often revenue or sales related), organizations should consider also rewarding staff for spotting a risk and bringing it to the attention of the senior leadership team. I have only worked in one organization that proactively ensured the performance scorecard included risk management conduct (beyond completing mandatory training), thus risk management was seen as a key enabler rather than a blocker to the business.

Performance metrics drive behaviour. Does the performance scorecard only focus on financial metrics or does it include behaviour and living the values? Fitness and propriety are also crucial and under the SM&CR there are safeguards to ensure those holding key roles are fit and proper.

Designing the cultural values, and living those in day-to-day operations, modelled by senior leaders, helps to embed a strong conduct culture. Demonstrating how this is embedded is important for the regulator if the fintech is asked. However, for a growing organization, setting the tone at this stage and having the right policies, procedures and values in place will support it when it reaches the next stage of growth. Instilling culture in people is not an easy thing to shift. Developing and spending time nurturing the culture the fintech wants from the early stages will have a huge benefit as it continues to grow.

Systems and controls

Systems and controls are at the heart of risk management. In any risk management framework, an organization keeps a risk log, where it identifies its key risks and develops controls within the risk appetite of the firm to manage those risks and keep the business safe. Controls are a front-line or first-line concern and should be put in place in the entire chain of the organization to be able to identify the points at which things may go wrong, manage those points of risk and reduce the severity of its impact. And it applies to all activities within the organization whether it's in product development, implementation, change management, operations or conduct.

The regulator wants to see that the fintech has thought of its business model, what the conditions may be by which it cannot fulfil its duties to its customers, investors, regulators or cause harm to the market in any way and that it puts in place the right measures to minimize or eliminate their impact.

It will assess the effectiveness of controls: the design and implementation, the frequency in which they are reviewed, whether they are dynamic and responsive to the changes, how consistent they are in identifying issues before they occur. The regulator will also assess that they are developed and implemented following an effective process that ensures they are the right controls for the businesses and they have the buy in from the leadership through to the rest of the organization. We will focus on areas that are important to a scaling firm when it comes to its controls.

CONDUCT

There are standard controls that can be put in place at all stages of the fintech's life cycle to deal with conduct matters. For example, an effective whistleblowing policy or framework that is used consistently and communicated on a regular basis to staff is one such control.

Others include policies such as conflicts of interest, anti-bribery and corruption and a general code of conduct. It is not enough to have a policy. It is more important that there are signs that it is embedded and understood across the organization. It must be able to pick up when there are breaches and deal with them. To that end, it doesn't have to be elaborate and extensive as long as it is understood and complying with it is part of the culture.

CHANGE MANAGEMENT

A scaling firm will have a lot of change going through the organization. From product development and implementation to leadership and staff changes, new teams being set up and organizational restructures, a scaling firm seems to be in a constant state of flux. A fintech should have a clear, documented description of the change programme for the organization that is endorsed by the senior leadership team. It should put in place a change governance framework supported by change impact assessments and an adequate risk assessments and risk logs to help with developing and monitoring the controls.

The key for a scaling firm is to build the frameworks for good change management programmes such that they can flex and be adapted to the dynamic conditions the organization faces. Feedback opportunities and lessons learned are good ways of ensuring controls are embedded in the next phase of action, so are risk tolerance levels and a clear process where escalation is needed. A firm that is scaling is adept to change. However, as it is growing in size, adding frameworks that will help identify and deal with risks as it grows will support it in the next phase of its life, therefore thinking about how systems and controls need to change and adapt at this stage will be very helpful in the long term.

PRODUCT DEVELOPMENT AND SERVICE DELIVERY

Scaling firms are adding new products at a rapid pace and dealing with increasing client numbers. The governance and frameworks that ensure product is being delivered in a way that will not cause harm to consumers is crucial. This can sometimes be a point of contention between firms and regulator. Firms are testing and rolling out products and services quickly. This is their DNA. Regulators want to see that there has been thoughtful consideration for the impact on a now larger number of consumers, that the fintech has considered the controls around product design delivery and customer service and that when things go wrong there is a process where they can be put right.

It's worth mentioning that many fintechs use 'Agile' techniques and ways of working. It has often been purported by some that 'Agile' doesn't follow traditional change processes and therefore, regulators don't understand how it works. That is no longer the case and the concept of controls in the agile process does not hinder the project team from delivering at pace. Rather, it sets the standard for what is the maximum level of harm or disruption it is allowed to create in its project delivery.

Controls around product and service delivery are more than just testing and pushing out product. They need to address points around target market and suitability of product, vulnerable consumers and whether they are being harmed, whether communications are consistent and easy to understand and how it meets the Consumer Duty requirements. These controls also need to address whether there are third parties involved in the design or delivery of the product or service and how the fintech ensures the right level of oversight.

OPERATIONAL RESILIENCE AND CYBERSECURITY

A scaling fintech, if it hasn't already, should start to think seriously about operational resilience and cybersecurity. Already there is an obligation on many firms to comply with operational resilience frameworks identifying key business functions, the risk appetite around failures and outages and the controls and contingencies in place to address these.

If this has not been considered previously, now is the time to do so. A fintech should think about the systems, software and processes that will ensure its operational resilience. They should also have an incident response process in place for when things go wrong. It does not have to be elaborate, but it should consider areas such as the IT risk management framework, business continuity planning and testing, managing third-party partners, incident management and threat vulnerability.

Getting into a mindset that this is a key function of the business will serve the fintech well as it moves to the next phase of its life cycle and maturity, as there is a lot of scrutiny placed on large institutions who do not have the right level of operational resilience and cybersecurity.

DATA MANAGEMENT CONTROLS

Effective and safe data management will continue to grow in importance as the fintech expands in size and scale. Adding more staff, adding more customers and increasing the size of overall operations means that there are more opportunities for vulnerabilities when data is not classified, managed and stored appropriately leading to breaches that can be costly for the fintech.

A fintech at this stage, should understand the nature of the data it holds, its sensitivity and put in place the right information security policies which must be shared with all staff. They should also classify the data it holds and ensure there are safeguards on who can access that data and a process for reporting data breaches.

Now would be the time to consider if any detection tools and software are needed to identify anomalies and address them, that password policies are understood, and monitoring and reporting tools are in place that are reviewed by the senior leadership team. Policies such as these should be embedded in the general operations and culture of the fintech.

SPECIFIC RELEVANT CONTROLS

There can be relevant activity that is unique to the fintech's business model for which the regulator expects the right controls to be in place. Examples of these are safeguarding for payments firms, client asset controls for any firms holding client assets such as peer-to-peer lenders, brokers or custodians, credit risk controls, trader controls or financial crime controls.

Often the specific controls are due to the regulator identifying that a particular business model has an area of risk that, without controls, can cause harm to consumers or the market. There should be safeguards for example on how client money is segregated, used and protected given that the risk in misusing funds or co-mingling such that reconciliation is difficult.

It is good practice for the fintech to think of what controls should be put in place that will ensure the right outcomes for consumer and the market. In one of our case studies in Chapter 10, Eigen Technologies, an artificial intelligence company that works with many sectors including financial services, outlines its controls framework for the safe and effective implementation of AI across business processes.

While I mention financial crime controls, most financial services firms will need to have appropriate financial crime controls. The type of controls will vary depending on the business model. For example, financial crime in a payments firm or a bank will be different from an insurance company. After all, the business model is different, and the type of financial crime conducted will be different. A payments company will need to ensure that money is not being laundered through its operations. An insurance company will need to combat fraud in the form of false claims.

We will cover financial crime in detail in the following chapter.

Governance

The board of directors should be effective in overseeing the strategic direction and performance of the organization. The composition of the board is crucial in ensuring that it is effective. For large organization which we will cover in the next chapter, this often means a large board with a level of diversity and skills that can oversee the organization effectively. Often boards of fintechs at this stage of scaling comprise investors and founders. Of course, this varies from one business to the next and is based on the scale of the fintech.

At this stage, the board of directors may be expanded to include one independent non-executive director. It is always welcome when a scaling firm starts to see that some sort of independent challenge in its leadership is a positive and sets out to achieve this proactively. The fintech has within its power to add more independent board members and to assess the skills it needs for the right oversight and advice at board level.

The assessment at this stage of the fintech's life cyle will be around the board demonstrating that it is having the right debates at the board meetings, that they are making effective decisions, that there is a good degree of challenge to get to the right outcomes and that the behaviour of board members is appropriate. The board papers often are the source of evidence and are often missed. The importance of the quality of the papers cannot be understated. The board reports and papers, including board minutes, show that the board is receiving an appropriate level of reporting for its members to have a meaningful debate and make effective decisions.

Do the documents sent to the board allow the board members to identify the financial position and the key risks? Do they allow the board to understand how the fintech is dealing with these risks? What are the key impact areas and is the fintech delivering on its purpose? These are important questions for the board to consider at this stage. The board must understand the regulatory environment in which it operates to ensure that the fintech is meeting its regulatory obligations. This cannot be left to the staff member responsible for 'regulatory affairs'. An example of this is the Consumer Duty which requires a sponsor or champion at board level to ensure that it is being delivered effectively.

Often board members can be interviewed by the regulator for fitness and propriety. Being able to articulate the regulatory obligations and how the firm is embedding a conduct culture in the organization will serve the fintech well. You may consider that this practice is only used for larger organizations. That is not the case. Scaling firms are more frequently subject to these enquiries.

Oversight functions (second and third lines of defence)

Oversight functions are the second and third lines of defence in any risk management framework. The relevant second line functions here are risk, compliance and legal. Third line is always an internal audit.

These functions are really important to a business that is mature or seeing exponential growth. The purpose of risk and compliance function as second line functions is not to single-handedly keep the organization safe; rather it is to provide the right challenge and oversight ensuring that everyone in the organization understands their role as a risk manager, the importance of compliance and how keeping the organization safe is everyone's job. This is one of the gravest errors organizations large and small make. Embedding a risk management mindset is not about hiring a bunch of risk managers or compliance officers and making it their task to deliver 'risk management'. Risk and compliance must be understood by the leadership and modelled for everyone across the organization.

A scaling firm should start to think about building a second and third line. There is no set formula for this. The size and seniority of the team will depend on the size and scale of the business. At the early stages of growth, a fintech may wish to add a few compliance officers of varying skills and experience. Getting the right expertise to develop policies across the organization should be an initial focus. It may also be sufficient to hire a strong head of risk or risk manager that can design an enterprise-wide risk management framework suitable for a growing business.

Often fintechs have thought of these, but in the sense of getting the experts to do it for them by outsourcing these functions. That's fine, as long as it is understood that the leadership of the fintech is accountable not the compliance third-party provider. Whatever model or size of team a fintech puts in place, an effective second and third line should be independent, have good flows of communication with the business, evidence of the right amount of challenge and debate and a dynamic approach to the function to be able to adapt with the business.

Summary and takeaways

Scaling businesses are at an inflection point where they need to ensure that the momentum of growth, but also consider what other areas of the business need to grow as well.

Ensuring that the fintech does not lose sight of the back office, risk management and governance requirements should be at the heart of their thinking at this stage. It is an exciting time which can be short-lived if the infrastructure and systems aren't developed to support the future size and scale of a fintech's operations.

Regulators are aware of this stage of growth. The FCA has developed a programme that oversees and supports firms in this stage of growth to ensure that there is minimal disruption to markets and consumers.[6] This is particularly important at this stage given the potential level of disruption grows with the size and scale of operations.

Fintechs should therefore think about the areas of their business that need investment at this stage. This is where fintechs can set themselves to move into maturity stage. It is an exciting time for any organization and getting this stage right can be a great foundation for its longevity and future impact.

Notes

1 J Chen. Growth Company. Investopedia, 2019. www.investopedia.com/terms/g/growthcompany.asp (archived at https://perma.cc/JVM4-NPKB).

2 S Galloway (2017). *The Four*. Bantam Press.

3 OECD. 'High-growth enterprises rate', *Entrepreneurship at a Glance 2016*, OECD Publishing, 2016. doi.org/10.1787/entrepreneur_aag-2016-23-en (archived at https://perma.cc/LAH5-Y5MT).

4 Financial Conduct Authority. SUP 1A.3 The FCA's approach to supervision, FCA Handbook. Financial Conduct Authority, London, 2023. www.handbook.fca.org.uk/handbook/SUP/1A/3.html (archived at https://perma.cc/2M55-FHBB).

5 D Piasecki (n.d.). The role of the chief operating officer. McKinsey. www.mckinsey.com/capabilities/operations/our-insights/stepping-up-what-coos-will-need-to-succeed-in-2023-and-beyond (archived at https://perma.cc/E569-6MFG).

6 Financial Conduct Authority. Early and High Growth. Financial Conduct Authority, London, 2023. www.fca.org.uk/firms/authorisation/early-high-growth-oversight (archived at https://perma.cc/9UWB-UEWE).

8

The responsibilities of maturity

CHAPTER SUMMARY

- Understand the changes a firm goes through when entering maturity
- The responsibilities placed on a mature firm go beyond internal operations
- The impact a mature firm can have on the ecosystem
- Growing the support functions to ensure safe and sustainable growth
- Keeping the spirit of innovation and agility alive while becoming a mature organization
- A proactive and open relationship with the regulators is key

From scaling to the next stage

Fintechs have a dream. When they start up, they believe in their idea and want to make a difference with their product. Many fintech stories start by finding a gap in the market and looking to close that gap. From our case studies in Chapter 10, OakNorth founders found through their experience running a previous business, Copal, that despite a cash flow positive and healthy business model, they were not able to get funding and many other similar businesses have suffered in the same way. So, they set out to change that by building OakNorth.

Insignis responded to a market gap identified by the regulator. They saw that a large number of people were not investing their savings. Modulr found a payments system that is disconnected and slow and resolved to fix it. Eventually, founders start to think of their 'exit strategy'. What is the strategy that will take them to the next level of growth? In some cases, the exit strategy is to sell to another owner or to exit the business. In ideal scenarios, founders will have created so much value that they will sell in the open market to allow for further growth. Some might even get to the stage that they will issue an initial public offering (IPO).

In all these cases, the founders and creators of these organizations are hoping to get to critical mass and to be able to add value to the market by scaling their business to the next level so they can truly compete with some of the largest names and become well-known names themselves. This is also the point at which the firms start to enter what I'm calling a 'mature phase'. They are making an impact, they are seen and known in the market and are starting to gain the position among other large players.

With maturity comes responsibility

That level of maturity brings a level of responsibility which can also mean that there is more scrutiny from its regulators. The reason is simple. A mature fintech can cause more damage to consumers and the market if things go wrong. It may gain market power such that it creates a monopoly or uses its position to distort competition in another way. The obligations on the fintech are now growing and the way in which it runs its business requires maturity and a balance of skills, resources and talent.

The same stakeholders will have similar expectations to those outlined in Chapter 7 for scaling firms. However, maturing firms will now be scrutinized under a market-wide lens. Reputation is important here because they have reached a point of visibility of brand that they must think about how they are being a positive market contributor.

Decisions the firm takes may have a higher impact on competition, or disruption which could cause lack of confidence in the sector. We outlined the three key stakeholders in Chapter 7 and how it is important for the fintech to increase the area of overlap in the Venn diagram of expectation.

At this stage, the fintech still deals with the same dynamics, but in addition, the market impact is wrapped around any decisions it makes. The fintech may have an impact in areas such as:

- **Competition:** a firm can grow to become a monopoly or engage in anti-competitive behaviour due to a position of dominance in which it may find itself.
- **Supply chain management:** Due to its size, the decisions it makes on how to deal with suppliers can make a large impact on the supply chain, including in areas such as pricing and terms of trade.
- **Market integrity:** Disruption to its operations of any kind, from operational outages to money laundering or fraudulent activity can send a wave of fear or concern in the market which will impact the reputation of the sector.
- **Cybersecurity:** The level of vulnerabilities it has may expose a wider part of the ecosystem to cyber-attacks.

These are additional market forces that a mature organization will adjust to. It can no longer only think in an internal focused way. Risks that the fintech will be considering are market risks and it has a duty to ensure it is playing the right role in maintaining a well-functioning market.

In Chapter 7 we introduced the diagram looking at the different stakeholder groups and the need to increase the overlap among the interests of these stakeholders. We now see in Figure 8.1 that the fintech looking to balance these interests must also ensure the market-wide impact is a factor in its decisions.

Mature organizations not only have gained market share, they also have a strong market brand and have hired many more people. The reason the fintech has got to this level is because it has invested in a strong vision and strategy. It has hired the right talent and has strong

FIGURE 8.1 The overlap of stakeholder expectations in maturity stages

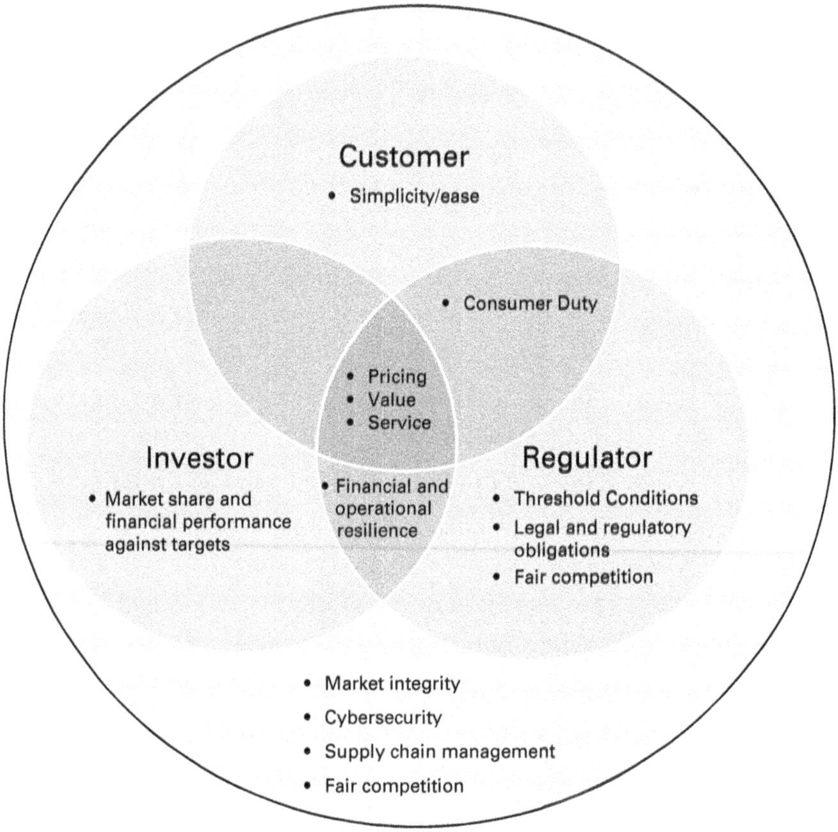

leadership at the top of the organization as well as in its key functions. These leaders will understand how to run a large organization, with the right systems and controls, processes, structures and financials.

It's important to clarify some of the characteristics of a mature organization. The definition here is not restricted to multi-product, multi-entity, multi-jurisdiction types of organizations only. A firm can significantly grow a single product line in a single market and be a mature organization, or it can grow a group of products and services while being limited and focused on a single market. Significant growth and impact in a single market also falls within the definition of maturity.

The links between regulatory risk and other risks

The links between enterprise-wide risks and regulatory risks are more important than ever for a mature organization. The better the organization is run with strong enterprise-wide risk management, the more regulatory risks are under control. Regulatory weaknesses and failures can be costly to the business. When they are identified by the regulator, and this is true for regulators around the world, there can be (depending on the specific matter) additional questions and remediation action to take place in a structured manner.

OakNorth puts it very well in the case study we present in Chapter 10. They recognized that if they focus on doing the right thing, they will get ahead of regulatory requirements which also ensures efficiency for the business. If they are proactive in meeting their regulatory obligations, they can avoid the potential of lengthy remediation processes and commitments that will divert their efforts and focus away from the strategic running of the business.

> OakNorth, the bank, has worked hard to develop what it sees as a good working relationship with its regulators. It is much better for OakNorth to anticipate the questions and address them proactively. They believe that getting this right first time makes their life easier. If they don't, they recognize that it will create too much focus and resource on remediation to fix identified issues after the fact. Too many issues identified by the regulator will create a loss of confidence and that is a risk they don't want to take. Their view is that a fintech doesn't have a business if the regulator isn't happy.

A regulated entity that is in maturity is under the spotlight. Regulators tend to have more resources dedicated to overseeing these firms for the reasons we outlined above. As we will see in the coming sections, regulation involves the sound running of the business across the board. There is no particular ring-fenced activity that will mitigate or address regulatory risks.

Risk management maturity

As discussed across the book, a strong risk management framework that is proportionate to the size and operations of a fintech will support its ability to meet its regulatory obligations. This is certainly the case with firms that have reached maturity. When a fintech has become sizeable in revenue and operations, it will need to ensure the size of its support functions around governance, risk management and systems and controls are adequate.

I set out below how a mature fintech can consider how to meet its regulatory requirements in line with the Threshold Conditions which it must always meet and in balance with its risk management practices.

Purpose, vision and mission

As the organization becomes larger, how the purpose is communicated and embedded becomes more important. Having a clear purpose that is understood by every employee will ensure the organization is delivering on its purpose and that any risks identified are mitigated and addressed. This is what will create and define the culture. Larger organizations are under scrutiny from the regulator and the ability to demonstrate how its vision and purpose is lived across all levels will be key.

A purpose and vision needs to be conducive to good outcomes for consumers and the market. Evidence of how the firm delivers its purpose while addressing any harms and mitigating them will be required as it engages with its regulatory bodies.

For a larger organization there are multiple ways in which it must communicate and deliver on its purpose.

- **Written communication** is consistent, clear and defines what the organization is and what it is not, as well as what it is willing to accept in terms of risk. Clear and punchy messages that are consistent across all mediums internally and externally are crucial.
- **Verbal communication** – Internal messaging, town halls, individual and group meetings all carry coherent and consistent messages.

External communication is also consistent, and staff can see that tone from the top does not change.

- **Behaviours** – Here, this is particular to the behaviour of the leadership, executive teams and line managers. Behaviours need to be fully aligned to the written and verbal messages. Decision-making on internal and external matters is a key area in which behaviours are displayed. The relationship with regulators is another key assessment of the right behaviours displayed by the organization. Being open and transparent, reporting accurate and timely information, disclosing information proactively and embedding regulation that meets the objectives of consumer protection and being a positive contributor to the market are examples of displaying the right behaviours that deliver the purpose and do not harm consumers.

- **Policies and procedures** –This is another way in which each employee understands their obligations of good conduct. Purpose and vision can be delivered via policies of good conduct, risk management and speaking up. The firm can use policies and procedures that demonstrate the code of conduct is in line with the purpose and values of the organization in delivering good outcomes as well as a risk management framework that allows for everyone to report risks, speak up and report what they see is contradicting the purpose and vision. It is important to offer training and effective tools to allow employees to understand their obligations and their role in delivering the vision and culture.

Leadership

The expectation of larger organizations is that it has individuals at the board and executive level that are fit and proper, experienced and have wide-ranging skills that cover the key functions of the organization. These are the individuals that are running the business.

We covered some of this in Chapter 7, here we explain how this evolves as the fintech matures.

A fintech here is at a stage where it must consider some of the key elements and close the gaps in its leadership appointments. Some of the things worth considering include:

Experience of leading large organizations. This can no longer be left to chance. Many organizations work to ensure that the founders are evolving their leadership skills. In some cases, we see how founders have passed on leadership to another individual who brings the right level of experience to take the organization forward.

Spans of control. Multiple roles performed by one individual will no longer be possible in a larger organization. Looking at the structure of the executive team and board and expanding the leadership team as well as the structure of the management teams with effective levels of delegated authority is an important evolution for organizations at this stage. Due consideration for decision-making and governance structures are important too.

Skills across the key functions. Identifying the impact areas or functions to keep the business running safely and ensuring that the leadership with the appropriate skills are brought in to run such functions is now necessary. Many organizations that are moving from the scaling to the maturity stage find that their functions evolve naturally, but in most cases a disciplined approach to identifying these and investing in the right people to run these functions brings the best results.

Independent oversight. Consideration for bringing in the right number and skillset of independent non-executive directors that will ensure that there is independence on the board to allow for scrutiny, debate and effective challenge will be needed.

The Senior Manager and Certification Regime in the UK is not just about appointing and having approvals for the senior managers in question. Now is the time to define and document the statements of responsibility for each function. These statements should articulate what responsibility and decision-making belongs to each executive, how delegated authority is implemented, what the decision tools are and how it is reported.

How a growing leadership team comes together, collaborates and delivers the purpose and culture with a single voice will be key to the effective and coherent running of the business.

Business model and strategy

Mature organizations often have a clear and deliberate business model and strategy which has worked well for them to get to this level. Often internal and external factors have played a role in getting it to this stage. Business model and strategy analysis should consider what the products the firm offers are, how internal and external factors influence the delivery of these products (or potentially create inherent harm) and how the firm will look to address these.

External influences   No organization operates in a bubble and the market conditions play a key role in the firm's growth and development over the course of its life. For a long time, markets in the UK and around the world experienced a low interest rate environment and businesses had easy access to funding.

In 2020, with the start of the Covid pandemic, the dynamics changed overnight. If an organization was not prepared for the various scenarios of 'shocks', it became vulnerable to the effects of those sudden and rapid changes to the market conditions and consumer behaviours. The Covid pandemic and subsequent market conditions meant that for the first time in a long time, interest rates started to rise and investment activity slowed down. As we discussed in Chapter 1, investment in fintech in the UK dropped significantly during that time (although it retained its position on a global scale, indicating that these new dynamics during and post-Covid are global in nature).

The FCA financial resilience survey in 2021 of approximately 19,000 firms solely regulated by the FCA (i.e. not regulated by both the FCA and PRA) reported that approximately 59 per cent indicated that they would experience a reduction in revenue due to the Covid pandemic. Of these firms, around 72 per cent estimated this reduction to be between 1 and 25 per cent, and close to 19 per cent estimated a 25–50 per cent reduction in income.[1]

Overnight, the digital became much more digital than before. The economy is still recovering from the aftermath with high inflation and high interest rates around the world. In the UK and in markets around the world, there have been big winners and big losers coming out of the pandemic. Firms that offered travel money suffered with lack of travel, payments firms thrived with digital payments growing exponentially, and many small businesses are still suffering, causing defaults and high rates of insolvency.[2]

The latest insolvency rates reported by HM Treasury in the UK (January 2024) show that there has been a steady rise in insolvency cases since Covid.[3]

An assessment of how resilient a business model is to these changes and what buffers the organization is putting in place to deal with these when they occur is a key strategy for a mature organization. Stress testing and scenario planning has to be performed by the firm. It's worth saying that while the expectation and level of stress testing have been lower or didn't exist for a smaller organization, it is now seen as important to demonstrate how every business offering financial services is thinking about its resilience and what it needs to do in case of external market conditions that will create a significant impact on their business.

The legislative, political and social environment   Legislative, political and social factors all influence what decisions firms can take and how they can perform their activities. In the UK, the most poignant example was Brexit. Firms had to make assessments and make decisions to deal with such a monumental change in the political and legislative structure of the UK. Firms had to consider how to separate their operations and various functions, and in many cases had to establish a second office in the EU or the UK depending on where their current office was located. The ongoing future divergence in these two regulatory environments will start to emerge. We are already starting to see this in the case of crypto asset regulation with two different regimes. In general, with significant political or legislative changes, regulators will ask firms to assess how these changes will impact their business model, the type of planning they are undertaking, and what they will do to ensure that there is no disruption of services to their customers while at the same time meeting their regulatory and legal requirements.

The geopolitical instability that has come with the Russia–Ukraine war means firms have to make decisions on their activities in affected locations. A fintech may not have physical operations in that region, but in a global and digital world, they may still offer services to the affected region or have suppliers in that region. The boundaries of the supply chain in a digital world are not always clear and due diligence is important.

As we discussed in Chapter 6, at times fintechs have to operate in an environment in which there are new and emerging technologies that are partially regulated or not at all. Fintechs need to consider their strategy in an environment if and when regulation will be implemented that they will have to observe.

The social environment is not always obvious when it comes to regulation in financial services. However, a mature organization will need to consider its operations in the light of how the social structure is changing, how it considers diversity and inclusion or other socially related matters such as financial inclusion and vulnerability. How are its operations impacted by an economic shock that has the potential to have many people move into a position of vulnerability such as the one we saw during the Covid pandemic?

Some of these matters would not have been issues raised 10 years ago and they would not have been at the top of the agenda for an organization that is at the start-up or scale-up stage. The changes which we have seen in the social, legislative and political environment in the past five years have been fundamental to the need for these matters to come to the fore. Fintechs who have reached a level of maturity must consider them carefully. This is particularly true for social matters with ESG dominating regulation in the last few years. In 2023 the European Banking Authority (EBA) provided guidance to financial institutions on benchmarking diversity practices[4] and the FCA consulted on a minimum standard for diversity and inclusion.[5]

Environmental factors Closely related to the social matters discussed above, the importance of environmental factors has been gaining more traction in recent years. The expectation is primarily on larger organizations to consider their carbon footprint, investment strategies and decisions they make that will contribute positively to a greener planet.

It is a nascent area of regulation. It's also a particularly complex one due to the lack of a uniform and consistent set of metrics that inform the expectations of government and regulators. There is currently a large degree of arbitrage as a result of the differing approaches by different jurisdictions. All these are topics the fintech needs to navigate. The key obligation on relevant firms in the UK is the climate-related disclosure requirements. Organizations in scope include premium listed companies, asset managers, pension providers in the UK and insurers of standard listed shares and depository receipts. Similar standards have been expected across the world with a drive to make these disclosure requirements consistent.

The Taskforce for Climate-related Financial Disclosure, better known as TCFD, has outlined four categories of disclosures for financial services firms in scope. In the UK, the Financial Conduct Authority has aligned its expectations against the TCFD's categories.[6]

Governance. Disclose the company's governance around climate-related risks and opportunities.

Strategy. Disclose the actual and potential impacts of climate-related risks and opportunities on the company's businesses, strategy and financial planning where such information is material.

Risk management. Disclose how the company identifies, assesses and manages climate-related risks.

Metrics and targets. Disclose the metrics and targets used to assess and manage relevant climate-related risks and opportunities where such information is material.

What is more important here than ticking the box of disclosure or regulation is how environmental changes affect the firm's operation across its value chain. Whether you fall in or out of scope of these rules, considering environmental impacts will serve the fintech well. In keeping with the spirit of regulation, and with the knowledge that this is a growing area of interest, organizations that are growing should start to think about their carbon footprint, their impact on the environment and the risks of climate change to their business.

So, while there are rules and standards set for in scope companies, the risks of climate change are real for any organization, based on its location, the location of its clients, and the possible economic and social impacts that climate events may bring. Therefore, considering this in your risk management policies and frameworks, discussing it at all levels of the organization is simply good practice for any organization.

Competition-related matters   Maturing firms as we noted are bigger in size, scale and market share. While all firms must adhere to competition laws, larger firms may start to develop a position of dominance or unfair advantage. Gaining market share in and of itself is not unlawful. The key points for firms to think about are whether they are using a dominant position of any kind to practise market pressure, price pressure or able to obtain unreasonable profit margins. This is an important time for the fintech to consider how its growth is contributing positively to competition and not finding itself in a legal risk of antitrust laws.

Suppliers, products, customers and distribution   Moving to the more operational side, business model assessment will consider all components of business delivery from product design and development, to target market, to how the product is delivered and supplier relationships.

Target market. Who is the target market? The nature and risk profile of the customers and whether the product is suitable for that target market are important considerations. Does the product attract a different market to the one intended? Does the product cater for vulnerable customers? And what is the approach the fintech takes to identify and interact with such customers?

Product design. A lot of this falls into the space of Consumer Duty which we covered in Chapter 2. How does the product take into account the target market? How does the fintech reasonably foresee and mitigate any risks?

Distribution channel. These must be appropriate for the target market. Is it direct distribution or does the fintech use intermediaries? If so, being a larger firm how does it ensure that it continues to deliver consistent standards and oversees the performance and delivery of intermediaries and distributors? It is important to note that when a fintech decides to use third-party distribution channels such as agents, distributors and intermediaries, it retains the responsibility for their performance to the regulator. Modulr, in our case study in Chapter 10, showcases the importance of this role and considers it when onboarding and managing its customer base who are firms using their platform to deliver services to their own end consumer.

Supplier relationships. This is important and sometimes overlooked for a number of reasons. If the supply chain is disrupted, how does the fintech cope? The key example to note here is when services are outsourced. Something we have touched on and will discuss under operational resilience, but it doesn't stop at technology providers. It also relates to shared service arrangements, staffing and operational suppliers. Ensuring due diligence is undertaken on how the supplier matches the values of the fintech, and how they are covered when outages or disruption in supply happens are key considerations for the analysis of business model resilience.

Financial resilience and prudential risk management

Financial resilience for a firm that has significant impact in the market becomes a key category that must be considered. The failure of firms is one of the biggest issues the regulators consider because firm failure causes significant consumer harm if not managed in a way that will minimize financial impact to its customers and stakeholders. It is important to note that regulators are here to ensure markets are functioning well and firm failure does not create disruption that will cause consumer harm. Their goal is to ensure that consumers do not suffer losses and that market integrity is maintained so as to not cause as loss of confidence in the market.

Regulators are not here to ensure that a business survives. As we mentioned previously, a sign of competitive markets is that you have firms entering and exiting the market, but regulators care about firm closures being done in an orderly manner, where consumers are made whole and markets have confidence in continuing to operate and trade in such environment.

There may be a paradox in the points I made above. During the financial crisis and in the case of Silicon Valley Bank in 2023, regulators and governments stepped in to avoid failure, thus ensuring the disruption was minimal for the market. When there is systemic risk and the result of failure would be catastrophic to the economy or a key part of the economy, there will be some level of interference to ensure markets continue to function well. We saw this during the financial crisis with actions by the UK and the US governments in relation to companies Royal Bank of Scotland and AIG respectively. It is well worth noting that since the financial crisis, there have been a number of measures that have been agreed and put in place to strengthen the resilience of financial markets and the systems operators within it. Capital requirements and financial stress testing are some of examples. This is part of the continued effort of the regulators and legislatures to ensure that they respond to market changes in this space.

Fintechs that have grown to maturity should be aware of the impact they have market-wide. They must ensure their financial resilience and stability, as well as put in place strong risk management frameworks for their financial management and a wind-down plan that is well funded and is triggered in clear circumstances to deliver a solvent wind-down should that be required. These are topics that require discipline and maturity in their own right.

Financial resilience is closely linked to business model particularly as it relates to the viability of the business model. A key factor that must be considered is whether the fintech in this stage can continue to have a viable and sustainable business model. In the case of financial resilience, it is linked to its ability to demonstrate strong returns, meet its forecasting and budget expectations, has a strong revenue pipeline, has adequate capital and liquidity, and meet its financial metrics.

The strength of how it manages its financial position and affairs is just as important. This includes demonstrating strong financial risk management frameworks, having full visibility of its financial position, the ability to review its financial performance on a regular basis and having adequate reserves to deal with shocks. There are various rules and expectations depending on the nature of the business that each entity needs to consider.

Capital considerations: Some capital requirements are set out in the regulatory rulebooks relative to each country depending on what type of business the fintech operates. This may not always be the case if the fintech is not regulated or if they operate multiple business lines.

It's important to consider what the capital requirements in the context of the business model are as well as the risk profile of the fintech and the value chain. Some of the considerations are:

- **Regulatory capital**
- **Material credit exposures**
- **Settlements risk**
- **Counterparty exposures**
- **Concentration risk**
- **Operational risks, business disruption, business continuity risks.**

This is not an exhaustive list. The firm will have to make an internal assessment on its end-to-end business model. It will need to decide where there are exposures that need to be considered when looking at their capital adequacy position.

This is also often a contentious issue and can be subjective. It is particularly the case when the firm has moved from a lighter model of oversight to one where there is an expectation from regulators on the role it plays in the well-functioning of the market.

The nature and source of capital is also important to consider, drawing particular attention to capital injections from a parent company outside the UK. The requirement that subsidiaries are, as much as possible, ring-fenced and are able to operate self-sufficiently in the UK market has been a key outcome of the financial crisis. It remains one of the requirements placed by the regulator on many financial institutions. One might argue that this has served the entity and the UK market well for example when the Silicon Valley Bank parent company entered financial trouble. The UK subsidiary was considered strong and resilient and a quick resolution following intervention from the UK government and regulators was found where HSBC acquired it for £1.

Working capital and liquidity   A company has to be able to pay its bills. Working capital management will be an important consideration for a mature organization. Evidence of how this is managed is important. Is the firm now profit making? Can it cover its working capital? Who does it rely on for its liquidity? These are all questions a mature firm will need to ask itself.

Often, but not always, firms at this stage have positive cash flow and some are even profitable. Both scenarios mean that working capital is covered by the firm's own resources, not by investor funding. Of course, this is not strictly the case if investor funding is used for expansion plans in product or geography. However, the organization can ask itself whether its core value proposition is offering positive returns.

In regard to liquidity, again a firm will have to think of readily available sources of liquidity and funding if needed. For example, the firm will need to think about the nature of the asset classes it holds and the liquidity profile of these assets. In the case where extra liquidity is needed, can the organization tap into liquid assets or funding options quickly?

Stress testing and wind-down plans   Stress testing and wind-down plans should be considered by mature organizations. They should consider the various risks to the operation of the fintech thus developing risk thresholds, the capital buffers and additional measures that might be triggered should a wind-down become necessary. The scenarios are varied in nature. Financial stress testing relates directly to the strategic and operational functions of the business and is an important form of risk management and mitigation.

Many large banks are already required by their regulators to undergo stress testing. These are often what are considered systemically important financial institutions for the running of the economy. As a general practice, it is worth any organization but particularly larger ones to consider what the stress scenarios relative to the business model are and how might a fintech in this stage conduct stress testing. Considering stress scenarios are easy when modelled on past world events. They are less easy and less pleasant when there is a need to imagine catastrophic scenarios that may or may not happen.

So how can the fintech approach this? A good way to start is by looking at the economic, environmental, social and political risks that have a large impact on the organization. This is core to the strategy and the enterprise risk management framework should the fintech have implemented one effectively. Then considering impact and probability of these scenarios and assigning a rating and considering what are the reasonable capital requirements, operational back up plans and when these need to be invoked as a clear and credible plan that is updated on a regular basis.

People and culture

As a fintech grows larger, it often grows in staff numbers and maintaining the conduct culture that will keep it safe will be a key deliverable the fintech must ensure it gets right.

It should have started to put this in place from its scaling stage and the building blocks at that stage will help in how to continue to ensure a strong culture that is understood and lived by all members of the organization. The people strategy, policies and behaviours all play an important part in the culture of the organization. There are a number of elements that can contribute to driving a high-quality conduct culture.

Financial incentives. This is an area that has had a significant amount of attention particularly following the financial crisis of 2008 and other misconduct related news stories in financial services. How staff are compensated and how this is linked to their behaviour is seen as an important component to driving the right culture. This starts with senior executives, but it sits across all parts of the fintech. Of particular interest are bonuses. How the board is compensated such that it maintains the integrity of independence and how the executive, senior and middle management are assessed to drive better outcomes for their staff, the environment and customers is critical.

Performance scorecards, formal or informal, can be a helpful tool here. If it only focuses on financial results but does not link performance scorecards to demonstrating a strong conduct culture then this can lead to behaviours that will drive higher returns for the fintech, but suboptimal outcomes for the fintech's customers.

Non-financial incentives. Non-financial incentives relate to recruitment, training, talent development, succession planning and other types of activities that don't necessarily link to pay and bonuses but are effective in driving behaviour.

- A fair and robust recruitment process brings in the right talent to the fintech for the roles that are now important to fill as a larger organization.
- Training and development ensure that staff have the right skills, tools and resources to perform their roles with minimal errors or anxiety.

- Resource management allows the fintech to oversee capacity issues, where there are areas of unreasonably high workload and plan accordingly. This is important because high workload leads to shortcuts and errors that can be costly to consumers and the fintech.

- Good support structures for employees such as employee assistance and coaching programmes are becoming an important component of supporting staff in performing their roles effectively. These are opportunities to drive a consistent and high conduct culture on an ongoing basis.

Policies and procedures. For people it starts with the code of conduct but of course it doesn't stop there. People policies link in strongly with financial and non-financial incentives. Having a consistent set of policies for performance management, reward and compensation, recruitment, and ongoing training and development is necessary. Policies should allow for a risk management, and a speak up culture. A whistleblowing policy implemented effectively is one of those important policies.

Regardless of what policies a fintech puts in place, what matters is the implementation of and outcomes of having these policies. It serves as a standard code that everyone must follow, but it is most effective when it links in with the vision and values, everyone including the most senior of staff refer to and follow it, and there are consequences linked to breaches of policies.

Diversity and inclusion. This is becoming an important component to any people policy in the UK and other countries around the world. How diverse is the board, the senior management team and the staff? The outcome for staff in minority groups is an area that is gaining particular increased focus from regulators. The benefit of diversity and inclusion has been argued and now there is a drive to ensure that organizations, particular those that are larger in size, are considering how to foster a diverse workforce and demonstrate inclusivity among their workforce starting with tone from the top.

Systems and controls

Systems and controls are the tools that will allow the firm to deliver its vision and strategy effectively. These can be technological or non-technological systems. On non-technological controls, a risk management framework that includes three lines of defence is a system and control mechanism that ensures there is effective oversight across the fintech's operations. A customer service and complaints team ensures that issues reported by customers are dealt with and managed in a timely and effective manner.

Technology plays a key role in the control environment of any organization. Fintechs in particular have considered how they use technologies to effectively run and oversee the business in areas that have not in the past had technology solutions implemented. Systems and controls should sit across all aspects of the business. Although there are many different systems and controls that a fintech could implement, here we will discuss some of the key categories that a firm should think about when growing their systems and controls in a way that will serve the growth it has experienced. This is also an area that should have been considered as we mentioned in Chapter 7, as the fintech is going through its scaling stage.

Product and customer   Fintechs are some of the best organizations when designing customer-centric products and services. User-centric design thinking is at the heart of their ways of working and they often exist to solve a real user need. Here controls ensure that the fintech has a clear definition of its target market and the design of the product caters for that target market. It starts with the product strategy being aligned with the vision for the fintech. It also identifies the target market and considers the elements of vulnerability and unintended consequences.

Controls such as product governance, effective testing, release stages, the use of behavioural science, the impact of the launch of this product on customer service and operational teams, managed technology capacity and an up-to-date risk register with risks and mitigations which are reviewed regularly can be effective. In the UK, the FCA's Consumer Duty is a key regulation that ensures the right outcomes are delivered to consumers from product design to implementation and customer service.

Change management   Change is a key theme that many large organizations have to grapple with. It is difficult to find a large organization that is not dealing with some kind of change whether it be structural, cultural or digital. For fintechs, change and how it is managed is another area of strength. They have seen and implemented change repeatedly and can be case studies for how to implement effective change. When they start to see growth, they can use their skill and disciplines to affect change safely.

Designing a change plan in line with the organization vision and mission, knowing why change is needed, having the right communication plans including change impact assessments and having the right governance which highlights and manages risks early are all controls that will ensure effective execution of a change agenda. Visibility of the change portfolio and how it is being implemented should be overseen at board level.

Data management controls   Information privacy and data protection is an area that every firm must comply with regardless of industry. While it is principally regulated by the Information Commissioners Office or the ICO in the UK, data protection that falls within the purview of cybersecurity and financial information is of the utmost sensitivity in nature, therefore financial regulators take it seriously.

As an example, data localization rules apply in around 75 countries which prevents businesses from storing customer data outside the jurisdiction in which the customer resides.[7] This, in turn, impacts data portability. It is a complicated area of law and regulation and fintechs who have started to expand globally must ensure they have a thorough understanding of their obligations in each jurisdiction in which they operate. Controls over data privacy and the flow of information in, out and within the fintech should be managed sensitively and carefully.

A data strategy is important to guide the implementation of the right controls and the creation of a data management framework keeps the company safe. Many organizations are moving to a paperless environment and technology can play a key role in a control environment for data management. Here are some of the areas that are important in a strong data management framework:

- Data strategy that maps the data flows and identifies areas where data losses may occur.
- A plan for closing the gaps of strong data controls and monitoring.
- Data classification – defining clearly the classifications but keeping it simple.
- Electronic means to identify sensitive data and track its movement thus acting with speed in the case of a breach or near breach.
- A data breach notification policy that is clearly communicated to staff regularly.
- Linking the organization's data strategy to the cybersecurity policies.

Financial crime   Fintechs at every stage of their development must ensure that financial crime controls are effective in advance detection of fraud, money laundering and terrorist financing. It is increasingly becoming an obligation to detect scams. We discussed financial crime controls in Chapter 7 which are applicable for financial crimes more generally. Fighting financial crime is an ecosystem-wide matter and mature organizations have a role to play in their own financial crime systems and controls as well as the influence they have in the driving forward the right behaviours and remedies market-wide. Managing financial crime effectively in large organizations ensures that financial crime is stopped at the remitting and the receiving end. A significant amount of discussion is going on in relation to new techniques that can stop financial crime and how collaborative efforts domestically and cross-border can support such efforts.

Some of the latest development in the fight against financial crime which are important for a mature organization are:

- **Confirmation of payee.** This is a rule required by the larger banks that connect into the payment rails to verify the sender details before the payment is made. This was implemented in the UK for the largest banks and now extends beyond them. The momentum of confirmation of payee is gaining traction around the world.

- **Information sharing.** There are ongoing efforts to find ways to share information along the payment chain in a way that does not breach confidentiality.

- **Information being carried on the payment chain.** There are also efforts to standardize payments messages carrying additional information such as ISO 20022 and efforts to strengthen sanctions screening and money laundering checks.

- **Authorized push payment fraud.** The regulators in the UK are looking for ways to deal with the increasing level of authorized push payment fraud, which deals with scams as a fraudulent activity, and have put in place compensation measures in specific circumstances but are now considering a number of other measures to spread the cost of fraud and incentive sender and receiver banks to combat fraudulent activity thus focusing on the chain rather than the sender side only. The model is being observed around the world to see how it develops and if it is effective.

- **Data analysis tools.** These are increasingly being used to spot mule accounts or fraud taxonomies. The use of AI in this field is gaining traction with considering network analytics, leading indicators of financial crime and privacy preserving tools to ensure compliance with data laws.

Money laundering and financial crime usually involves payments which is why the focus is on the payments chain. However, it often starts before the payment where verification checks, KYC, appropriate due diligence and customer classification is carried out. It is the responsibility of all firms to ensure that they are playing a part in fighting financial crime. This extends beyond obvious providers of financial services into audit and accounting.

Specific areas of controls   Similarly to firms in any stage of their lifecycle, there are some areas of control which are unique to fintechs and may not apply across the board. A few examples are:

- For trading firms, these include market abuse, insider trading, price controls, exposure controls and trader risk controls to name a few.
- For payments firms, they include controls to ensure the correct reconciliation and safeguarding of customer funds and for lending firms, credit risk and exposure controls.
- Each fintech must consider and implement the controls unique to their business model in addition to those we discuss here.

General controls   General control could range from conflicts of interest, to anti-bribery and corruption, whistleblowing, code of conduct and anti-slavery. All policies within the organization should have a set of controls that ensure that they are implemented effectively. When there is a breach, there should be clarity on the action and outcome.

New technologies to implement controls

Fintechs are known to solve problems using technology, so it is no surprise that they many are looking at using technologies to enhance how they run their business. This applies to systems and controls. In many cases, these can be effective. However, they are new approaches that are not familiar to regulators. At times, this can create friction with regulators as the proven and tested approach has not been adopted. Some examples are KYC processes that use new technologies, or AI tools to spot and stop fraud trends.

It is important to have an open and transparent relationship with the regulator, particularly at this stage of the fintech's life cycle. When considering a novel approach to how to apply systems and controls in a fintech's operation, particularly on an area that may differ from the convention and that may raise questions, an early dialogue with the regulator explaining how the new approach will be implemented, over what stages, how will it be tested, what are the back up plans if things don't go well and how can the fintech prove that it is an enhancement to the current process is critical.

Operational resilience and cybersecurity

Operational resilience and cybersecurity in a digital economy, while it can fall under systems and controls, is becoming an incredibly important area of focus for industry, policymakers and consumers. Operational disruption can cause far reaching harm therefore operational resilience is important for the stability of the financial system.

For larger organizations a major outage or a cyber-attack can impact a large number of customers as well as other companies in the supply chain. The impact is felt across the chain and can affect confidence in the ecosystem. A strong financial sector is a resilient one. As we noted earlier, a mature organization has a responsibility towards itself and its customers, but in addition it holds a responsibility to market. The stakes are higher here, and there will be a strong focus from regulators on large organizations getting this right. Below are some of the key areas for a firm in maturity to think about. Note that they are not mutually exclusive and should be considered in connection with each other.

Operational resilience planning and testing   This follows a very similar fashion to the risk management we described earlier. A fintech should identify their key business services and set tolerances levels for disruption in line with their risk tolerance framework thus identifying what the maximum disruption they are willing to accept is. This should include the mapping of such services to identify where weaknesses and vulnerabilities may occur and what scenarios will take them outside their tolerance levels. Putting in place controls to mitigate these and testing regularly is key.

Business continuity plans   Business continuity plans should be tested on a regular basis to ensure that they operate effectively in case of disruption. It goes hand in hand with resilience planning and testing. It includes technology backups triggered as and when needed as well as people and governance frameworks.

Crisis response framework   Does the fintech have a structure around crisis response management? Earlier in the life cycle, this may well be the few people at the top of the organization but for mature organizations, a crisis may occur anywhere in the business and there should be a framework that staff are familiar with to invoke a crisis response action. A crisis response framework should be clearly linked to tolerance levels and regulatory obligations.

Levels and severity of crises should be defined and each level should have clear definitions of who is the crisis team, who is the decision-maker, what level of escalation is needed, what is the communication strategy to customers, to suppliers, to regulators and any press related communication. A well-documented and rehearsed crisis management framework is a tool to minimize any damage when the harm has crystallized.

Another reason firms in maturity should have a crisis response framework is because, depending on the severity of the issue, in the UK the regulators might invoke what is called the **'Authorities' Response Framework'**. It is a crisis management framework market-wide where regulators can now oversee the effective resolution of the issue. If a firm is ever at the centre of an authority's response, it serves it well to have its own crisis management in order.

Third-party outsourcing   Many organizations in maturity start to consider third-party outsourcing for key operational functions. This is not uncommon as it makes sense for an organization to focus on its core competency and allow another party or partner to offer the services for a function. There are a number of points under operational resilience a fintech must think about when looking at these arrangements. The overarching point here is that the fintech remains accountable for its operational resilience regardless of whether it outsources to a third party or not.

- Does the fintech have adequate understanding of the subject to be able to effectively oversee the operations and delivery of the outsourcing partner? We discussed this under AI as one example in Chapter 6.

- Do they have the right service-level agreements in place to ensure the level of performance expected? Does it align with the company strategy and how are operational disruptions dealt with?

- Does the outsourcing partner have concentration in the market? If so, where does the fintech rank in the priority of issues being sorted when there is disruption?

- Is the outsourcing provider in the same jurisdiction and time zone? If not, what is the impact on providing the services?

- What is the nature of the relationship with the outsourcing partner? Do they demonstrate that they understand the regulatory obligations for mature organizations and do they share the same conduct culture and risk management ethics?

Most outsourcing arrangements work well because the above items have been given due consideration and the relationship is one of partnership.

Cybersecurity at the heart of the organization   It's not only about the systems and controls and technology. It's about the people and an end-to-end holistic approach. Cybersecurity will only work if everyone in the organization is on board with their role in protecting the company's information. It also requires a well thought through cybersecurity policy and framework.

I can't understate the significance of cybersecurity as a topic in its own right. However, I offer below some points to consider when a fintech is looking to develop and enhance its cybersecurity strategy.

- Start with a strategy. Based on your business model and risk taxonomy, what is the cyber strategy that is most applicable?

- Understand the threat landscape that exists for the business model. What are the types of ransomware or attacks that the fintech or similar businesses have experienced?

- Map out the key systems and processes used by staff and customers and identify any vulnerabilities that need addressing. Key areas here include identity and access including password hygiene and two factor authentication and access rights for new joiners, leavers and those changing roles.

- Define the cybersecurity maturity of the organization and establish the target a fintech wants to reach. This can be done using a known cyber resilience framework such as NIST, COBIT or ISO 27001.

- Based on the strategy, prioritize where attention is needed most.

- Develop and implement the cybersecurity policies, systems and controls and monitoring frameworks in line with the strategy. Monitoring and detection capabilities should spot anomalies in the environment. Other tools such as warning indicators and reminders to report anomalies could also help.

- Communicate the strategy to all staff effectively and repeatedly. Offer training and awareness campaigns.

- Develop key performance indicators, and report against them up to board level and monitor the changing threat level and how the organization is responding to it.

- Learn from the information uncovered. Log incidents, understand their nature and frequency and strengthen the cybersecurity environment with that knowledge.

Implementing a well-known global framework is one of considerations for a fintech reaching maturity. Attaining a level of accreditation gives regulators and the market confidence in the anti-cybercrime environment the fintech is maintaining.

Cybersecurity is changing and dynamic, and the organization needs to ensure it is responding to this changing environment proactively. Having a risk-aware culture of the impact and consequences of cyber-attacks is important to be well understood by all members of staff such that the job of fighting cyber-attacks does not fall on the leadership and technology alone. Rather, each staff member should play a part in keeping the organization and its customers safe.

Governance

Regulators care about the effectiveness of the governance of an organization particularly at this stage. Governance frameworks need to develop now to cater for an organization that is growing is size and scale. It is what will keep it safe when direct oversight from the founders or a small leadership group is no longer possible.

Some of the key questions that a fintech must start to ask itself in this stage sit around two key categories.

Board composition and effectiveness in overseeing how the fintech manages risks   Is the board of sufficient size, skillset and independence to ensure that it is able to challenge the leadership team and each other to make effective decisions? Below are some of the important things to consider for boards:

- It is important to have a diverse group of board members that come with various areas of expertise for the effective oversight of the organization. After the financial crisis, there was an emphasis on the board accountability of financial management and the need to have specific expertise in that regard. The same occurred with digital transformation programmes and we are starting to see the need for understanding new technologies such as AI.

- Appropriate behaviour that demonstrates company values and sets the tone from the top.

- Effective communication of the risk appetite statement, the conduct culture and values of the organization.

- Evidence of an appropriate level of discussion, challenge and debate to ensure decisions are in line with strategy, risk appetite and culture.

- Appropriate committees set up with appropriate delegated authority with their effectiveness reviewed annually.

- Board information at an appropriate level of detail and quality to provide the right level of reporting and allow effective discussion and decision-making.

- Outcomes at the heart of the discussion at board meetings. How the fintech's customers are being treated fairly, are vulnerable customers identified and treated appropriately, is the firm making a positive impact on the market are all questions the board should discuss.

- Conduct risks are identified and managed. The board is responsible for setting the conduct culture and expectations. Ensure that policies and decisions drive the right behaviour.

- Environmental, Social and Governance is tabled on a regular basis and matters of diversity and inclusion are considered not only at board and executive levels but across the organization.

- Operational and financial resilience is understood and within board risk appetite, noting any events or circumstances that may impact resilience such as transformation or external factors.

- Consumer Duty sponsorship at board level ensuring that it is implemented effectively.

These are usually evidenced by board packs and minutes, reports, terms of reference, board strategy, risk appetite, and internal and external communication.

The list is not exhaustive, and the needs and effectiveness of the board must be reviewed regularly in the light of changes to the landscape in which the firm is operating as this will change the risk environment.

Regulators will often meet and interview board members as another way to gauge the effectiveness of the board particularly in its oversight, advisory and fiducial responsibilities. Effective boards will allow the executive teams to run the fintech but have sufficient oversight to oversee and direct the company.

The biggest mistake a board can make is getting too detailed or offering arm's length oversight. A balance needs to be struck and committees can play an important role in overseeing the key functions. Appropriate training for board members and having a mix of experience helps. Often fintechs that see themselves as disruptors and more agile than large incumbents pride themselves on the ability to move quickly and minimize governance. However, when they start to enter maturity, many recognize the need for experienced board members to support the oversight and direction.

Governance processes, frameworks and accountability structures   Good governance is supported by the processes and accountability structures. A good understanding of these structures across the organization means that the right decisions can be taken by the right people at the right time and there is clarity on roles and responsibilities.

The SM&CR has played an important role in offering a framework for how good governance can be implemented with Statements of Responsibilities for each of the key functions. Documented policies and procedures on how decision can be taken in which forum and implementing what is known as a RACI (Responsible, Accountable, Consulted and Informed) framework designed within agreed risk tolerances helps the fintech implement strong governance.

This starts and is demonstrated by the board. A risk appetite statement is defined by the board and while it is a broad statement it is usually underpinned by the key impact areas that have been identified for the safe operation of the fintech. These impact areas will have specific risk tolerances and clear definitions of what scoring applies to what is inside or outside tolerance levels.

Setting that at board level ensures that the policies, risk register, risk reporting and mitigations are driving towards the risk appetite set by the board.

Any governance framework for a fintech in maturity is also supported by oversight functions often referred to as three lines of defence.

Oversight functions (three lines of defence)   This is a stage where the organization should consider implementing three lines of defence for its risk management.

First line is your front-line team. Sales teams, product owners, customer services, operations teams are all examples of front line. They are the first to deal with customers and products and this is where the right processes and policies will drive behaviours aligned with the culture of the fintech.

Second line of defence is your support teams: risk, compliance, legal, HR. They are the teams that design and deliver the policies, engage in the various activities of front line in an advisory capacity and conduct reviews to ensure that processes are followed and risks are managed.

Third line is the internal audit function. Up to this point, firms may have outsourced the audit function. When a fintech reaches stages of growth and maturity, it should consider the need for an internal independent audit function that can conduct formal audits of various functions (there is often a cycle) that identifies gaps, breaches and systematically reviews the activities needed to close these gaps or deal with the breaches. Audit results are often reported to the board. Breaches should always be reported.

The balance of risk and innovation

As companies grow from start-ups to maturity, we've seen how the need to mature their processes, policies and governance frameworks is important to ensure sustainable growth. Sometimes, it can be observed that the innovation and entrepreneurial spirit is lost and that the burden of governance, regulation and risk management can turn the organization into the kind of organization that they entered the market to disrupt.

Finding the right balance that doesn't lose the agile and innovative spirit is both difficult and critically important. Fintechs are professionals at cutting through governance and getting to the right answer. There is no reason why this cannot continue as they mature. At the same time, they must recognize that the responsibility they have to build their governance and risk frameworks will support the business in the long term and that is not just about satisfying the regulator.

Efficacy of a governance structure is often conflated with having a committee for everything. In reality, this is not efficient governance.

For example, OakNorth in our case study in Chapter 10 identified that their governance frameworks needed to mature as they started to see substantial growth. However, there came a point where they realized it was holding back decision-making and the agile approach that made them successful in the first place. They are now trialling how to implement a proportionate level of governance that allows flexibility and keeps the spirit of innovation and agility alive. The same goes for systems and controls and the use of technology for more accuracy and efficiency. In all cases, testing that the new approach works, ensuring a back-up is available and having an open and proactive dialogue with the regulator will help get the balance right.

Key takeaways

Every fintech start-up has the dream of becoming a large organization that has grown in size and scale and is delivering its vision of real value to the market. This is the stage, however, that puts the fintech in a space of impact and the decisions it makes will have a bearing on more consumers and how the market operates. The contribution it makes beyond internal decisions will make a difference and recognizing that role will ensure that it plays its part in a strong industry.

This also requires a heightened focus on the sound running of the business. This is not only for its own survival but due to the additional regulatory expectations. These are not at odds. We have again demonstrated here that while there is a higher expectation of regulation, the ability for the fintech to implement its risk management and regulatory obligations effectively will help its own viability and sustainability. The themes throughout the various stages of growth we've outlined so far are the same. The level of focus on how back-office functions, policies, governance, systems and controls and the right people in the right roles will change as the fintech goes through its growth cycles. Therefore, the way in which a fintech adapts its risk management framework and considers its regulatory obligations should be dynamic and revisited as part of the normal course of its strategy and operations.

Notes

1 Financial Conduct Authority. The coronavirus (Covid) financial resilience survey data. Financial Conduct Authority, London, 2021. www.fca.org.uk/data/coronavirus-financial-resilience-survey-data (archived at https://perma.cc/9UWB-UEWE).

2 S Galloway (2020). *Post Corona: From Crisis to Opportunity*. Portfolio Penguin.

3 The Insolvency Service. Commentary – Monthly Insolvency Statistics December 2023. The Insolvency Service, London, 2024. www.gov.uk/government/statistics/monthly-insolvency-statistics-december-2023/commentary-monthly-insolvency-statistics-december-2023 (archived at https://perma.cc/E569-6MFG).

4 European Banking Authority. Final report on the guidelines on benchmarking of diversity practices, including diversity policies and gender pay gap, under Directive 2013/36/EU and Directive (EU) 2019/2034. European Banking Authority, Paris, 2023. www.eba.europa.eu/activities/single-rulebook/regulatory-activities/internal-governance/guidelines-benchmarking (archived at https://perma.cc/2M55-FHBB).

5 Financial Conduct Authority. Diversity and inclusion in the financial sector – working together to drive change. Financial Conduct Authority, London, 2023. www.fca.org.uk/publications/consultation-papers/cp23-20-diversity-inclusion-financial-sector-working-together-drive-change (archived at https://perma.cc/LAH5-Y5MT).

6 Task Force on Climate-Related Financial Disclosures. 2023 Status Report. The Task Force on Climate-related Financial Disclosure, 2023. assets.bbhub.io/company/sites/60/2023/09/2023-Status-Report.pdf (archived at https://perma.cc/QGM3-LYMM).

7 McKinsey and Company. Localization of data privacy regulations creates competitive opportunities. McKinsey and Company, 2022. www.mckinsey.com/capabilities/risk-and-resilience/our-insights/localization-of-data-privacy-regulations-creates-competitive-opportunities (archived at https://perma.cc/JVM4-NPKB).

9

An international perspective

CHAPTER SUMMARY

- Global organizations need to consider fragmented regulation

- There is no one organization that regulates 'fintech'. The activities and outcomes dictate what is required to achieve regulatory compliance

- Fintechs are developing in various jurisdictions in different ways and at different speed levels

- Crypto asset regulation is also fragmented despite global efforts to coordinate it. Some jurisdictions are further advanced (such as the EU and UK) and will potentially set the standards which other jurisdictions will follow

- AI regulation goes beyond financial services and will have a myriad of existing and new regulations that need to be considered when operating in this space, whether building or implementing AI models

Fintech is recognized as a necessary ingredient in advancing financial services around the world. The effort of every country to look at how technologies can modernize their financial systems, create competition and fuel innovation has been an ongoing for many years and will no doubt continue in the future.

Technology is also creating a paradigm shift in globalization. The potential of what it brings is endless. From a purely technological standpoint, there are no borders; products and services can be offered cross-border seamlessly. While the technology allows that, the legal, governance, taxation, capital markets and regulatory frameworks place standards on how organizations must set themselves up, and how they offer services.

This creates a dilemma. On the one hand, fintechs who want to expand need to navigate the legal, tax and regulatory expectations on a country-by-country basis and find capital markets that will support their growth ambitions. On the other hand, governments and legislators in each country need to think about their role in a set of services that are more global than ever. This requires them to find a balance between setting the standards they believe are important for the market, which can only apply to the jurisdiction for which they are responsible, while attracting new fintechs to innovate and thrive.

All of this is happening in a dynamic environment that continues to change. The speed of AI advancement and adoption cannot be underestimated. Meanwhile, the concept of tokenization and its applications in financial services is gaining significant traction as applications are deployed in real life. All this means that the financial, legal and regulatory frameworks for the industry are trying to catch up. This creates another level of uncertainty for organizations looking to expand geographically.

Deciding where to operate or how to expand the company's services relies on a number of factors. It starts with the market potential and demand for the service. However, it also includes the factors we discussed around financial markets and the ability to raise funds, legal and governance structures and how liberal or restrictive they are, tax implications or incentives and of course, the regulatory framework in the potential new geography.

Regulation plays an important role in the decisions an organization makes regarding its international expansion. Questions such as how stable the regulatory environment is, how easy is it to obtain a licence, the capital requirements, the expectations on the type of entity that can be set up or the level of staffing required, and finally the ongoing regulatory obligations that would need to be met.

Fintech regulation around the world

As mentioned throughout the book, financial services regulation is largely activity-based. This means that regulation depends on the activity and outcome of that activity rather than what the organization largely does. A utility company who decides to issue credit cards will need to obtain a licence under financial services regulations to be able to conduct that business despite the fact that credit cards would not be considered its core service.

Like other financial institutions that fall under regulation, a fintech does not have a specific regulatory regime. Depending on what the activity it is doing, it will need to obtain a licence pertaining to its activities. However, over the years as new business models in fintech have emerged, regulation has emerged with them. A prominent example is the regulation of payments and e-money or wallet services where unique regulatory regimes have been developed across the world.

Today there are payments and e-money regulatory regimes in the UK, the European Union, Australia, Singapore and in some parts of the Middle East.[1, 2, 3]

Frequently, payment regulations applicable to fintechs vary across different countries in a few ways:

- The licensing regime itself may vary. Some jurisdictions like the United Kingdom, Singapore, the European Union, the United Arab Emirates and Saudi Arabia have rigorous licensing in place. While others focus on narrow components such as anti-money laundering requirements.

- Some countries may look at the narrow identification of risks and bring particular activities into existing regulation. An example is deposit-taking licences in Australia. Under Australia's prudential regulator, APRA, if a fintech offers stored value services, such as

PayPal top-up wallets, where these payment institutions resemble deposit-taking institutions (like a traditional bank), then they will need to obtain a licence as a deposit-taking institution.[4]

- The type of oversight from regulators can vary. Some jurisdictions are more active than others in the supervision of firms in the early stages or start-up and scale-up.

- The requirements to obtain and operate a licence varies. For example, the level of capital and liquidity requirements, requirements around the safeguarding of client money, the risk management frameworks and the governance requirements including the appointment of specific roles may depend on the jurisdiction.

Despite these variations, there are similarities across regulatory regimes. In general, this tends to be around issues such as money laundering and fraud prevention, data protection and cybersecurity. That is not to say that there aren't differences in implementation. Rather, it is the case that there are more similarities in how these have been decided and implemented than differences. Cybersecurity and anti-money laundering efforts tend to follow standards that have been accepted internationally recommended by institutions such as the Financial Action Task Force (FATF).

In recent times, the reality is that it has started to get more complex. With the dynamic of rapid technological innovations, regulation around areas such as crypto assets continues to evolve on a national level with MiCA[5] in Europe, the Cryptoasset regime in the UK, and the US's differing responses. Where the activity stops and starts is becoming blurred. AI is economy-wide. When will AI technologies start to impact decision-making and how does it help the less abled or vulnerable? Are there questions of liability and ethics that society needs to contend with? This is especially the case in financial services. Additionally, open banking, open finance or open data can touch on more than pure financial services as we saw in the example of a company that uses open banking to calculate carbon footprint.

When there is uncertainty in what regulation applies or whether it applies today, a fintech can draw on existing regulation with the principle of same risk, same regulatory outcome to guide the firm in how to approach the regulatory risk and achieve the best outcome. We are seeing this in the development of regimes such as crypto and AI.

Nevertheless, these developments create uncertainty and can be a lot to deal with if a fintech operates in more than one jurisdiction. There are similarities in some of the regimes that develop in different countries, but the detailed requirements and application of the rules can be significantly different.

When the second Payment Services Directive (PSD2) was implemented, there were a number of differences in how strong customer authentication was implemented in the UK vs the rest of Europe. Furthermore, there were differences in how it was implemented in different countries within the Eurozone. Examples include strong customer authentication of transactions, payment instructions and transaction limits on contactless cards.

Not only is regulation country specific. In some cases, such as the US, a fintech must navigate both federal and state legislation. Due to the dynamics, we have seen that regulatory arbitrage is alive and well in the industry. How each individual fintech decides to engage with this landscape is a choice it must make.

A key question a firm needs to ask itself is what their priorities in choosing the jurisdictions in which they want to operate are. Jurisdictions with strong regulation are sought after and many fintechs believe that a licence in said jurisdiction gives them credibility and a reputation of high standards with the consumers. Strong regulation jurisdictions have refused a race to the bottom concept and therefore the expectations are higher on how firms need to meet regulatory obligations in these markets.

Jurisdictions with a lighter touch regulatory regime offer an alternative, particularly in the conceptual and testing stages. So fintechs need to weigh up the different options based on their business model, stage in their life cycle and growth ambitions. Most large markets such as the US, the Eurozone and the UK expect high standards of consumer protection and high standards to protect market integrity. Other large markets such as China are following suit.

A 2018 research paper by the UK's Department of Business, Energy and Industrial Strategy looked at effective regulatory regimes across various advanced economies and the outcomes they drive.[6] The paper found that effective regimes had a 'heavier regulatory touch'. Perhaps not surprisingly, a heavier touch approach contributed to better risk management and higher standards embedded in the operations of the business. Interestingly, it also found that this created better consumer outcomes in terms of protection, quality of products and services and pricing. In fact, it did not stifle innovation. As we discussed earlier, this is an ongoing debate that is had regularly in financial services. What is the right level of regulation that supports innovation? The 2018 research paper is interesting in showing that more robust regulation contributed to better outcomes.

While this paper did not focus on financial services regulatory regimes per se, the findings mentioned applied to all industries and regulation on a general basis.

Who regulates fintech?

The primary financial services regulator in each country is generally responsible for licensing and regulating fintech. In the UK, this is the Financial Conduct Authority. Other relevant regulators to observe include data and information privacy regulator (the Information Commissioner's Office in the UK) and for larger institutions the prudential regulator (Prudential Regulation Authority in the UK). In Australia it is largely the Australian Securities and Investment Commission (ASIC), the Australian Prudential Regulatory Authority (APRA) and the Office of the Australian Information Commissioner (OAIC).

In Europe, similar expectations exist with the added benefit of a harmonized regulation across the Eurozone. Of most relevance to financial services are the European Banking Authority (EBA), the European Central Bank (ECB) and the European Securities and Markets Authority (ESMA). Then, depending on the actual country of operation, they are overseen by the relevant financial services regulator, commonly known as competent authorities, in that particular Eurozone country.

Regulatory authorities in many western economies tend to be numerous with differing roles. The central bank is often responsible for monetary policy, financial stability and financial services' licensing. The supervision and enforcement element is often left to the financial services regulators. The primary regulator for fintechs therefore is often the financial services regulator/supervisor.

In other smaller developed countries or in developing countries the central banks are the regulatory authorities and often set financial services regulation, supervise and enforce. Examples of such an approach occur in Singapore and the United Arab Emirates. Singapore is a jurisdiction which is open to innovation, fintech and has a forward-looking approach to new technologies. The Monetary Authority of Singapore operates as both the main regulator and central bank.

The US is the leading market for fintechs starting up and scaling up. This is due to many factors such as the size of the market, capital markets flexibility, liquidity and taxation regime and incentives. What is interesting is this position is achieved despite the regulatory regime in the US being extremely complex for firms to navigate.

Most fintechs fall under both federal and state regimes and must comply with the laws and regulations of each. A few of the federal financial services regulators in the US are:

- The Securities and Exchange Commission (SEC). It is the principal authority responsible for regulating the securities market from bad practices, market manipulation and other behaviour that may harm consumers.

- The Office of the Comptroller of the Currency (OCC) – which regulates and supervises banks in the US including branches of foreign banks.

- The Commodity Futures Trading Commission (CFTC) which regulated futures and options markets.

- The Financial Industry Regulatory Authority (FINRA). An example of self-regulation, FINRA is a non-government organization that regulates the broker–dealer industry.

- The Federal Deposit Insurance Corporation (FDIC). This is another organization that regulates banks and deposit-taking institutions.
- The Financial Crimes Enforcement Network (FinCEN). The financial crime and anti-money laundering agency.
- The Consumer Financial Protection Bureau (CFPB). It is the principal consumer protection agency receiving and dealing with complaints across all areas of financial services.

As mentioned earlier, these are only the federal agencies that a fintech may need to engage with based on their activities. State regulation will also need to be observed. If a fintech operates in more than one state, this adds to the complexity in engaging with regulators in the US.

Open banking around the world

Open banking as mentioned in Chapter 3 is a '*simple, secure way to help you move, manage and make more of your money*'.[7]

There are many definitions of open banking that largely differ in the use of words rather than the meaning. What is important to note is that these definitions are simply a description of what open banking does. All definitions describe the scenario where consumers are enabled to take control of their data, share it with organizations that can analyse it, and offer more choice and a variation of services that will allow them to make better choices and potentially improve their financial lives.

For ease, we will call this open banking although the efforts are now going well beyond banking data to other financial services. The key benefit is data. The ability to unlock consumer data from places where it is trapped, in this case in banks and financial services institutions for the benefit of consumers is the aim of open banking/finance/data.

We highlighted how open banking is being developed around the world in different markets and the various different goals for which open banking is seen as the solution. These include improving competition, encouraging innovation, fostering inclusion and enhancing consumer protection.[8] These outcomes are not mutually exclusive and interlink closely.

Innovation fuels competition. Competition delivers better consumer outcomes from fair value, better prices, more choice and higher quality. New and better services to consumers can lead in many ways to financial inclusion. Quality services in a competitive landscape deliver consumer protection.

Open banking agendas in the UK and Australia had competition and innovation as the core objectives. Other markets such as Brazil and many countries in the APAC region see this as an important initiative for the unbanked and underbanked. It's important to note here that depending on the market in question, open banking regimes have to consider the kind of data sets that must be accessible in order for open banking to be effective.

Payment data in the UK, Australia and Europe is seen as rich data sets that, if accessed by third parties can offer a variety of new solutions and services. This seems logical as most people in these markets already have a bank account. There may be many underbanked consumers, but there isn't a large population that is unbanked (i.e. consumers who do not have access to a bank account through a traditional financial services provider).

Payment data is ineffective if a market has a large population of unbanked. This is the case in markets such as Indonesia where half the population in unbanked. In fact, according the World Economic Forum, in 2022 six in 10 South East Asians are either unbanked or underbanked.[9] In this case, other sources of data will have to be considered to take advantages of the benefits of open banking.

The approach open banking has taken differs from one market to the other. In most markets such as the UK, the EU, Australia, Brazil and Saudi Arabia open banking was a regulatory initiative.

In APAC, open banking has been largely market-led with encouragement from the regulators seeing its benefits. In the cases of Singapore and Hong Kong, regulators offered guidance on the standards set for open banking. However, unlike the UK and Australia, banks were not mandated to participate.

In countries such as the US and Canada, it has been a market development that has relied on the idea of screen scraping to collect data and offer services that could be of greater benefit to consumers.

Regardless of the variety of ways in which open banking was triggered, it is widely agreed that there are numerous benefits to supporting and growing an open banking ecosystem in a way that will instil trust and confidence in consumers. As such, a general expectation of open banking around the world is that it needs standards around technology and rules of access and engagement.

Technology-related standards on how data can be shared, and the security of those channels I specifically call this technology-related standards because it is associated with technology as opposed to technical standards which could be related to an interpretation of a particular law or regulation. The technology underpinning open banking so far is Application Protocol Interfaces or APIs. They need to follow common protocols of security and resilience. The question left open is the type of APIs used. Standardization supports interoperability and lower barriers to entry. In other words, it makes sure everyone is using the same technical standards.

Some regimes defined standard and others didn't. The UK's open banking framework launched in 2017 by the CMA looked to standardize APIs for the nine banks initially in the scope of open banking. The rest of the market did not fall under the same obligation. Instead, they were within the scope of PSD2, the European directive which did not prescribe API standards and left it to the market. However, the market in the UK has been converging on the open banking APIs standardized by the CMA and open banking continues to gain momentum as described earlier in Chapter 3.

In Australia, these standards were largely prescribed by the Data Standards Body and took the approach of open data and consumer data rights, which could then be implemented across each industry. Australia is another market that is further advanced in its open banking implementation and adoptions compared to the rest of the world. Standardization may have played a role in its adoption across the market.

Without this technical standardization, the need for some of the smaller fintechs to develop multiple APIs to connect to multiple providers of banking data can create a barrier to operating with the scares resources they have.

TrueLayer, as discussed further in a case study in Chapter 10, have looked to offer a solution by building their own API that allows their customers to connect to other parts of the open banking chain by connecting to TrueLayer. Other technology standards include data specifications, security standards and speed of responsiveness of the API.

Rules of access and engagement   It is important that rules of access and engagement are well defined to ensure the expectations of various parties and their accountability. While these link to the technology-related standards, they also relate to the adherence to laws and regulations that will ensure trust and confidence in the service. A key component of open banking is data. How it is collected, stored, used and shared must be well defined. Another crucial component is consent. In the UK, this is explicit consent from the account holder ('account' usually relates to a traditional bank account, but it could be any other account that participates in open banking. Credit card and e-money wallets are some examples). In jurisdictions where open banking is regulator led, it follows that fintechs who wish to offer these services must be registered or regulated. They therefore must follow a set of standards expected by their regulator.

Again, looking at TrueLayer's experience, they found that the regulatory focus from one regulator to another, sometimes in the same jurisdiction may differ. The focus of the Financial Conduct Authority in the UK differed from the focus on the Central Bank of Ireland. This was at a time when the EU's PSD2 was implemented across both jurisdictions equally.

Open banking today

Today open banking continues to gain momentum and it is either being implemented in countries that have not done so or expanded to other products and services in financial services and beyond.

Globally, it is fragmented and there is no coherence around outcomes or standards. Each country is considering the benefits of open banking for its own application. The headlines are similar, but the detail of the expectations placed on firms in the open banking chain as well as the varying approaches of each regulatory authority makes it a challenging exercise for a fintech looking to operate globally in this space. The expectation is to consider the implementation of open banking in each country and comply with those standards.

Open banking on a cross-border basis has not come to the fore yet although some dialogue is starting to take place. The challenges that need to be addressed before open banking can take a much more international direction include some of the following:

- How will data be accessed, processed, shared and stored?
- What law does a fintech fall under at what point in the delivery chain?
- Who is accountable when things go wrong?
- The varied consumer protection laws in different countries.
- Who will set the technical standards, such as rules, schemes and technology?

We can apply laws on open banking within one jurisdiction, drawing on existing regulation around data protections, explicit consumer consent, and other financial services regulation such as payments regulation. We can also pass legislation to support an enhanced legal and regulatory framework. However, the ability to do this on a cross-border basis has become highly complex.

Crypto assets

Crypto assets regulation is starting to emerge in various markets at a varying pace. The European market has been one of the first to introduce regulation with its Market in Crypto Asset Regulation or MiCA. The UK has also pushed ahead with regulation while other markets have implemented a restricted or total ban on crypto activity.

The most widely known ban was that of China which prohibited cryptocurrency transactions in 2021.[10] Previously it had prohibited crypto mining. But China is not the only market banning crypto activities. Saudi Arabia, Egypt, Argentina and many more ban all or some crypto activity citing reasons of financial crime and market stability due to extreme price fluctuations. And in the case of China, according to the World Economic Forum, the risk of capital outflows.[11]

In many cases, jurisdictions are banning crypto activity until regulation is implemented. Given these risks, regulation is increasing becoming a desired state for crypto advocates and critics alike.

However, time is of the essence. Regulation and standards, preferably at a global level are needed. The crypto asset market is becoming wide and varied and the type of activities are growing. Activities akin to traditional finance, such as payments, deposits, lending and capital market activity such as initial coin offering, derivatives and trading have grown in popularity. Additionally, the crypto market is recognized as being borderless. The varying pace of regulation in different markets can give rise to regulatory arbitrage as well as inconsistent regulation that doesn't adhere to similar standards on a global level.

However, crypto assets and the speed in which it has grown, has caught the attention of global organizations such as International Organization of Securities Commission (IOSCO), the Bank for International Settlement (BIS) and the Financial Stability Board (FSB).

All these organizations have been consulting and looking to issue standards on how crypto assets can be regulated while allowing each jurisdiction to tailor it to their markets. The key areas of concern are the same: market integrity and stability, consumer protection, minimizing arbitrage and combating money laundering and other financial crime such as terrorist financing.

International Organization of Securities Commission's (IOSCO) recommendations

IOSCO's consultation regarding crypto assets in May 2023 looks to make 18 recommendations for the regulation of crypto assets.[12] It has taken a principle-based and outcomes-focused approach and suggests that regulation should offer a level playing field with traditional finance. This is a similar approach to 'same risk, same regulatory outcome' we mentioned in Chapter 5 in the UK's suggested regulatory approach to crypto asset. We see it repeating itself in recommendations by the Financial Stability Board and the MiCA regulation.

As an international organization, IOSCO also calls for consistency in standards to avoid room for arbitrage. The IOSCO consultation covers six key areas:

1 *Conflicts of interest arising from vertical integration of activities and functions*

   Recognizing that business models are emerging to cover more than one activity such as operating an exchange trading, custody, settlement and margin trading, there is a need to have the right governance frameworks in place to avoid conflict of interest arising. This may go as far as separate legal entities for each activity.

2 *Market manipulation, insider trading and fraud*

   Here, due to the cross-border nature of crypto assets, it's important to have effective controls to mitigate fraud, market abuse, market manipulation, conflicts insider dealing and effective disclosures.

3 *Cross-border risks and regulatory cooperation*

   The recommendations around cross-border and regulatory cooperation are designed to deal with matters of anti-money laundering, financial crime and regulatory arbitrage.

   It is also a benefit for crypto asset fintechs who are looking to operate in multiple markets to have consistency of approach.

4 *Custody and client asset protection*

   In a similar fashion to existing custody and client asset requirements, the recommendations set out how regulation should ensure effective controls on segregation, safekeeping, handling of client money as well as ownership and liability considerations.

5 *Operational and technological risk*

In a very similar approach to operational resilience in any organization, effective controls and disclosure on operational resilience, cybersecurity and technological risks should be documented, effectively managed within effective governance frameworks.

6 *Retail access, suitability and distribution*

This recommendation addresses those that are idiosyncratic to crypto not covered above, particularly with the recent failures of crypto asset firms and the onward negative impact on retail consumers. The asymmetry of information, a particular market failure here, is seen as a key reason to implement regulation that will ensure retail consumers have adequate protections. The paper particularly calls out the behaviour of many fintechs in this market as taking *'an ambivalent approach to regulatory compliance'*.

These recommendations are exactly that. The role of IOSCO is to encourage collaboration and standardization. While there is no expectation that they will be implemented, they offer guidance to jurisdictions that are considering regulation of crypto assets that fintechs should consider.

The Financial Stability Board's (FSB) recommendations

The Financial Stability Board or FSB is another organization that coordinates global efforts on supervisory and policy matters that relate to market stability. In July 2023 it published a paper setting out a global approach to the regulation of crypto asset activities.[13]

The focus of the paper was on market stability given the price fluctuation seen in the crypto market and some of the high-profile failures witnessed.

The principles that underscore its work are:

- Same activity, same risk, same regulation. Current regulatory frameworks may be suitable for crypto activities and should be applied.

- Technology neutrality. Regulation should consider the activities and the outcomes rather than the technology used. Of course, this is consistent with outcomes-based regulation the UK adopted with its Consumer Duty and the approach IOSCO have taken regarding regulation that is 'principle-based and outcomes focused'.

- Flexibility and high-level view. The FSB aims to work with the regulators in the local jurisdictions to design a framework that can be implemented in their respective markets. Therefore, it needs to allow for a degree of flexibility to allow this to be effective on a large scale.

The recommendation follows a very similar approach to those issued by IOSCO. There is a lot of collaboration among these bodies so that shouldn't be a surprise, but equally, regulation as a field of practice as described in Chapter 2 is naturally the baseline for the work of these regulatory bodies.

The FSB has made nine recommendations. Some of the notable headlines in addition to those set out by IOSCO are:

Risk management: the FSB calls out risk management frameworks and the need for regulators to ensure crypto fintechs have a comprehensive risk management framework with effective controls, monitoring and reporting. It recognizes that it should be proportionate to the size and scale of the fintech, and effective risk management should apply in cases where the activities of a crypto fintech pose financial stability risks.

Collaboration and information sharing among regulators: The FSB suggests that regulators work together on consistent application of regulation and in cases where it is possible, share information. The collaboration and sharing will go a long way in strengthening local regimes and ensuring that some consistency is applied to the regulation of business models that can be global and offer services that are borderless in nature.

Data collection recording and reporting: This is a similar requirement to those operating in traditional finance where there is an expectation that a regulated fintech has policies and procedures on how to collect, store, process and use data. Regulators should also have data reported to them and use it to fulfil their supervisory duties.

Risks to financial stability arising from interconnectedness: This is a key risk called out by the FSB. It suggests that there should be an understanding by the regulators of the interconnectedness of a crypto business to the wider financial system and how disruption to the crypto business might have a knock-on effect to the financial system.

Other areas highlighted are governance, regulatory powers and regulatory frameworks, disclosures and effective regulation of crypto providers with multiple activities.

The FSB in a similar fashion to IOSCO offers guidance and encourages adoption of similar standards.

A word on MiCA regulation

Covering every regulation emerging on crypto assets requires its own book. But MiCA regulation is worth a comment.

The European Securities and Markets Authority (ESMA) is taking a phased approach to developing and implementing crypto regulation. This is being delivered in three packages, the first (MiCA) has already been delivered.

There are two clear messages from the ESMA's work on developing MiCA:

- The rationale for developing this regulation was all the reasons we discussed so far pertaining to consumer protection, market integrity, anti-money laundering and financial crime. In addition, there was a clear outcome regarding competition. MiCA regulation seeks to lower barriers to entry, allow new fintechs to operate and there is a consistent message of proportionality across MiCA.

- It addresses the convergence of MiCA with other similar regulations by the national competent authority (these are often the financial regulators in each country) of the EU countries. It also sets out a plan on how to deal with that divergence which can be helpful to fintechs operating in multiple markets in the EU.

Are we heading towards convergence?

Despite seeing a fragmented and multi-paced approach to crypto regulation, we can see that the themes and expected outcomes are very similar. This can give crypto fintechs some consistency on what it needs to operate in multiple markets. It does remain complex, and the pace of progress differs. However, like regulation over the years, it tends to catch up. Payments regulation is one such example. There will always be differences in the specific rules applied in each jurisdiction. The essence of what we have discussed in this book is to look at the compliance obligations in spirit and how they link to sound risk management. In crypto, this is no different. It seems that with a few global organizations such as IOSCO and the FSB offering recommendations as well as regulators such as the UK and Europe sharing their approach, local regulation of crypto should evolve with a bit more consistency.

From a high-level practical perspective, if a crypto fintech is looking to operate in multiple jurisdictions, it has a number of options to consider as shown in Figure 9.1:

FIGURE 9.1   Options for crypto fintechs looking to operate in multiple jurisdictions

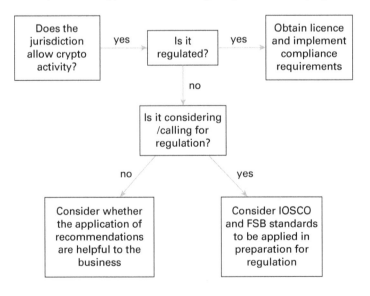

- The first question is whether the jurisdiction allows crypto activity. If it doesn't then it is a breach of the law to operate in that market.

- If it is regulated, then understanding the licensing requirements is the next step. It might be a registration or be a comprehensive process. The outline in Chapter 5 can assist in helping you.

- If it is not regulated but considering regulation, it is worth considering what you need to do to prepare for it. How soon it will come is a helpful question to ask but ensuring the mindset and skillset needed to operate a regulated entity will help in the lead up to regulation coming into force, allowing you to be the first to be successfully licensed.

- If the jurisdiction allows crypto activity and has no intention of regulating it, there are many questions that should be asked around the ecosystem and how it is developing from a competition and stability standpoint. It is important for the fintech not to dismiss the principles set out in regulation as it is based on risk management and governance frameworks. It is also worth noting that if a fintech is operating in multiple markets, there is growing interest from regulators on the overall business model globally. It may not escape regulatory, reputational and other relevant risks if one of the jurisdictions in which it operates does not plan to regulate crypto activity.

Nathalie Oestmann, long-term practitioner in the Web3 crypto space, sets out approaches for how fintechs can move the conversation forward. It includes education of the public, self-regulation, engaging with existing fintechs and engaging with regulators. We'll discuss this in more detail in the Outlier Ventures case study in Chapter 10.

Artificial intelligence

Artificial intelligence (AI) has been taking the world by storm. It specifically took off when OpenAI developed ChatGPT in 2023, a generative AI model that is based on what is now referred to as Large Language Models or LLMs.

What is specifically unique about AI, which gives rise to the significant opportunities and equally significant risks, is that it is borderless. It can be everywhere, it travels seamlessly and globalization could take on a different meaning under the possibilities of AI. New services can be offered by robots from anywhere in the world, or perhaps in the metaverse. The possibilities can be endless.

Therefore, the excitement around AI tends to be on the two ends of the extreme. One is the possibility of a world where everyone can be in charge of their financial lives through the use of AI. As discussed earlier, there's a tremendous amount that eye-gazing technology can do and there's excitement about how robotics can be put in place to enhance quality of life. The other extreme is the negative impact. The deep fakes, identity theft, cyber-attacks and human intelligence reimagined that could come with AI.

AI is not neat. AI in financial services will not necessarily change the actual purpose of financial services and the role it plays is much broader and much more blurred with other industries.

AI today

From a point of where we are today globally on the topic of AI, it is possibly more fragmented than ever, highly politicized and views may cover two ends of the extreme and everything in between. How this translates into financial services is no different from other industries. Is it helpful, is it harmful, how can it can be controlled? When fintechs are considering using AI to offer unique services, these questions need to be considered carefully.

AI as an opportunity that cannot be stifled   In the context of regulation, one extreme is that AI needs to develop to create innovation and opportunity and any regulation will simply restrict it. After all, it has been around for a long time and self-regulation has worked well. Open AI's foundation is to develop AI for good. Google have put out their AI principles publicly which outline the use of AI for good outcomes:[14]

1 *Be socially beneficial.*
2 *Avoid creating or reinforcing unfair bias.*

3 *Be built and tested for safety.*

4 *Be accountable to people.*

5 *Incorporate privacy design principles.*

6 *Uphold high standards of scientific excellence.*

7 *Be made available for uses that accord with these principles.*

They are clear in that they will not engage in AI where it causes harm.

AI as an existential threat   The other end of the spectrum is that AI is an existential threat to humanity, and it must be put under control. This sees AI and robotics, if left unchecked as taking over our lives, creating intelligence that can surpass human intelligence given the speed at which it learns. And while we've seen what is coined 'hallucination', which is the phenomenon that after a while LLMs start to produce output that is out of context and nonsensical, there is a belief that AI will continue to develop to overcome this, that it is only a matter of time before robots take over our jobs and our lives.

HOW IS IT REGULATED GLOBALLY?

Such fragmentation creates differing views on how to regulate it. Some of the key considerations fall under a number of buckets.

To regulate or not to regulate   The question of whether to regulate AI comes from the same angle of decentralization and the fact that technologies that are controlled by regulation will stifle innovation. The fact that AI is economy-wide, it is not industry specific and can have cross-cutting effects across many industries means that restricting it will significantly limit the opportunities it can create.

For example, limiting AI in health care, may put a stop to opportunities for it to be beneficial in decision-making.

The use of digital twins is another such example. Creating a digital twin can allow an inordinate number of simulations that allow experimentations not possible or even ethical in real life today. Experimentation on a digital twin rather than real life is more acceptable due to unknown consequences that can heppen in an experiment on real people and real lives.

Proponents of no regulation argue that we cannot restrict these technologies from developing by placing rules too early. Perhaps the key point here is when is the most effective time to introduce regulation?

It is fair to say that this approach is becoming a minority. Elon Musk, founder and chairman of Tesla and SpaceX, has been very publicly warning of the existential dangers of AI together with other leaders such as Steve Wozniak, Apple co-founder.

As of 2024, there is a recognition that regulation is needed. It cannot be left to the market to self-regulate. The question is how and to what extent.

Comprehensive or low touch   Adding to the question of when, is the question of how much.

Comprehensive regulation will look at AI in every industry and consider rules that will ensure risk management is applied across the board. An overarching and comprehensive approach to AI regulation should ensure that an end-to-end set of outcomes is considered when considering how AI develops.

This is complex, but important. Harmful AI will obviously have second order effects elsewhere.

Critically, beneficial AI may have positive or negative effects in other industries if not considered across the spectrum of industries. For example, AI that prolongs our lives, without ensuring that we remain healthy, will put a larger amount of stress on the health-care system, the pension system and the environment.

Considering low touch AI regulation, it is important to ensure it is proportionate to the outcome. As we explained throughout the book, AI is more than just generative and has been used for a long time. Many of its applications are low risk and therefore a proportionate response to what is expected should follow. The expectations can then grow as the level of threat grows.

Existing regulation or new regulation   Like all new technologies, regulators consider whether existing regulation may serve the needs of ensuring the risks are contained. This has been the approach as we've seen in crypto assets and it seems that it is the approach with AI in many jurisdictions.

Drafting new legislation is time- and resource-consuming, it can create uncertainty for fintechs in the transition period and creates a new layer of compliance burden for fintechs.

The principles here are same risk, same regulatory outcome as well as following the scope and nature of existing regulation. Outcomes-based regulation can be adapted for similar risks as we've seen with the UK's Consumer Duty launched by the Financial Conduct Authority in 2023.

Rules based could be more prescriptive and specific to a defined business model or activity although that doesn't automatically mean the new regulation must be created.

When looking at same risk, same regulatory outcomes, a frame of reference for comparison is a prerequisite. Activities such as crypto assets which perform similar roles to markets, payments and lending activity already have a framework for comparison.

I mentioned earlier in this section how AI does not fit into a neat box. We've already seen the interaction and blurring of lines between financial services and other industries. As an example, telecommunications companies are involved with dealing with financial scams that are done via a mobile phone and social media companies must confront false advertising of financial promotions. Now the need to collaborate cross industry is more important than ever.

So are we heading towards new regimes, existing regulation across industry or combination of both? It seems that each of the EU, the US and the UK have taken different approaches based on their legal and regulatory structures and what they deem appropriate for their markets when it comes to AI and financial services

Regulation around the world

Regulation of AI is a pressing theme in US, UK and EU as they are markets where there are large fintech communities, there is fintech investment and a big drive to promote innovation in general.

So far in this book we've looked at regulation from a strict financial services angle. AI goes beyond this. Here, it is important to reiterate that regulation of AI is beyond financial services regulation specifically but applies to the sector depending on the activity.

Therefore, we will discuss the approach to AI regulation beyond financial services regulation.

THE EU AI ACT

The EU AI Act was the first of its kind when it was announced in 2023. It looks at AI holistically and considers the risks that AI brings.

It then attempts to take a proportionate approach to the level of risk defining it on four levels:

Unacceptable risk – activity that creates harm to individuals and society. Any AI development is strictly banned.

High risk – these are defined as '*AI systems that negatively affect safety or fundamental rights*'[15] and fall under the EU product safety legislation or a further eight defined categories. None of these categories fall strictly within financial services. That is, they are not financial products or services. But many of them can be used in how we offer financial services. For example, biometric identification, employment related matters and AI that assists in the interpretation of the law.

Generative AI – here the proposal is to introduce disclosure rules that oblige fintechs to inform users that the content was created using generative AI as well as disclosing copyrighted material used in training the model. There is an expectation that the model is not producing illegal material.

Limited risk – the expectation is that users are made aware that they are interacting with an AI model. This is seen as minimum transparency expectations, ensuring that the user is fully informed and is thus making an informed decision.

We will see more from the EU regulation as it develops further. As of early 2024, the EU is considering a supervisory body to monitor the adherence to the new regulations. It is worth noting that Brazil has taken a similar approach to the EU in its attempt at AI regulation.

THE US: A COMBINATION OF APPROACHES

The US is a highly complex market for regulation with federal and state laws governing financial services. As we previously discussed, AI is economy-wide and therefore regulations span across multiple industries in addition to the federal and state set of rules.

The US therefore, is considering various activities within AI that can be covered in existing legislation. Labour laws may cover any bias in models used in recruitment. Transparency laws may cover the need to disclose that an AI model is being used. Cyber risk and practices of risk management and governance in each sector can also be applied. However, many gaps remain and the US has looked at a combination of approaches:

- Existing regulation where activities within AI naturally fall under legislation with minimal or no updates.
- Executive orders to close gaps in certain areas.
- New agencies that could be set up to deal specifically with coordinating the risk management approach to AI.

THE UK, DEFINING AN APPROACH TO AI REGULATION

The UK government has been active in developing the right regulatory framework for AI and delivered a consultation paper in March 2023 outlining their ambition on how to regulate AI. It does acknowledge that existing laws are also applicable to many areas of AI. As highlighted across this book, a consistent approach the UK takes is to regulate the use, not the technology. Existing regulation in financial services such as the Consumer Duty, an outcomes-based regulation, can work effectively for managing AI risks on a fintech level.

However, the UK government sees there are gaps, and a more rounded approach to AI could close those gaps. In its consultation, it considers the need to take an 'innovative and iterative' approach and ensure that flexibility is maintained so as not to stifle innovation. The paper sets out guiding principles that AI fintechs should consider when developing or implementing AI solutions. Of note, the approach clearly sets out that in the first stages, it is not rushing to develop legislation. The UK government considers it important to allow for monitoring how AI is developed and allow for flexibility to ensure the right legislation is eventually delivered.

The UK believes that the right regulation will ensure that innovation will thrive and therefore set out the characteristics of the regulatory framework to be *'pro-innovation, proportionate, trustworthy, adaptable, clear and collaborative'*.[16]

For fintechs, the principles it sets out offer guidance on how to think about using and developing AI:

- *Safety, security and robustness*
- *Appropriate transparency and explicability*
- *Fairness*
- *Accountability and governance*
- *Contestability and redress*

How to approach AI regulation globally

Regardless of the regime or the jurisdiction, we can already see the similarities between the different regimes. The principles underpinning the safe development and delivery of AI make sense and the spirit of what they are trying to achieve is aligned.

The difficulty for global fintechs is when they need to consider what regulation exists in some jurisdictions, what is being developed in others and how to deal with jurisdictions which are still assessing AI.

Regardless of country, fintechs should consider laws around:

- Data protection and privacy
- Operational resilience and cybersecurity
- Consumer protection and consumer rights
- Any particular AI regulation that is being considered.

Overlaps between these regimes are already emerging. Fintechs will find that there is some form of convergence on issues such as disclosure and transparency, governance and accountability, and copyright and Intellectual Property (IP) laws.

Matters of consumer protection diverge and are very different in different jurisdictions today thus it is fair to assume that this remains a topic that is unique to each jurisdiction.

International standard setters such as IOSCO and the Bank for International Settlements have also issued papers outlining views and recommendations on how to look at AI from a global perspective. In 2024 the BIS issued a bulletin on AI in central banking and concluded that central banks are early adopters of AI, that it has many benefits that can support the role of the central bank and that collaboration and information sharing will be key to ensure they stay current with the developments in AI.[17]

IOSCO offered measures for regulators to consider when supervising intermediaries and asset managers using AI.[18] These measures include governance, accountability at board level, ensuring the model is tested periodically, that there are the relevant skills within the fintech to test and oversee the AI activity and that they define what disclosure is required for transparency of the use of AI model.

Summary and takeaways

Global regulation of new technologies is at nascent stages. Each jurisdiction is tackling them differently. For fintechs operating globally, this is an issue they face. Certain regulations have been around for a long time and there have always been global efforts to standardize and harmonize regulation on matters of cross-border interest. Open banking, AI and crypto assets are global in nature. While they are in their early stages of development, they are all recognized as candidates for greater global standardization where possible.

Despite the many suggestions and recommendations on how regulation should apply, it remains the responsibility of each jurisdiction to implement final rules and standards for that jurisdiction. This poses challenges for fintechs operating in multiple jurisdictions.

There are multiple ways fintechs can consider handling this depending on the business model and the countries in which they wish to operate. In general, they could choose one of the following approaches:

- Hold high standards across all jurisdictions as the direction of travel will likely be similar across the jurisdictions in question.

- Apply minimum standards but ensure that capacity is built in the system to scale if needed.

- Consider its strategy and business model and apply minimum standards and a selection of additional standards on an outcome-based approach relevant to its strategy.

Another option is to do nothing and wait and see. This may be appropriate depending on the stage at which the fintech is at. Nevertheless, it might be useful for the fintech to ensure planning and capacity building is able to respond quickly when AI regulation develops.

Notes

1   Monetary Authority of Singapore. Payment Services Act: A Guide to the Essential Aspects of the Payment Services Act 2019. Monetary Authority of Singapore, 2020. www.mas.gov.sg/-/media/MAS/Regulations-and-Financial-Stability/Regulations-Guidance-and-Licensing/Payment-Service-Providers/Guide-to-the-Payment-Services-Act-2019.pdf (archived at https://perma.cc/R75C-GREA).

2   Central Bank of the UAE. Payment and Settlements Regulations and Standards. Central Bank of the UAE, n.d. www.centralbank.ae/en/our-operations/payments-and-settlements/regulations-and-standards/ (archived at https://perma.cc/8PKY-SGHE).

3   Saudi Central Bank. Law of Payments and Payment Services. Saudi Central Bank, n.d. www.sama.gov.sa/en-US/LawsRegulations/DocLib/Law_of_Payments_and_Payment_Services-EN.pdf (archived at https://perma.cc/F5PE-PFHK).

4   Reserve Bank of Australia. Regulation of Purchased Payment Facilities, Reserve Bank of Australia, 2000. www.rba.gov.au/media-releases/2000/jmr-rba-apra.html (archived at https://perma.cc/DYZ8-A9TM).

5 European Securities and Markets Authority. Markets in Crypto-Assets Regulation (MiCA), European Securities and Markets Authority. n.d. www. esma.europa.eu/esmas-activities/digital-finance-and-innovation/markets-crypto-assets-regulation-mica (archived at https://perma.cc/UYG3-9EGS).

6 J Etienne, K McEntaggart, S Chirico and G Schnyder (2018). *Comparative Analysis of Regulatory Regimes in Global Economies: BEIS Research Paper Number 19*. Department for Business, Energy and Industrial Strategy, London. assets.publishing.service.gov.uk/media/5bea9751ed915d6a1e83911f/CAoRR_final_report1.pdf (archived at https://perma.cc/WKX6-P4HF).

7 Open Banking Limited. What is Open Banking? Open Banking, n.d. www. openbanking.org.uk/what-is-open-banking/ (archived at https://perma. cc/3NZX-R2F2).

8 S Farrell (2023). *Banking on Data: Evaluating Open Banking and Data Rights in Banking Law*. Wolters Kluwer.

9 K Lim. How to close Southeast Asia's financial inclusion gap. World Economic Forum, 7 February 2022. www.weforum.org/agenda/2022/02/closing-southeast-asia-s-financial-inclusion-gap/ (archived at https://perma.cc/W4GE-SKAN).

10 BBC. China declares all cryptocurrency transactions illegal. BBC News, 24 September 2021. www.bbc.co.uk/news/technology-58678907 (archived at https://perma.cc/E9BZ-EJND).

11 F Shin. What's behind China's cryptocurrency ban? World Economic Forum, 31 January 2022. www.weforum.org/agenda/2022/01/what-s-behind-china-s-cryptocurrency-ban/ (archived at https://perma.cc/7BRE-UVVS).

12 International Organization of Securities Commissions. Policy Recommendations for Crypto and Digital Asset Markets: Consultation Report. International Organization of Securities Commissions, Madrid, 2023. www.iosco.org/library/pubdocs/pdf/IOSCOPD734.pdf (archived at https:// perma.cc/VXN8-TXMV).

13 Financial Stability Board. FSB Global Regulatory Framework for Crypto-Asset Activities. Financial Stability Board, Basel, 2023. www.fsb.org/wp-content/uploads/P170723-1.pdf (archived at https://perma.cc/B9UM-X4LN).

14 Google. Our Principles. Google, n.d. ai.google/responsibility/principles/ (archived at https://perma.cc/7ZWL-W2PV).

15 European Parliament. EU AI Act: first regulation on artificial intelligence. European Parliament, 8 June 2023. www.europarl.europa.eu/topics/en/article/20230601STO93804/eu-ai-act-first-regulation-on-artificial-intelligence (archived at https://perma.cc/9M7U-3RUC).

16 Department for Science, Innovation and Technology. A pro-innovation approach to AI regulation. Department for Science, Innovation and Technology, London, 2023. www.gov.uk/government/publications/ai-regulation-a-pro-innovation-approach/white-paper (archived at https://perma.cc/8GR4-A3FF).

17 D Araujo, S Doerr, L Gambacorta and B Tissot (2024). *Artificial Intelligence in Central Banking*. Bank of International Settlement, Basel. www.bis.org/publ/bisbull84.pdf (archived at https://perma.cc/3D9U-52YD).

18 International Organization of Securities Commissions. The use of artificial intelligence and machine learning by market intermediaries and asset managers. International Organization of Securities Commissions, Madrid, 2021. www.iosco.org/library/pubdocs/pdf/IOSCOPD684.pdf (archived at https://perma.cc/RC39-MH3Y).

10

Case studies in the real world

The case studies in this chapter reflect examples of companies looking carefully at the challenges of fintech regulation and how they have opted to implement it via different stages to their life cycle. The companies covered are operating in areas such as payments and lending, open banking, crypto assets and AI, and we also offer the perspective of traditional large institutions in the sector.

OakNorth: A success story in UK fintech. In our case study, Nick Lee explains how the relationship with the regulator is something they focus on and nurture for the benefit of the business, their customers and the ecosystem. The company has a regulated and unregulated arm, and the case study discusses how this is a real benefit in understanding what it means to operate a regulated entity for both business activities. It also highlights the challenges of growth while trying to keep an entrepreneurial spirit.

Modulr: A payments company authorized and regulated in the United Kingdom. Modulr has innovated to streamline the payments process and provide efficiencies for its customers. It believes that regulation is something to be embraced and talks about its ability to navigate the regulatory requirements. Crucially, it sees an opportunity to operate as an e-money provider in the UK and Europe.

Insignis Cash: A start-up begun by two ex-capital market bankers from large global organizations. Giles Huston, CEO and co-founder gives a perspective on navigating regulation that did not exist for his business model. He also explains what it means to be a fintech founder and how the roles he and his staff deal with change as the company grows.

TrueLayer: One of the first adopters of open banking read and write functionality. TrueLayer operates globally and has been a driving force in pushing the open banking agenda forward in the United Kingdom, Europe and other locations. In this case study, TrueLayer offers useful views on how to navigate regulation and why it is important to them. They are an active participant in the open banking ecosystem.

Outlier Ventures: Offers a view from an investor in web3 and crypto assets. The case study offers a perspective from a COO who is seasoned and experienced in the fields of fintech and crypto web3. As an investor, Outlier Ventures needed to understand the regulatory environment and operate within it actively to ensure that the regulatory developments were considering all perspectives. Seeing a large number of start-ups in this space offers a unique insight into their operations and challenges.

Eigen Technologies: This case study offers an interview with Dr Lewis Z Liu, co-founder and CEO, on implementing AI for a large institution and practical ideas on how AI governance can be applied. While AI is economy-wide and Eigen Technologies naturally work with multiple industries, its unique perspective can offer learnings on how to approach AI in any industry.

Visa: The perspective of a very large financial institution on fintech. Visa sees the benefit of fintech and has many programmes to support and partner with fintechs to offer better solutions to end-users. A significant organization with global reach, Visa is able to offer a perspective on the development of fintech from start-up to scale-up and maturity as well as across multiple jurisdictions.

Fintechs in areas of payments and lending: OakNorth

Launched in September 2015 and founded by entrepreneurs Rishi Khosla and Joel Perlman, OakNorth is a fully licensed UK bank. It provides the UK's fastest growing and most ambitious businesses with the fast, flexible debt finance (loans of £250k up to tens of millions) they need to scale, while also helping savers make their money go further, via a range of award-winning and competitive savings accounts.

Nine years on, OakNorth has lent over £10 billion to businesses across the UK and throughout a wide range of sectors, achieving performance metrics that place it among the top 1 per cent of commercial banks globally in terms of ROE and efficiency. Its data-led approach allows it to look at the future, rather than just fixating on the past, meaning it avoids making decisions based on outdated financials. Using data and analytics, it builds up a granular view of every business in its portfolio, combining this with forward-looking scenario analysis, to enable it to be a trusted funding partner as the business scales, and continue confidently lending through economic cycles and unprecedented events.

Identifying the market opportunity

How did the technology support the proposition and how was the thinking around the USP developed? OakNorth's co-founders, Rishi Khosla and Joel Perlman, identified a market opportunity following the frustrations they faced when trying to get financing for their previous business, Copal. The company was profitable and had good cash flow; however, none of the high-street banks were willing to give them a loan unless they put their homes up as collateral. Over the next 12 months, they went to the US several times and one of the special situations desks of a large US bank offered to give them a $10m dividend recap. So, they were unable to get a bank loan of £100k, but they could get a dividend recap for $10m. Over the next few years, they met countless entrepreneurs who'd had similar painful experiences when looking for finance, so when they sold Copal to

Moody's in 2014, they set out to address the gap they'd experienced first-hand.

Why does this gap exist? One of the main reasons behind this is that innovation in commercial banking has been limited to loan origination systems and modern core banking systems, which means the way that scale-up/mid-sized businesses are served has not evolved for decades and much more innovation is needed.

Compare this with what has happened in the consumer and micro-business space, where the customer experience has dramatically improved over the last decade, and where there are now highly customized products at the point of sale and embedded within other journeys. The issue is that most lenders and financial institutions simply do not have the data and analytical capabilities to bridge the techniques used in the consumer and micro-business space, with the analytical rigour of corporate lending – i.e. taking a granular, forward-looking view of each business. As a result, they default to the same approaches that have been used for decades relying on broad sector assumptions, and a heavily manual approach that provides an (a) inconsistent; (b) slow; and (c) poor experience for customers.

OakNorth is addressing this gap by empowering scaling mid-sized businesses with proven and profitable business models, but unmet or overlooked banking needs. Its USPs focus on four core areas:

- Speed: it aims to complete transactions in days or weeks vs the months it takes with a traditional high-street bank.

- Flexibility: every loan is designed for the business and its unique needs. No off-the-shelf solutions or 'computer-says-no' decisions.

- Transparency: businesses are kept in the loop throughout the application process and may even be invited to meet its Credit Committee (i.e. the decision-makers).

- Entrepreneurial: as a bank founded by entrepreneurs *for* entrepreneurs, its entire proposition is designed with the customer in mind to create a delightful experience for businesses.

NAVIGATING THE EARLY-STAGE START-UP AND THE VARIOUS
GROWTH PHASES

OakNorth has been able to successfully navigate its early-stage start-up phase, and its current scale-up phase by focusing on the following:

- Delivering outsized customer outcomes: everything it does is with the customer in mind. It does not tell them what it offers, it asks them what they need and then sees what it can offer them to address that need. Its customer-centric approach has resulted in around 50 per cent of its new lending coming through referrals and more than 50 per cent of its borrowers being repeat customers.

- Building a robust business: OakNorth reached cash flow break-even just 11 months after launch and it has been profitable every year since. It has always focused on building a robust business model as this was essential for ensuring it would be able to continue to serve its customers through economic cycles.

- Product–market fit: OakNorth ensured it had a strong product–market fit and that it was solving a real problem faced by businesses on a daily basis across the UK.

Focusing on these by default meant that OakNorth is meeting the new Consumer Duty which launched in July 2023 in the UK. This is not surprising. When it comes to how to navigate the regulatory obligations, OakNorth's founders believe that if you do what's right for your customers, you're doing what's right for your shareholders, and generally doing what's right for the regulator. They ensured that they take the regulator on the journey with them. As a result of this approach, in May 2016 OakNorth became the first UK bank to have its core systems fully hosted on the cloud. This was done in close discussion with the regulator.

Financial resilience has been key   OakNorth recognized that some fintechs have chased valuation and customer numbers over profitability and hoped that financial sustainability will follow. This is not an approach the founders wanted to take. Instead, they believed that it is much better to grow when you are profitable rather than try to grow before that point. This has served OakNorth very well given investors are expecting a shorter time to profitability. It also put them in good stead with everything that they had to face from Brexit to weathering the economic cycle.

EMBEDDING RISK MANAGEMENT THROUGH YOUR VARIOUS STAGES AND WHY THIS IS A BENEFIT

Risk management at OakNorth is something that has continually grown and matured over time. OakNorth focused on developing risk management in a way that reflected the risk profile of the organization. When it first started, risk management was relatively straightforward but appropriate for what was effectively a zero-balance sheet. Risk management frameworks evolved as the business has grown, this is a result of internal reflection, the advice and challenge of the Board, and staying informed about the regulator's expectations, priorities and feedback. For example, there is no need for banks to set up a loan workout team until their licence is granted and they are offering loans.

As OakNorth matured, via the same approach the risk taxonomy grew and frameworks were developed continually across all the areas of business from financial crime, conduct risk, cybersecurity, credit, prudential and operational risk to name a few. With that evolution, the resource and expertise around governance and risk grew and became more detailed and with enhanced effectiveness.

Governance becoming bureaucracy OakNorth found that there comes a point where a fintech ends up doing too much and shifts its focus to risk management and governance, which runs the risk of ignoring the entrepreneurial culture that got it to this point in the first place. Governance cannot become too cumbersome and slow down decision-making and hinder the agility of the fintech. OakNorth identified this and deliberately went through a reflection process to ensure it kept appropriate levels of governance while not losing the entrepreneurial spirit and mindset.

The challenge is trying to make sure it is able to explain what it is trying to do and bring the regulators along with it. This involves explaining the products upfront, how the development of the product will work, how the risks have been identified, what the controls are and how the testing is being done. In addition, they explained that this would be done in small steps, and if the development did not work that they could be turned off with minimal disruption and harm. It is crucial, though, that it did not start with a heavy and burdensome governance framework.

The right talent at the right time   As OakNorth evolved its risk management function and frameworks, it brought in and developed the right talent to deliver them. It was also important to ensure that everyone in the organization understood the spirit and the importance of a good conduct and risk management culture. OakNorth found that attracting and developing the right talent for this could sometimes take time.

Often people coming to a fintech do not always want to work in a highly regulated organization, so finding the balance to ensure everyone thinks of risk management is critical. OakNorth's leadership team spent a lot of time with staff to explain the need to find this balance and develop a culture that is agile and entrepreneurial, yet cares about risk, regulation and conduct.

The regulated and unregulated businesses   OakNorth group operates two main business lines. OakNorth, a digital bank, which is a regulated entity with a banking licence, and OakNorth Credit Intelligence (ONci), a software service business that is an unregulated software provider where other commercial lenders in the US are its clients.

OakNorth and the regulators have a good working relationship, and they work hard to achieve and maintain this. It is much better for OakNorth Bank to anticipate the questions and address them proactively. They believe that getting this right first time makes their life easier. If they do not, they recognize that it will create too much focus and resource on remediation to fix identified issues after the fact. Too many issues identified by the regulator will create a loss of confidence and that is a risk they do not want to take. Their view is that a fintech does not have a business if the regulator is not happy. ONci is the software OakNorth uses. While not regulated, it takes steps to introduce itself to overseas regulators because its clients are regulated. It believes the confidence in this service comes from the recognition that OakNorth understands what it takes to be a regulated entity and the service it offers will therefore meet those expectations.

Nick Lee, Head of Governmental and Regulatory Affairs at OakNorth

What have been the regulatory challenges?

To date, the PRA and FCA have delivered successfully on their aim of reforming the authorization process for bank applicants. However, what we have yet to see in the UK is any of those new entrants being able to scale to a size to meaningfully compete with the large incumbent banks. Its goal of creating a major shift in prudential regulation of banking start-ups is still a work in progress. While I'm incredibly proud of the impact OakNorth has had on the British economy in terms of job creation, home building and GDP growth since 2015, none of us new entrants have yet to scale enough to be considered significant competitors to the incumbents.

A key reason for this is that the burden of regulation falls more heavily on challenger banks than it does on larger, systemic institutions. That is evidenced by higher capital and regulatory requirements per pound of risk exposure. These risk and reporting requirements don't generally differ between small, new banks and global multinationals. With an ever-broadening scope of regulatory requests and requirements, it seems counterintuitive to competition to disregard size and status. Furthermore, capital requirements at present penalize banks that only lend in the UK, which many scaling banks do as obtaining licences in other markets is a time and resource-intensive process.

What do you want to see next?

What's needed in the UK is not less regulation, but better regulation – i.e. regulation that is agile, proportionate and focused. This is the sweet spot that we should encourage our regulators to achieve. In a post-Brexit environment, UK regulators must take advantage of the flexibility that comes from our exit from the EU. They need to regulate in a way that removes the barriers to growth and scaling, develops a more proportionate and risk-based regulatory framework in an agile manner, and allows innovation and competition to flourish. This will benefit consumers and business with lower costs and better services without sacrificing financial stability or consumer protection.

However, in the UK, the ability for new banks and existing mid-tier and specialist firms to scale, grow and deliver genuine competition for the incumbent, high-street banks, is being hampered by barriers to growth, particularly the MREL regime. In the UK, one of the main MREL triggers is activated when a bank's assets pass the £15bn level. However, to ensure the MREL regime captures only the largest 'systemic' banks, the Bank of England could increase the MREL trigger to £50bn of assets. By doing so, it is estimated that mid-tier UK banks could unlock additional lending capacity over the next five years, potentially up to £62bn. With an estimated multiplier effect of three to four times to the real economy, this change could be fundamental to the future growth prospects of the UK economy, without significant impact on financial stability. Moving the trigger to £50bn would also bring us more in line with our partners in Europe and the US.

Furthermore, I believe that we should never see the banking sector as a zero-failure regime. This is not how a healthy and competitive market economy operates. To support this new approach, along with the changes to MREL above, I suggest that the funding of the Financial Services Compensation Scheme (FSCS) should be reviewed. At present, our scheme is only funded to deal with very limited bank failures and cannot recapitalize banks. It is not able to cope with failures from systemic banks which is why when they failed during the financial crisis, they had to be bailed out by the taxpayer through HM Treasury. This model makes government and regulators more risk averse, seeking ever higher requirements to ensure they are not blamed for any kind of failure.

While no one is seeking bank failures, it should not be a taboo subject. Just as in the US, we should look at a more robust and fuller funding model for the FSCS and give it the ability to use more tools including bank re-capitalization. These changes should be funded by the banking sector with those who bear the most risk paying the highest contributions. That would give regulators and government confidence to make the necessary changes to the system for more proportionate and risk-based regulation to enable competition and economic growth.

Fintechs in areas of payments and lending: Modulr

Business payments are a complicated mix of processes, permissions, batch files and delays that we in the consumer world would not tolerate. Consumers expect payments to be embedded into apps so that they do not notice them. Meanwhile, even the most automated business processes have to stop and send a payment request to the finance team or request to see if a payment has been received. Few businesses would consider designing payments into their internal process flows because they would not even be aware it would be possible.

Think of the lending company with its complex risk and approval system that sends an email to a customer saying, '*your loan is approved*', followed by a day or more wait for the money. Wouldn't it be great if the platform instead emailed '*your loan is approved and paid out*'. Or the car dealership that sends out a rep to buy a car and has to stand on the seller's driveway waiting for payment to go through. Better surely to inspect the vehicle and then tap a button on the in-house app to make the purchase. Or salaries paid instantly rather than after a three-day wait.

The problem is that finance and product professionals, especially outside the financial services industry, aren't aware that there is another way. Not only can payments be made via a software call, but also accounts can be created and made to trigger actions when money is added to or moved from the account. Those not in the financial services industry assume the only option is legacy bank-provided payment processes, based on a non-real-time batch payment framework, business hours only, and with no service-level agreements. They certainly do not consider an API suite that can be integrated into their tech stack.

Modulr, today, solves these problems for its customers. It calls the service it provides **Embedded Payments**. Modulr's Business Payments offering enables microenterprises, SMEs, corporates and enterprise customers across the UK, and Europe to efficiently pay in, collect and disburse funds instantly into a range of accounts, wallets and cards – all accessible via API calls. Modulr has created an industry-leading platform that provides a range of product capability, deeply integrated into an expanding network of accounting and payroll platforms.

Building on its business payments offering, Modulr also leverages its deep payments expertise and extensive product capability to solve specific problems in certain industry verticals, including travel, merchant payments, lending, wage advance, and investment and wealth. Through its software-driven product modules, integrations into industry ecosystems and a rigorous approach to compliance and risk management, Modulr is building the modern FinOps Hub to enable payments to work for businesses. The benefit to customers could be reduced complexity and cost, new revenue streams, better end-customer experience or a combination of all of these.

One simple example of the benefit Modulr provides is shown in this without/with Modulr payment flow diagram in Figure 10.1.

The market opportunity

The global revenue opportunity from payments is massive and estimated at over $2trn. Therefore, it has attracted significant investment

FIGURE 10.1 Modulr diagram

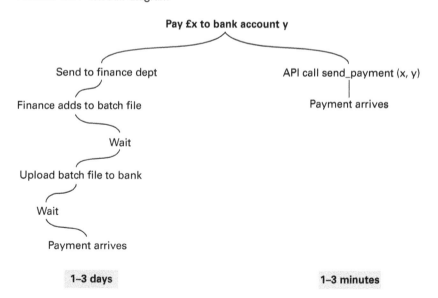

and has powerful incumbent providers. Modulr was founded by Myles Stephenson with an initial small expert team who had worked together previously experiencing the challenges of building businesses without the technology enabled access to payment services. Modulr was created in late 2015 to fix the problems in business payments outlined above by bringing together a purpose-built technology platform, regulatory permissions and direct access to the payment networks with the core design principle of clients being able to select the components ('modules') they require to solve a specific problem. This focus on solving specific problems leveraging deep payments expertise, extensive product capability and developing expertise in specific market verticals has enabled Modulr to be successful in a large competitive market.

This broader market experience combined with having seen the regulatory landscape open to new participants and market demand for API-based payments infrastructure not being addressed by incumbent providers led to 2016 being the ideal time to launch Modulr. Indeed, regulation in the EU at the time, pre-Brexit, had only recently permitted non-banks to provide payment services in the way Modulr planned. Business payments were seen as a standalone service, not something that could be deeply integrated into any company's tech stack.

APPROACHING REGULATION

For most of Modulr's customers, a key benefit is that they can use, integrate and deliver payments products without being regulated themselves. Modulr enables this key benefit using a number of deployment models delivered to rigorous standards in risk management and regulatory compliance. Modulr's Partner model requires a thorough upfront and ongoing assessment of how the client's business operates, the business plan and financials as well as the client's risk management and compliance controls.

Modulr obtained its UK Electronic Money Institution (EMI) licence with the UK's Financial Conduct Authority (FCA) and with the Netherlands' De Nederlandsche Bank (DNB) to operate across the EEA. In addition to its EMI status, Modulr became a direct participant in the UK Faster Payments and Bacs payments schemes meaning it settles directly to the Bank of England without needing an agency bank relationship. In addition, it has become a principle issuing member of Visa and Mastercard.

Regulation provides a vital opportunity, but also an operating obligation on Modulr that most technology companies do not have to bear. However, it is also the investment that unlocks Modulr's value to customers. Technical integration to Modulr is quite straightforward, but customers have to accept that Modulr must ensure they uphold the strict requirements required by its regulators. For customers that only need to manage their own money via Modulr accounts and services, this is an operating model which is more familiar to businesses. However, where the customers wish to offer accounts to their own customers, they must submit to an onboarding, ongoing partner oversight and then an annual audit to cover end-customer onboarding, fraud prevention, money laundering and so forth. Their customers must accept terms and conditions that are required by Modulr.

Modulr takes its regulatory responsibilities extremely seriously. Its licences are its most valuable asset. For this reason, Modulr does not hesitate to take appropriate action on customers when they do not meet their obligations. Like most tech businesses Modulr does suffer some client churn, but unlike most, the main churn reason has been Modulr requiring clients not meeting its strict partner oversight and supervision requirements to cease payment activities.

ATTITUDE TO OVERCOMING REGULATORY CHALLENGES

The notion that regulation is something to be overcome is alien to Modulr. Modulr exists because of, not in spite of regulation in Europe and the UK that aimed to spur competition in payments. The UK and Europe are two of the few large economic regions in the world that permit non-banks to become payment participants. Modulr could not operate the same business model in the US, for example, without a partner bank. This has forced Modulr to focus, initially at least, on the UK and Europe, but this has also been a benefit. The potential market is huge, and it has stopped Modulr from losing focus by trying to become a global player in a payments market that is notable for wide regional variations in payment schemes and local regulatory requirements. International overreach with early expansion has been one of the causes of fintech failure.

An unexpected challenge has been the perception of regulation as an EMI as being lighter touch than for banks by some of those entering the sector, within the sector and to some extent understandably those outside the sector. Modulr's view is that this has damaged the sector by giving the impression that rules are more relaxed. In reality, EMIs have a tighter set of products they can offer (they cannot, for instance, lend money like banks) but within these rails, they need to operate to the same standards as banks as they relate to providing payment services. This has allowed the often incorrect position of fintechs operating to a lower standard and level of scrutiny. This simply should not be the case.

THE STAGES OF GROWTH

Modulr used the network of its venture builder seed investor Blenheim Chalcot to prove its business model which provided there was a receptive client base. This was quickly followed by ambitious fintechs looking for a partner to fast track their business idea. The first customer was a merchant cash advance business, which remains a top client today. Without Modulr, they would be unable to receive their customers' point-of-sale revenue on which advances are secured, and in real time pass them on, less a pre-agreed split, to their customers. Modulr began transacting in late 2016 and within a year had hit the all-important £1m recurring revenue milestone.

The key strategies that help build a solid business were:

1 Staged product development, both in terms of services offered, and how the service was delivered initially via payments partners but over time bringing services in house to drive gross margin.

2 A vertical approach to sales and marketing, with an initial focus on financial services customers, creating industry vertical

knowledge rather than attempting to offer payments to anyone. Focus verticals have since expanded to accounting and payroll software providers, travel and marketplaces.

3 Rock solid risk and compliance services and teams.

WHERE SHOULD REGULATION GO NEXT?

Modulr's financial services client base remains its largest, but the big opportunity is to unlock the broader market. Modulr's platform can benefit any business, or indeed organization (such as a government department) that runs on a software platform.

There are also market reforms needed to truly enable the competitive levelling intended by electronic money institution legislation as part of the broader regulatory change including the second Payments Services Directive in the EU ('PSD2'). EMIs and Payment Institutions (PIs) have been a great way to stimulate competition and innovation. As the sector and individual institutions are now reaching scale, progressively deeper integration with the core regulatory environment becomes key alongside direct access to the core payment scheme and central bank infrastructure, increasing robustness of the whole system while promoting competition and innovation. The UK's legislation was based on the same (pre-Brexit) regulation, but the UK stepped ahead of the EU by also permitting non-banks to directly connect to payment infrastructure. It is good to see the early drafting of the third Payment Services Directive (PSD3) drafts are discussing the same for connection to SEPA payments, but this will take some time to come into force.

EU regulation remains shackled by in-country practices and rules that contradict the EU-wide laws. Accounts in the EU should be acceptable to use across the EU but in many countries, there are limitations on the use of accounts that do not have the same country code as the country in question. In many countries it is impossible to have salaries paid into an account with a different country code. This practice is called IBAN (International Bank Account Number) Discrimination. Things are slowly moving in the right direction, but it will take time.

Fintechs in areas of payments and lending: Insignis Cash

In this case study, Giles Huston, CEO and co-founder of Insignis, provides his views on navigating regulation that did not exist for his business model.

Summary of the Insignis Cash business model

Insignis was never designed to be a disruptor. We see our business as an enabler for the UK savings market. We see benefits for all parties including banking partners, our financial advice partners and most importantly our mutual clients. We are trying to get the blood pumping in the UK savings market.

FIGURE 10.2 Insignis model

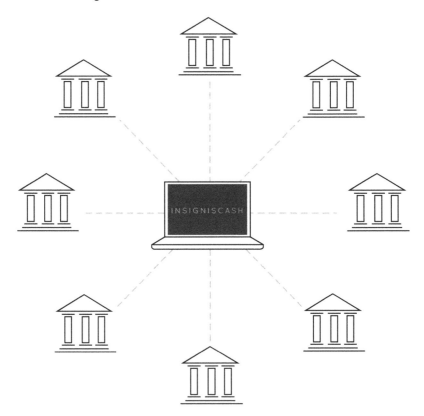

IDENTIFYING AND DEVELOPING THE MARKET OPPORTUNITY

There were two major catalysts that ignited our focus in building this business. The FCA report about the UK savings market from 2015 was the first. The report highlighted a lack of dynamism and motivation and the customer inertia that came with the cash savings market. Consumers were not shopping around or switching, and a gap existed to help.

We saw this as the opportunity. When considering how to solve this, we modelled our solution on a version that has been successfully launched in the US. Cash saving products tend to be local and local solutions are important. We looked at that model, adjusted it for the UK market and applied that concept to the problems best highlighted by the FCA report.

The platform is digital. It is a hub that connects into multiple cash savings product providers. The idea is that our customer is able to access multiple product providers through a single application and execution interface. The customer doesn't have to do the shopping around across multiple banks and will be able to diversify risk and get the best deals on an ongoing basis with one onboarding process. The concept uses technology at its heart. It's a simple concept, but we then set out to identify how best we do we do this and balance all our obligations as we go.

WHAT HAVE BEEN THE REGULATORY CHALLENGES?

Our challenge was mainly that it became very apparent we needed to be regulated but our business model didn't really have a neat box that we fitted into at the time. We had good conversations with the FCA which we proactively initiated. The initial response was that cash is not a regulated asset class and we didn't need to be regulated.

However, the business model relied on us having the right level of credibility with customers and with the product partners, often highly regulated entities that expect high standards from their partners. Given the proposition relies on these partnerships, we felt regulation was necessary for the comfort of the market generally with a business model such as ours.

It nevertheless created difficulty because we hadn't yet completed the platform and launched the product but needed to be regulated to set up the right accounts and infrastructure. Our initial solution was to set ourselves up as an Appointed Representative of another entity to get us into the regulated sphere. Another important reason is the learning that we benefit from by being a regulated entity. We expected regulation would come down the line and this was our way of recognizing this up front.

Then the second Payments Services Directive arrived (PSD2) and we went back knocking on the door of the FCA to be authorized under that regime. We applied in May 2018 and were approved in September 2018. The process was smooth and the FCA were extremely helpful. We believe regulation is here to help our proposition not hinder, so we embraced the spirit of it before we started the authorization process.

HOW DID YOU OVERCOME THEM?

We identified proactively what the challenges were and set out to have the right conversations proactively with our regulator. Open and transparent conversations with all parties in the ecosystem gave us an idea of what we needed when it came to risk and regulation. For example, it was imperative that we build and maintain strong operational resilience and cybersecurity. Our platform had to be the best it could be. Minimal down time and full trust in how it operates.

We also gave ourselves a very clear flavour on what to expect as a regulated entity by becoming an appointed representative first. There was also the element of empathy. Coming from very large institutions meant that we could empathize how long things take and how to navigate the banks themselves. We were a small fintech relative to their size and lots of wailing from small companies doesn't help – we needed to recognize the reality of the world and work with them on how to get the right outcome.

HOW DID YOU NAVIGATE THE EARLY-STAGE START-UP AND THE VARIOUS GROWTH PHASES?

Swallow one's pride. We came from long careers in large financial institutions. A founder of a fintech will have to let go of their pretensions and do things that they haven't have to do for the last 20 or 30 years. The early stages mean that founders are the visionaries, strategists and operations people. We had to get hands dirty. In those early days we simply had to do everybody's job. This also meant going the extra mile for something that may not seem like it is worth the effort. I would drive 600-mile round trip to help an elderly lady with the application process. But having to wear many hats has a lot of benefits. The founder gets to know the business and can make the right decisions.

Decisions were divided into must haves and nice to haves. We focused on the must haves in the first couple of years as we were developing the value proposition and making sure it worked well for our partners and customers. Many founders fall foul of too many nice to haves in the initial stages. Version 1 has to be good but also 'good enough'. For example, there are a large number of banks in the UK with which we can partner. We launched with 12 banks only. Nobody asked why only 12. We thought that 12 is a much better outcome for our clients than one or none.

Our risk management was tailored for the various stages of our life cycle. At the start, we drilled down on operational resilience and cybersecurity. This was very important to get right since we are responsible for large amounts of money moving around the system. Our payments model is to move a relatively small number of tickets but large amounts and a payment simply can't go wrong.

The model reinforced the necessity to double down on payments and security infrastructure. We looked at our options and considered outsourcing to be our best option. We work with Barclays and HSBC payments infrastructure where we get full access to the UK payments infrastructure while having the full functionality that we need with a reasonable fee. Outsourcing this functionality has been a good outcome for our model so far.

AT THE SCALE-UP STAGE, WHAT HAS CHANGED?
We are seeing great growth, and the most important thing is to make sure that the various functions are moving at the same pace and that our risk management is adapting to that change in a dynamic way. We use the metaphor 'keep the trains moving at the same speed'. It doesn't help when one business unit gets too far ahead of the others.

Our business has three core components that have to move at the same pace: Product, Distribution and Operations and Risk, which sits in the middle.

These three pieces have to be built at approximately the same speed. We built in parallel with becoming a regulated entity and continued after being regulated. It's not a cliff edge and the way we thought of our risk management and regulatory requirements was partly driven by the regulatory requirements and also about embedding the culture of doing the right thing for our clients and our partners. The new Consumer Duty has come in and we feel we have been prepared for it for a long time. This is a mindset. It's the culture we live and our model at Insignis.

There were a number of themes that helped us in our scaling journey:

- Our founders are older than the average fintech founder. This may sound controversial but with our long careers in banking and going out to make a difference we had the confidence to recognize what we don't know.

- Conscious incompetence. Find people who compliment you and recognize what you can't do. We realized that we were a fintech company with two 'fin' people running the business, so one our early and critical appointments was a great Chief Technology Officer.

- As the business scales, recognize what skills are needed to free up the founders for leading the strategic direction of the business. It may be a chief risk officer or a COO. Increase the board to the level that allows the founders to do the things that they are supposed to do.

- Our risk management framework wraps itself around all aspects of the business. Product, technology, operations and distribution. We have structured our executive team to lead these functions effectively. When we started, cyber and regulatory risks were the key risks we focused on. Now the risk matrix has become more complex as the business has grown to include reputational and further operational risk.

WHAT DO YOU WANT TO SEE NEXT?

Insignis is now at the scaling stage of the business and is roughly doubling each year. We now have three key areas of focus:

- Firstly, to ensure that all aspects of the business continue to be truly scalable.

- Secondly, to continue to demonstrate to our constituents – our banking partners, our financial advice partners and our clients – the value of the service to the UK savings market.

- Thirdly, to ensure that we have right people as part of our team, and that they have the training opportunities and growth path to thrive.

With these themes in mind, we see very significant growth all aspects of the business but especially our technology and marketing teams.

Open banking: TrueLayer

Introduction and summary of TrueLayer's business model

TrueLayer is a fintech payments company specializing in connecting to open banking APIs (application programming interfaces), and 'aggregating' these connections to enable other businesses to more easily access open banking, through a single TrueLayer API.

HOW DID TRUELAYER SEE THE OPEN BANKING OPPORTUNITY AND DEVELOP THEIR PERSPECTIVE AROUND IT?

TrueLayer's founders, Francesco and Luca, saw an opportunity in 2016 to enter the market following the second Payment Services Directive (PSD2). The opportunity was born from requirements on banks and other payment account providers, to open access to customer payments accounts, via so called 'dedicated interfaces'. In practice, banks were required to build APIs, to allow third parties to access account data and initiate payments. This was intended to increase competition and innovation.

The problem the founders set out to solve was that in order for businesses to make use of open banking, they need to be connected to *all* the banks that their own customers use. TrueLayer realized early on that businesses would not necessarily want to dedicate resources to connecting to the many banks, which is a technical task, requiring engineers and a high degree of expertise and maintenance. Therefore, TrueLayer's initial business priority was to connect to all the APIs provided by banks across the UK and EU aggregating these connections. TrueLayer then built its own API, so that businesses could connect to all banks via a single integration with TrueLayer. This is how TrueLayer developed its open banking network – offering businesses (from investment platforms to car retailers), an easy way to access the benefits of open banking.

WHAT WERE THE REGULATORY CHALLENGES?

TrueLayer came into the market following the introduction of a brand new regulatory regime. From the beginning this meant overcoming regulatory 'grey areas' where the practical aspects of the regime were not yet tested and working closely with the FCA and broader industry to overcome the challenges. Some of the challenges included the following.

Applying to the FCA for a new type of licence and being among the first companies to receive the licence   TrueLayer was among the first firms to apply to the FCA for permission to carry out account information and payment initiation services. Because open banking was so new, in our application, TrueLayer focused on visualizing what our services would look like to the consumer, by creating 'mock-up' user journeys in our application and by giving examples of real-world companies we would partner with. Additionally, while the FCA usually expects 'flow of funds' diagrams, we also provided 'flow of data' diagrams, anticipating that this would be a key focus of the regulator, as open banking data was a new aspect of their regulatory regime.

One particular challenge was meeting the authorization condition of obtaining professional indemnity insurance – there was very little awareness of PSD2 in the insurance industry at that time – and as a result insurance policies were difficult to obtain. TrueLayer worked closely with the insurance industry to educate them about the PSD2 requirements and obtain appropriate cover.

Innovating within the constraints of a new open banking regime   Initially TrueLayer was focused on 'data aggregation' – accessing customer account data and sharing it, with the customer's permission, with businesses, who could use the data to provide value added services to the customer. For example, TrueLayer partnered with Credit Ladder in 2018, which accessed open banking data to help consumers build their credit score. Early on, TrueLayer came up against a limitation of regulation which was holding back innovation: businesses who wanted to display consumer bank data back to consumers; for example, accountants or personal finance management apps, needed to be licensed by the FCA as an AISP – even if they were using TrueLayer to access the underlying data. This was burdensome for smaller firms and prevented them from operating in the market. TrueLayer worked with the FCA during the development of an agency model, where authorized AISPs like TrueLayer could appoint firms as their agents to allow them to access and provide data back to users. This helped to bring many smaller innovative firms into open banking. TrueLayer currently has over 60 AIS agents.

Obtaining additional permissions to further innovate   One of the limitations of open banking payments is that it was not developed with refunds in mind. PISPs initiate payments in one direction – from sending bank to receiving bank. TrueLayer developed a product where we provide our clients with their own merchant accounts, so that they can receive funds into them, and we can initiate payments back out of them in the form of refunds. It was necessary to apply to the FCA for additional e-money permissions to enable this feature. This came with a number of challenges:

- Increased capital requirements.
- Safeguarding requirements (as a PISP, TrueLayer did not hold user funds).
- Securing a safeguarding partner bank – having a bank account is necessary to obtain an e-money account, but many banks have withdrawn from providing these services to fintechs in recent years).

- Changing our open banking certificates – changing our regulatory status meant a change to our firm reference number (FRN) – but FRNs are 'baked into' open banking identification certificates. This meant a major project to re-enrol with all the UK banks with which we were connected with new certificates using our new FRN.

EU withdrawal   The UK's withdrawal from the EU posed major challenges for TrueLayer. With much of our activity taking place in the EU, we opted to obtain a licence in Ireland, which would allow us to continue to passport services into the EU. This required developing a physical presence in the country, and building our compliance, legal and operational teams to have the capacity to operate in two jurisdictions in parallel. The experience of becoming authorized in Ireland was different from the experience of being authorized in the UK, with the Central Bank of Ireland (CBI) focusing on different aspects of our application. Overall, this was very positive for TrueLayer, leading us to strengthen certain aspects of our governance and compliance approach. For example, while 'three lines of defence' is not a requirement under PSD2, the CBI expected TrueLayer to be operating under this model. Consequently, we have built out the three lines of defence, across the TrueLayer Group.

TrueLayer places a large amount of importance on anticipating major regulatory changes. We achieve this through horizon scanning, regulatory engagement and maintaining a risk register with senior management oversight. Information on external risks is escalated and discussed at senior levels which means that when changes like Brexit take effect we are in a position to implement a planned response, limiting the impact on our customers being one of our key objectives.

HOW DID YOU NAVIGATE THE EARLY-STAGE START-UP AND THE VARIOUS GROWTH PHASES?

TrueLayer has grown rapidly since it was founded with two people in 2016. During the Covid-19 period, TrueLayer grew to a company of over 400 people, with offices in UK, Milan, Dublin and Australia. Throughout this growth phase our key focus has been on scaling safely, being customer-focused, and plotting a course to profitability.

Scaling safely and sustainably   The fast-paced scale-up environment has required TrueLayer to develop and embed governance frameworks and controls that are fit for purpose, targeted and effective. It has been important for the risk and compliance functions within TrueLayer to work with the business to explain the requirements of providing regulated payments services, improve its risk posture and embed a compliance culture.

Scaling safely requires an effective compliance culture to be embedded company-wide at TrueLayer with:

• Senior management buy-in.

• An experienced risk and compliance team.

• Engaged employees that respond to changes as the business scales and matures.

Being customer-focused   TrueLayer's early customers were nimble, modern businesses that could quickly integrate and deploy our services. This allowed us to rapidly grow our coverage across the UK and Europe, and our product benefited through close dialogue with our merchants. Once open banking grew in adoption, larger and more sophisticated merchants added open banking to their platforms.

Integrating with FTSE100 merchants is very complex and demanding. Serving these enterprise merchants has been a competitive advantage for TrueLayer over the past few years but has required the company to grow in many ways. For example, many large enterprise companies expect TrueLayer to adhere to the highest security and risk management practices. As a result, TrueLayer has obtained SOC2 accreditation, as well as Cyber Essentials Plus.

Plotting a course to profitability   While TrueLayer has grown rapidly in recently years, we maintain a firm focus on the path to profitability, monetization and sustainable growth. As a scale-up, TrueLayer currently relies on venture capital investment. Recent economic conditions have meant difficult decisions, for example, a 10 per cent headcount reduction. This decision was taken in order to give the company the maximum amount of time to deliver on our strategy. When making this decision it was key to act quickly and decisively, to put us on the best possible path.

Crypto assets: Outlier Ventures

Outlier Ventures is the global leading Web3 accelerator, with a renowned reputation as the go-to authority for Web3 founders, investors and partners. With a portfolio of over 300 start-ups from every region of the world across its accelerator programme Base Camp and token launch advisory Ascent, Outlier Ventures has helped raise over $350m in seed funding across its various accelerator programmes. Outlier Ventures portfolio includes leading Web3 companies including Agoric, Biconomy, Boson Protocol, Brave, Cheqd, Cudos, DIA Data, Fetch.ai, Futureverse, Ocean Protocol, and Secret Network.

Outlier Ventures partners with global industry protocol leaders, including Aptos, Filecoin/IPFS, NEAR, Wormhole, Polkadot and Polygon, along with leading global brands to design bespoke programmes by its team of experts that help refine business strategy, product–market fit, community growth, token design and governance as well as investor and mentor networks.

A COO's perspective – Nathalie Oestmann, former COO of Outlier Ventures

As the former COO of Outlier Ventures, I have seen first-hand the implications of importance of regulatory clarity to ensure proper business growth. Outlier Ventures is one of the first VC firms dedicated to investing in the emerging Web3/Crypto start-ups since 2014. In 2019, Outlier Ventures introduced a pre-seed accelerator programme and, since launching, Outlier Ventures has received over 7,000 applications, supported over 300 Web3 projects and has helped raise over $350 million in seed funding for high-profile projects from across the world.

In my time at Outlier Ventures, I have seen some of the most high-profile crypto business scams uncovered, including Terra Luna, Celsius, Three Arrows Capital and FTX (to name a few) in 2022 as well as the costly $4 billion dollar fine in 2023 on Binance for not properly performing compliance checks which ultimately led to Founder and CEO Changpeng Zhao losing his job. These collapses have resulted in an estimated loss of $70 billion to investors and customers. Many of these 'scams' could have been avoided, with the correct regulatory oversight.

Outlier Ventures has always viewed its portfolio as an open stack of technologies on the blockchain that contribute to a new web paradigm, referred to as Web3. The accelerator programme has supported the launch and growth of notable projects across defi, NFTs and blockchain infrastructure with a focus on emergent metaverse use cases such as NFT-based digital couture fashion brands, avatar marketplaces, decentralized music publishing platforms, play-to-earn games, augmented reality social positioning protocols and more.

REGULATORY AMBIGUITY IN WEB3 AND CRYPTO ASSETS

Because the Web3/crypto space introduces completely new business models, it is true that there has been a lack of a clear and consistent global regulatory framework for blockchain and crypto assets. This certainly can create challenges for companies that are building in the space as they navigate different rules in different jurisdictions globally. It can also make it difficult for new companies to not only enter the market but also to grow, as investors and even customers are not always clear on what they can or cannot do.

Globally, some of the regulatory ambiguity still facing blockchain and crypto companies into 2023 includes:

1 **Classification of crypto assets:** Regulators are still grappling with how to classify crypto assets, such as Bitcoin (BTC) and Ethereum (ETH). Are they securities, commodities or something else? Even different regulators in the US can't fully agree. In August 2023, a New York district court delighted the cryptocurrency community by calling them a Commodity, while the federal Security and Exchange Committee (SEC) is calling them a Security.

2 **Consumer protection:** Due to the decentralized nature of the blockchain, there are concerns about how to protect consumers, particularly if the transaction is completely decentralized (meaning

not managed by a single company but rather by the consumer's own wallet on the blockchain). The rules around implementing robust risk management and consumer protection measures still need to evolve.

3 Licensing: Some countries require crypto companies to obtain a licence in order to operate. This can be a complex and time-consuming process, and the requirements vary from country to country.

FINTECHS' ROLE IN MOVING THE DEBATE FORWARD

Getting clarity on these topics will require communication and stress-testing of ideas between the Web3/Crypto Ecosystem, regulators and established businesses and is currently happening:

1 Engaging with regulators: It is becoming increasingly important for the more established Web3 organizations and industry groups to engage with regulators to learn about their concerns and to advocate for sensible regulation. For example, the Global Digital Asset Exchange Association (GDAX) is a trade association that represents some of the world's largest crypto exchanges. GDAX works with regulators to develop and implement best practices for AML/CTF and consumer protection.

2 Developing self-regulatory standards: Crypto companies are also developing their own self-regulatory standards. For example, the CryptoCurrency Certification Consortium (C4) is a non-profit organization that has developed a certification programme for crypto exchanges. The C4 certification programme assesses exchanges on a number of factors, including security, AML/CTF compliance and fairness.

3 Educate the public: One of the biggest challenges facing crypto companies is that the public is still largely unfamiliar with blockchain and crypto assets. Crypto companies are investing in education and outreach programmes to help people understand the benefits and risks of investing in crypto assets.

4 Collaborate with Web2 (traditional) industries: There is an increase in collaboration with 'traditional' industries, such as the financial services industry to develop new products and services that have compelling use cases. Adoption by regulated industries will drive crypto companies to invest in compliance to meet the requirements of regulators around the world. This includes hiring experienced compliance professionals, implementing AML/CTF procedures, and conducting security audits.

START-UPS FACE UNIQUE CHALLENGES

The reality is different for early-stage start-ups. They will be taking risks to get a new business model or product to market – it's commonly known as a risk-based approach. The premise is that start-ups are inherently of high risk, and it's better to fail fast in trying to understand if your product has the PMF (Product–Market Fit) that investors are looking for. If an idea indicates low market traction the team will iterate, pivot or just try something new. So, in the very early stages, setting up for the best compliance and or regulatory processes (with the exception of things that are absolutely illegal) will be minimal until the PMF is attained.

For many years, crypto was not yet classified as a financial product and therefore not regulated. Herein was the problem that is currently being rectified by clear definitions, starting with the definition of a Crypto Asset and what constitutes a financial transaction.

CONSIDERATIONS FOR REGULATORS

From my vantage point of seeing hundreds of Web3/crypto start-ups, here are some specific things that regulators can do to support innovation in this space:

1 **Create start-up friendly regulatory sandboxes** which allow start-ups to test new products and services in a controlled environment.

2 **Provide clear and concise guidance to start-ups on regulatory compliance** which is tailored to the specific needs of start-ups and should be easy to understand.

3 **Work with start-ups to develop new regulatory frameworks** that support innovation and protect consumers. This could involve holding stakeholder consultations or establishing pilot programmes.

4 **Support start-up incubators and accelerators** by providing funding or by offering other forms of assistance.

By taking these steps, regulators can create a more supportive environment for start-ups to innovate and grow in the Web3/crypto space, which will benefit the economy as a whole.

Artificial Intelligence: Eigen Technologies

Eigen is an intelligent document processing (IDP) company that enables its clients to quickly and precisely extract answers from their documents, so they can better manage risk, scale operations, automate processes and navigate dynamic regulatory environments.

Eigen's customizable, no-code AI-powered platform uses machine learning to automate the extraction of answers from documents and can be applied to a wide variety of use cases. It understands context and delivers better accuracy on far fewer training documents, while protecting the security of clients' data.

Eigen's clients and partners include some of the best-known and respected names in finance, insurance, law and professional services, including Goldman Sachs, ING, Bank of America and Deloitte. Almost half of all global systemically important banks (G-SIBs) use Eigen to overcome their document and data challenges. Eigen is backed by Goldman Sachs, Temasek, Lakestar, Dawn Capital, ING Ventures, Anthemis and the Sony Innovation Fund by IGV.

In an interview with founder and CEO Dr Lewis Z. Liu, Eigen Technologies outlined their view on AI in financial services and what some of the benefit and pitfalls that need to be thought through are. Below is a summary.

How do you see the role of AI in financial services?

In starting with finance, banks make money by allocating capital and managing deposits and loans. The simplest example is a retail bank. What is unique about financial services is as long as a capitalistic society continues, the movement and allocation of capital won't change. We saw some of the disruptors in the defi and Web3 space, but we also saw that it quickly fizzled out.

The act of allocating capital as a fundamental part of finance is not going to change, which is very different in other industries, for example photography, which has at its heart the act of taking a real photo. AI can disrupt that fundamental activity, blurring real with fiction. Eigen Technologies look at where AI fits in the most macro level by breaking down the activity:

- Sourcing of capital and customers
- Manufacturing and distribution
- Operations and support
- Regulation.

Eigen Technologies do not see a change to the act of allocating capital but the way capital is allocated does, from sourcing to manufacturing to distribution and regulation. These are the areas where AI can disrupt.

DOES EIGEN TECHNOLOGIES SEE FINANCIAL SERVICES STRUGGLING WITH THE RISE OF AI?

Financial services has a long history of using applied statistics and machine learning which we now call AI. Financial services is one of the first industries to commercialize what we see today as machine learning. Decades ago, banks were first to use automated credit decision algorithms, and the credit scoring schemes are all sophisticated machine learning models.

For example, there is a reason quantitative hedge funds were all concentrated in Jersey City. It happened to be right next to the internet cable so they could do quantitative trading. So, all of these things we market today as AI, back then, we called systematic trading.

Of course, AI has significantly progressed since then and the latest advances open up more possibilities with many more examples, from onboarding to document streamlining and increasingly intelligent applications. Much of the need to use AI is to automate and find efficiencies in the current process to offer efficiencies and/or offer a better user experience. If we take the private wealth space, AI can cut down time to onboard customers from one month to hours. This is significant result for the financial institution in its ability to offer a great service to its private wealth clients.

AUTOMATION VERSUS INTELLIGENCE?

It's important to make this distinction because both are important and both have their applications.

Starting with a standard automation example, let's say one applies for a mortgage. We fill out a bunch of forms online. That is regular automation. The forms used to be paper and are now online. But there are additional documents we now need – bank statements, rental slips and so on.

These are traditionally read by humans. That has been difficult to automate by traditional means because each document is different. In one example, a mortgage broker wanted the mortgage applicant to physically highlight the rent payments on their bank statement in the last 18 months. A long, manual and onerous exercise. Using Eigen Technologies, it gave the output in seconds.

This is a simple, tangible example of how AI is useful, and automation simply can't cope when dealing with the heterogeneity of information and documents. Digital automation works well when everything is deterministic and there are a set of rules that are clear. Once it requires the need to deal with complexity and heterogeneity to emulate a human process, then AI comes in to play its role.

DO PURE AUTOMATION AND AI INTERACT?

They do interact. Eigen Technologies likes to use AI first then use rule-based automation second to check the AI, using the same example of extracting rent payments from a bank account. Regular automation can check the validity, accuracy and consistency of the information that has been extracted. For example, is the amount a Pound Sterling or US Dollar amount? If it produces a name, then it's an incorrect extraction. Is 1mil reasonable as a rent payment? Rule-based to automation can sense check that the AI extraction has been effective.

This starts to lead to a model for AI governance and in fairness, financial services as an industry was one of the first to use AI type technology, and dealing with the financial crises across the years; it's an industry that has thought through governance better than other industries. In banking today, there is something that is called model risk management which has a couple of different roles:

- Bank doesn't lose money.
- That the output of the model is consistent and doesn't spit out crazy numbers. It therefore looks at who trained the machine, and how the output is being tested regularly.

Having said that, further refinement is needed as they have been perfect. A known example for which we've seen banks getting into trouble is gender and racial bias. Notwithstanding that, these are rules that are more akin to automation that can be placed on top of AI. In summary, use AI first then use traditional automation to check its accuracy, which Eigen Technologies have used in their governance framework.

CAN AI BE GOVERNED?

Eigen believes that to build trust in AI technology and the way in which it is applied to real problems, a governance framework should be established, something that they have developed and use with all their applications. They govern AI using four lines of AI defence.

- Model Risk Management (MRM) – test AI results against a test set, so it can automatically score the accuracy rate of the AI model. Eigen uses three different types of accuracy score.
- Setting confidence levels – Eigen marks answers as highly confident when two separate models agree. What level you set for high confidence may differ for different use cases. Typically, low confidence answers are sent for manual review.
- Automated verifications using rules and exceptions.
- Manual review – humans check the exceptions that are flagged as low confidence. Typically, in many use cases >90 per cent of answers are sent for straight-through processing with only the remaining <10 per cent requiring human review.

WHAT ARE AI RISKS?

'*AI does come with a ton of risks but we are nowhere close to the terminator scenario.*' Dr Lewis Z Liu, founder and CEO of Eigen Technologies. There are more salient conversations around real issues such as cyber, bias, social media echo-chamber, liability, and IP and Liability. The issues around cyber, biases, social media are being debated extensively. What is not being thought through and considered carefully is IP and copyright issues.

WHAT ABOUT IP AND COPYRIGHT?

The way that training is being done today without consent of the owner of the data or flat-out ignoring terms and conditions. There are deep civilizational issues with this but from a practical perspective, mature financial institutions that are really thinking about this don't want to get sued for having an AI Chatbot powered by generative AI model such as GPT that as Dr Lewis Liu puts it: '*starts to get data from a Taylor Swift song, which is totally possible. They don't want to get sued for that!*'

Dr Liu talks about live examples he sees where senior staff of large financial institutions don't want to get sued in the future for putting in an entire business model of open AI which may in future become illegal due to copyright laws catching up. This is an example of outcomes-based regulation where a company is thinking ahead of what they are prepared to tolerate under laws that are not yet introduced but can see where the harm may lie.

A WORD ON LIABILITY

This goes back to model risk management question. We, as humans, see that the systems and model seem so smart and getting smarter (in our judgement) then there is a risk that our inclination is to trust them. But generative AI is simply taking data from a very large set of data, organizing the same information in different ways and presenting it back. It has no tool to check validity and accuracy. Yet.

Furthermore, if an AI Chatbot is used in a particular application where it causes the wiring of a payment to the wrong account or makes a trade that is unwindable, who is at fault?

Even the most powerful version of GPT 4 is not consistent enough to deal with the very high level of accuracy that is required for financial transactions. This is why we must tread with caution.

CHATGPT IN A CLOSED ENVIRONMENT

There are some experiments using generative AI in a closed and controlled environment. For example, for internal use. An important consideration here is the difference between discriminative models and generative models. With discriminative models, the data on which the model is trained are data sets that the organization knows and with which it is familiar.

But generative models need much, much bigger datasets in order to actually 'understand language'. That usually doesn't exist in one organization no matter now big, because generative AI is based on the entire internet as its database. So, unless you have something comparable, it won't give you the same results. Further, the systems are not really well understood. In taking an example of a big bank in the US that trains their billion+ documents. That is still a tiny part of the internet. It doesn't even register. It's a size question – bigger is better. The message, again, tread with caution. Understand these models, apply governance and keep testing accuracy and reliability.

Large financial institution's view of fintech: Visa

In this case study, Visa offers their perspective on the state of fintech.

Introduction

Visa is one of the world's leaders in digital payments. Our purpose is to uplift everyone, everywhere by being the best way to pay and be paid, enabling individuals, businesses and economies to thrive. We are a payment technology company facilitating secure, reliable and efficient transactions between consumers, issuing and acquiring financial institutions, and merchants across more than 200 countries and territories.

In 1958, Bank of America launched the first US consumer credit card programme, BankAmericard, based on a decentralized transaction processing system, which later evolved into Visa in 1976, revolutionizing global payments over the past six decades. Visa's role in the payment ecosystem is to facilitate the transactions between the cardholder and its bank (the issuer) and a merchant and its bank (the acquirer). As the payments ecosystem continues to evolve, we have broadened this model to include digital banks, digital wallets, governments and non-governmental organizations (NGOs). We provide transaction processing services (primarily authorization, clearing and settlement) to our financial institution and merchant clients through VisaNet, our advanced transaction processing network.

THE IMPORTANCE OF FINTECHS AND THE ROLE OF REGULATION

Customer needs are always changing, and fintechs have a critical role in meeting those changing needs. Visa and the industry are constantly working to adapt to the underpinning technological changes. Visa made a conscious decision to become an open network, not to just serve our bank customers. This decision brought forward by a combination of vision and innovation rather than regulation has helped Visa to deliver benefits to an ever-increasing number of players in the ecosystem, including fintechs.

Fintechs have an impact far beyond finance and play a key role in addressing today's major socio-economic challenges, they have changed the way traditional financial services are delivered, playing a crucial role in boosting productivity, economic growth and job creation. Fintechs are now increasingly embedded into many cross-sector economic issues and interactions, as the economy becomes more digital, payment innovation has played a pivotal role in economic growth – that helps businesses and consumers to access financial services, improve their financial literacy and access personal finance, while addressing environmental risks and climate change.

The shift in customer behaviours and the new digital first mindset have increased the imperative for businesses like Visa to work and support the growth of the fintech ecosystem. Visa pioneered this transformation in digital payments, opening our network to extend new payment methods and product features to the benefit of the broad payment ecosystem, helping the financial lives and well-being of individuals all around the world. The resilience, safety and security of our network, combined with good, smart regulations and the trust of the Visa scheme rules enable new participants to access payments innovation on a global scale supporting both existing and new market participants in fintech.

Regulation must be thoughtfully designed and future-proofed to deliver against emerging risks and opportunities. Visa contributed to the Kalifa Review of UK fintech, published in February 2021, which helped to set out a strategy to enhance the resilience of UK fintech which recommended:

1 Increased collaboration between regulators and the sector.

2 Mutual commitment to banking competition and innovation.

3 Focus for better financial outcomes and end-customer needs.

A critical challenge for regulation is to encourage new players in the ecosystem while ensuring that risks are addressed. Both regulators and the industry have an important responsibility to set minimum standards, and to keep pace with innovation and customer demands, while maintaining the resilience and reliability of its infrastructure systems. To achieve this, it is critical for regulation to focus on outcomes, providing clarity to payment firms and fintechs on the outcomes that industry should deliver. Outcomes-based regulation is adaptable to dynamic and fast-moving sectors and can therefore best achieve the safe growth of the payment sector. Overly prescriptive regulation can limit the market's ability to innovate, resulting in negative or slowed customer outcomes.

VISA'S SUPPORT FOR FINTECHS, THE BROADER ECOSYSTEM AND THE ECONOMY

Visa is a long-standing champion of the fintech sector. We run an open network working with fintechs from digital banks to seed stage start-ups and other to create new value for our customers while reducing frictions in commerce for everyone. Our Fintech Fast Track programme allows fintechs to engage with us, benefit from Visa's payment network, and engage with our global clients to expand their scale and reach.

By sharing our Application Programme Interfaces (APIs), fintechs have been able to launch their start-up, and also expand and grow their operations, helping them to bring their innovative ideas to life for their customers with increased safety and speed, protected by Visa's world-class security measures. When we partner with fintechs, we work closely with them to understand their unique challenges and opportunities.

Visa's Fintech Fast Track programme supports fintechs globally to improve their customer offerings. It assists start-ups in developing new payment solutions and allows our global clients to connect with this growing fintech community. With hundreds of global companies now participating in the fintech programme, year on year, we provide fintechs with partner toolkits and certification programmes which makes it easier for them to connect with certified partners for digital issuance and other key services across the payment ecosystem, including digital wallets, digital banking, but also cross-border remittance areas and person-to-person payments.

Visa works with global fintech companies to enhance their scale and reach:

- Visa enabled the UK based fintech and Neobank to expand its services globally.
- Visa supported a multi-currency account and online payments fintech to transition from a coffee business in Melbourne, Australia to a fintech platform enabling businesses to manage and transact money internationally.

Visa collaborates with partners to empower cardholders and drive financial inclusion:

- Visa Corporate credit cards allow a UK credit card provider to offer business credit cards and loans with flexible repayment options to small and medium-sized enterprises (SMEs) in the UK.
- Visa functionality allows a global market leader for subscription management in Sweden to help people manage their subscriptions with ease and take charge of their bills within their banking app.

- Visa's client-reach allowed a marketplace commerce tech business in Latin America to partner with financial institutions to bring banking services like digital wallets, prepaid cards and micro-loans to the underbanked population.
- Visa cards power a debit card app for young people in the UK, providing an intuitive financial education app and prepaid debit cards for young people to learn to manage, save and spend money in a responsible manner.

Visa partners with businesses to support sustainability:

- Visa partnered with a UK circular economy fintech, so users can sell or trade in electronics and clothing in return for instant funds to use for future purchases.
- Visa's partnership with a sustainability technology business in Germany helps financial institutions to empower their customers to take climate action, educating them on more sustainable payment choices.

INDEX

NB: page numbers in *italic* indicate figures or tables.

Looking for another book?

Explore our award-winning
books from global business
experts in Finance and
Banking

Scan the code to browse

www.koganpage.com/finance

More books from Kogan Page

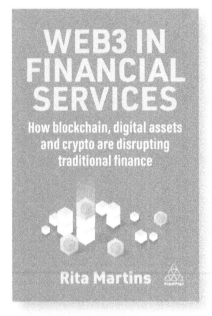

ISBN: 9781398615717

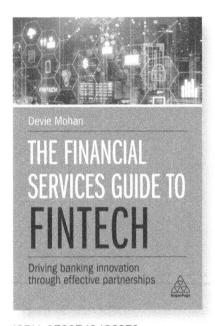

ISBN: 9780749486372

ISBN: 9781789667752

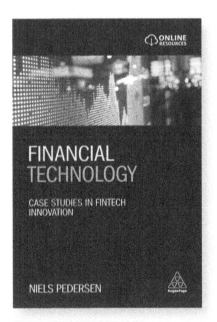

ISBN: 9781789665437

www.koganpage.com

Printed in the USA
CPSIA information can be obtained
at www.ICGtesting.com
JSHW070135240724
66915JS00005B/20